KIVA PUBLISHING

MAGDALENE CODES

DIVINE FEMININE FREQUENCY KEEPERS
WHO LIBERATE AND DISRUPT

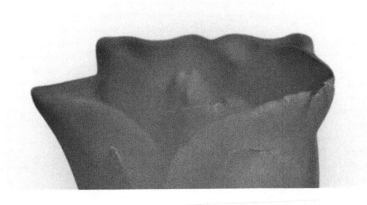

D1221712

MAGDALENE CODES
DIVINE FEMININE FREQUENCY KEEPERS WHO LIBERATE AND DISRUPT

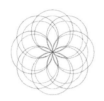

SHANNON VAN DEN BERG

AGNIESZKA GOLASIK · ALLIE MARIE
ANCA LAVINIA · ANGELA ROSENOW
CARYN TERRES · CASSANDRA FINCH
CATHY HO · CHELSEA BOISSONNEAULT
COLLEEN M COYNE · CRYSTAL LYNN PRIVETT
DAINA GARDINER · DHYANA KLUTH
EHRIN PARKER · ILONA POKA
ISABEL MORALES · JENNA BROWN
JESSICA SAGE · JULIANA LAVELL
KATHY ELLER · LISA CURTIS
MĀRCIA DĀROMCK MERMA · MELISSA ANN
MONIQUE VETTE · NICOLE ISHTARA KATZ
NICOLE MARIE ROSE · REBECCA COLLINS
SAMONE MARIE · SHONA KEELI ROSE
STELLA GRACE · VICKI LATTER

KIVA
PUBLISHING

Copy Editing: Christy Carlson
Formatting: Talya Pardo
Cover Design by Muse Designs

CONTENTS

INTRODUCTION

THIS BOOK HAS BEEN CALLED INTO EXISTENCE BY WOMEN around the globe and co-created by incredible Magdalene women who stepped forward to share their codes and embodiment with you. Since Magdalene Rising released over a year ago, I knew there would be a second and possibly more Magdalene books in our future. Her deep unconditional medicine is needed on the planet.

Mary Magdalene is a mystery to most people. She has a few brief, not so great mentions in the widely used Bible and a deliberate projection she's shouldered for centuries from the patriarchy dimming her light and all who would rise because of her.

She is the Feminine Christ, the Divine Feminine, sacred disruptor, and liberator. She is the fierce feminine, and unapologetic heart centered leader we can aspire to become.

Magdalene Codes tells the inspiring stories of sacred feminine disruptors leading the way forward with their unconditional love.

They know who they are and why they're here at this pivotal ascending time on our planet. They come to elevate humanity through their fierce devotion to their soul mission which overflows into how they BE in the world.

They are priestesses, mothers, grandmothers, healers, teachers, shaman, witches and divine feminine frequency keepers.

Their heart consciousness and expression of the sacred feminine mysteries are their gifts to future generations.

Come take a journey with us.

Let these divine women show you the power and liberation of the heart.

In these pages you'll find the presence of fierce feminine leadership who lets nothing and no one get in the way of her sacred knowing and mission. Leading from the heart with truth and connected to the entire Rose Lineage wisdom.

I invite you to grab a cup of tea or coffee and read a chapter at a time. Soak it in, integrate, feel it. These are life-changing stories these brave authors have poured their hearts into and bared their souls within. After each chapter you'll find the About the Author page and how to work with them if you feel drawn to deepen your relationship to Mary Magdalene and your inner sacred disruptor, or want to witness more of their expression of it.

Before you turn the page and dive in, place one hand over your heart and one over your womb. Close your eyes and breathe in and then out a few times. Connect to these women who bring forth these potent codes for you to receive. Open your heart and be present with each chapter. There is so much wisdom and expansion here for you.

Listen deeply. You'll hear Her beautiful medicine whispered to you through these pages.

With Love,

Shannon xx

THE JOURNEY TO RE-REMEMBER

AGNIESZKA GOLASIK

"For I am the first and the last,
I am the honored one and the mocked one.
I am the harlot and the holy one.
I am the wife and the virgin
I am a mother and daughter.
I am her...
Do not be afraid of my power...
I am the awareness of my own name.
I am the name of the sound and the sound of the name."
Unknown
The voice of the Divine Feminine - Nag Hammadi
Scriptures

EVERYTHING IS ENERGY FIRST

TO BE HONEST WITH YOU, WHEN I STARTED WRITING this chapter, I had no idea where the writing process would take me, and I was clueless about where I was going to take you. For a variety of reasons, while attempting to write this chapter, I was experiencing obstacle after obstacle. Being familiar with states of creative flow and energy movements in intuitive creation, I just knew that this energy stream was blocked. Even though I was familiar with Mary Magdalene as a biblical figure, working with Mary Magdalene's energy seemed so foreign to me.

The experience of writing for Magdalene Codes was so unlike writing for Jaguar Medicine and Isis Mother of Magic – the two international bestsellers by Kiva Publishing I co-authored. I strongly encourage you to read them if you haven't come across them yet. I am convinced that you will find them of great value. Born through energetic writing, those books are filled with inspirational stories containing potent medicines. It is the energetic writing process that makes them unique and so different from other books.

What is energetic writing?

Let me sum it up for you.

Since everything in the Universe is made out of energy and mentally created first, all things–both physical matter and spiritual energy–hold a specific vibration frequency. At first, this book was just an idea, a thought of a particular frequency in a channeled message. That frequency is key when it comes to energetic writing because the whole point of energetic writing for multi-authored collaborations is to connect to that frequency and channel it through writing in your chapter to share the message. With Kiva books, the titles and covers usually carry the frequency the books will hold. Therefore, both the titles and the graphics are always very activating.

The activation is like a calling to contribute. It ignites the energy you already embody by connecting it to the frequency of the book, or it activates the gateway to that frequency. In my case, it was the latter. I didn't feel like I embodied Magdalene's energy, but I definitely was curious about and open to holding it.

A GIFT TO UNPACK

With Jaguar Medicine, once I said "YES," everything unfolded quickly. Just like Mama Jaguar is known for pounces that kill fast, the jaguar energy came very strongly for me. When it showed up, I could feel Mama Jaguar's strong presence in an instant. It was one week-long writing pounce, and my chapter for Jaguar Medicine was created.

When I wrote for Isis Mother of Magic, the Black Madonna's presence was even stronger because I have always had a powerful connection with her. Without hesitation, the "YES" to co-authoring it came out of me at the speed of light, and so did the story.

But writing for Magdalene Codes was different. First, the opportunity came to me as a gift in a package with a Multi-Author Quantum Creatrix Oracle Deck I said "YES" to, so I didn't feel like I chose her. In a way, Magdalene chose me. The frequency gateway to her energy has been activated in me, but the timing couldn't have been worse. My mental space was occupied by decision-making concerning major areas of my life, so my focus was on making those crucial decisions. My energy was also highly scattered because I was traveling overseas visiting with family and friends. On the one hand, it was awesome but, on the other, exhaustingly overstimulating.

Because of the pandemic, it has been three long years since I visited my hometown. This trip was supposed to be a trip back to my roots, yet somewhere deep down, I felt so uprooted and out of place. A lot of things stirred up within me. I was observing my healed wounds, distant memories, and old triggers bubbling up to the surface of my awareness.

I couldn't find that sharp mental focus or a quiet place to write, let alone the dedicated time. I felt guilty for taking time away from my family. I couldn't find myself to be just by myself.

From adjusting to the time change, dealing with summer heat waves, problems with internet connections, attending a funeral, spending time with my relatives and getting entangled in their drama, observing my internal landscape and processing what was going on there, to having fun partaking in creative workshops and expanding my coaching skills, everything felt intense – as if the forces were against me when it came to writing for Magdalene Codes. The writing muse had left me. Just like me, she went on vacation.

REMINISCENCE OF MAGDALENE'S ENERGY

After many failed attempts to write and two missed deadlines, I finally said to myself, "It's time to bring the big guns and help this writing process by summoning my creative energy back to me. It's time to call on Mary of Magdala because Divine Intervention is needed here if I am destined to be a co-contributor to this book. The feast of Mary Magdalene on July 22 seemed to be a perfect day to do that. I had no freaking idea about what I would write, but I was determined to write. I found a rose-scented candle. I took out the beautiful icon of Saint Mary Magdalene that I bought in a small gift shop in a gothic cathedral church of her name that I stumbled upon while visiting my brother during the recent trip. After my kids went to bed for the night, I went outside to sit on the balcony. I lit the candle, whispered my favorite protective prayer, and asked Mary Magdalene for guidance and help.

I opened my laptop. To get my creative juices going, I started reading through all the research material I had gathered about Magdalene. The night was beautiful. I was sitting outside, covered with a blanket of a dark, starry sky. The cold, fresh air felt like a saving grace after a day of tropical temperatures. Slowly I could feel the energy starting to shift. It felt so damn good that I decided to take out the blanket and lay down to drop into it entirely. The feeling was so delicious that I started slowly drifting into the realms of dreams. Half awake and half asleep, I was aware of my body relaxing. My mind, on the other hand, was sharp. It worked intensely on retrieving memories from the past and searching its internal storage for all the encounters with Mary Magdalene.

The mishmash of recollections of random happenings and echoes of distant events filled my mind. It was all soft, blurry, and yet I was slowly starting to realize that this wasn't the first time I interacted with Magdalene's energy, which no longer seemed as foreign to me as I previously thought. On the contrary, the energy that filled that luminous dreaming mirage of mine was familiar…and it was intensifying. The more my mind was immersed in it, the stronger my conviction that I had encountered it before. I couldn't bring the sharp details of specific encounters back to my memory, yet to my surprise, I knew that Magdalene had been present in my life for quite some time. About an hour later, I found myself drifting back to the state of full consciousness while lying on the balcony floor. I realized that I must have drifted into a light sleep and was lucid dreaming of all the distant memories of encounters with the energy of Magdalene.

AN URGE TO WRITE

When I woke up the next day, I felt the strong urge to write. I followed that impulse and found a secluded spot, took my laptop, the rose candle, and the icon. I lit the candle, took out the icon and started examining it closely. The more I focused

14

my awareness on Magdalene's beautiful image, the more clearly she started speaking to me. It seemed like the icon came to life – the transmission of energy through the vividness of colors and the power of symbolic attributes was intense. When I realized that Magdalene was speaking to me through her attributes, I started connecting the dots.

One item, in particular, caught my attention. The bright scarlet egg she was holding in her right hand. An egg!!! One of the most potent symbols of all time linked by cultures of east and west to all of creation. The symbol of fertility, new beginnings, new life, resurrection, creative potential, and so much more. The symbol of the Goddess. When I noticed it, I could not believe it. For quite a few years, collecting eggs has been a big obsession of mine. It started when I got myself a beautiful gold and blue porcelain egg at a flea market a few years back. I kid you not, that egg spoke to me to get it. I could not take my eyes away from it. I had no idea WHY but I just had to have it. The impulse to get it was more potent than any reasoning.

I can bet you have those moments, too.
Strong urges that want to be followed, impulses with no answer to WHY? Those impulses when you don't understand the urge to get things, or do something, go somewhere, but the pull is so strong that you have to surrender. What usually happens is that you connect the dots much later and the WHY becomes apparent after some time passes when you can gain a deeper perspective. With time, it becomes evident to you how good or bad a decision it was to follow the urge or not.

Throughout my life, I have learned that following these strong impulses is about surrendering to the Higher Power. By acknowledging and following them, I immensely strengthen my intuition and connection to my Inner Wisdom. Following one intuitive impulse after another, no matter how strong or subtle, is like building an invisible intuitive muscle memory.

THE GOLDEN THREAD OF DESTINY

This was precisely the case with those two eggs. Two events separated vastly in time but connected through the golden thread of destiny. I follow the solid internal impulse to get them both: the gold and blue egg and the icon. I am convinced that the bright scarlet egg would not have caught my attention if this was not for that gold and blue egg and many more eggs that follow after it. While looking at it, something cracked open inside me.

Glimpses and hints of images from what was a lucid mirage the night before started coming back and passing before my mind's eye. I felt energy shifting. This time the mirage was different because some random elements of it became vivid and sharp. To my astonishment, they were all bright scarlet red, just like the egg Magdalene was holding, as if the color of crimson was a messenger. This realization came upon me suddenly, and order was created from the mirage of dreamy chaos as mental puzzles started falling into place. Magdalene was present in my life, I just did not connect the dots before. I realized that all those red things were not random at all. They all had one other thing in common – the way they came into my possession.

The memories about the circumstances of getting those items started flooding my mind. I realized that just like the opportunity to contribute to Magdalene Codes, they all came into my possession as gifts. This newly gained awareness threaded together "incidental" events and "random" things with a golden thread. An array of items from everyday use to those of more healing, ceremonial, ritual, and spiritual nature – they were all gifts. Gifts I either got for myself following the strong intuitive impulses connected to that primal part of me that just *knows*, or they were gifted to me by other wise women with strong well-wishing protective intentions.

There was a piece of Palo Santo covered in a bright red fabric that I have been using for all cleansing ceremonies gifted to me by my dear friend Dhyāna, whom you will also have a chance to connect with later in this book. Then a red string that wise woman Donya ceremonially knotted on my left wrist to protect me from everything of evil nature.

There was a bright scarlet fabric-covered journal I got in my late twenties and still have. Journaling in it kept me sane during my journey to motherhood while dealing with the struggles and insanity of unexplained infertility. Next, a red wallet I got myself for one of my birthdays. I saw it on the display, and a strong impulse came upon me to get it. Then a big, red leather tote bag with a humongous rosy flower of life motif on the front that I got myself with money gifted to me on my birthday. I saw it on display and knew this bag belonged to me. This bag has become my go-to tote ever since. Also a red dress that I fell in love with at first sight and got for myself as a gift for Mother's Day. Then came my everyday companion…a small crossbody handbag that I call my lucky miraculous bag because when I accidentally lost it, it was returned to me with my wallet intact.

What struck me even more was a realization that with all of those gifts I got for myself, I often went through some internal struggle when considering buying them. There were the thoughts of: *What do you need it for? You don't need it. It's a waste of money. You don't even like red.* The intense, intuitive urge to get them had fought with mental reasoning of arguments against it—the strong frequency of two forces pulling in opposite directions.

And yet the impulses to get them, even though the red seemed to be the least of my favorite colors, were always stronger. They won every single time. The potency of that energetic field to which the intuitive urges were connected was always more powerful. There was something primal about it. The reasoning mind had to surrender to it. It became apparent that through all those years, item by item, I was opening myself to embracing the vibration of scarlet – the color traditionally associated with Mary of Magdala. Just like talking through attributes in the icon I was holding in my hands, through all these years, Magdalene's energy was coming strongly to my life through all those favorite items of mine.

Then more memories flooded my mind. I realized she wasn't always about establishing her presence through material things. She came strongly through experiences. It hit me that Magdalene made her strong presence during the time of this recent "trip to the roots" I was taking.

First came a flashback of a womb healing ceremony from a few years back and then all that I had experienced during "Discover The Treasures Of Femininity" workshop I recently gifted to myself following the same primal, intuitive impulse. Her energy was strongly present in a red dress, a flower crown-making, and an oracle card-pulling ceremony. She came in strongly through acts of creative expression when, following the intuitive urge, I made a mobile sculpture that took on a form of mandala with a motif of Divine Yoni made out of random intuitively picked items: a rose-gold metal ring, a tear-shaped scarlet crystal ball, and red beaded wooden necklaces.

Moreover, this whole process of writing for Magdalene Codes was one significant experience of reconnecting with her and realizing her in myself. This was my journey to re-

remember. It was not until this very moment I am writing those words that I had this epiphany. Magdalene was the primal, intuitive force behind all the impulses!!! She was the voice of Intuition–the pure and mighty energy of connection to my Inner Wisdom!!! I was strongly connected to Magdalene because I was strongly connected to my Intuition.

...Or so I thought.

THE POWER OF THE CONDITIONING

After that insightful soul and heart-warming discovery, my energy shifted again. The mirage of red droplets that became crystal blue hit my mind, followed by a vision of a vast water dam built between two mountains. The dam was holding an immense amount of crystal blue water. Since it had no water bar, the water was pushing its way through cracks making its way to the other side, dripping down on the dam's wall. At first, I couldn't make sense of that vision. Then another insight hit me like a ton of bricks.

I only had access to droplets of my intuitive knowledge and droplets of Magdalene's energy. Deep down, I was afraid to fully embrace all my instinctive urges, just like I was afraid of becoming who I was taught Mary Magdalene was. You see, years of catholic upbringing had a tight grasp on my mind. Somehow, despite how pure Magdalene's intuitive energy felt to me, part of me still believed Magdalene was a sinful woman–a devil-possessed prostitute.

The voice in my head was very stubborn, insisting that I did not want anything to do with a harlot possessed by seven demons. I did not want to be a bad girl. I wanted to be a good girl, the one I have been told to be and have been for so long. Then a potent long-forgotten fear bubbled up to the surface of my consciousness, the fear of a little girl who was afraid to be bad because being bad equaled being possessed by demons. While sitting and observing with full awareness of what was coming through for me, I could feel the fires of Divine Feminine's Holy Anger rising to burn away all that conditioning engraved in my brain. When the sacred fury seceded, the veil was lifted.

I realized that I couldn't fully embody Magdalene's energy and be utterly fearless in following my Intuition because my subconscious mind was hyper-focused on protecting me from everything my subconscious considered bad. To my subconscious, the embodiment of Magdalene's energy equaled an embodiment of dirtiness and evilness because this narrative about Magdalene was magnified when I was a child. My subconscious had put up the dam because it got fixated on that one aspect.

You see, everything that your subconscious catches on in your younger years stays as a program that will run your life unless it comes up to the surface of your matured consciousness to see the subconscious program for what it was–a child mind's mental defense mechanism.

I can only speculate when the cracks started to appear in the dam.

It was when I got tired of being a good girl and started to question what seemed illogical and search for my own answers. When I started spending a lot of time meditating to gain understanding and insight into myself. When I stopped pleasing others and started pleasing myself. When I stopped burning myself out to prove myself to others. When I understood that people could only see as much good in me as they see in themselves. When I said, enough is enough and strongly put up my boundaries. When I befriended my demons and started integrating all my shadow parts. When I started loving my shadow parts for they are the gifts in disguise.

When I dropped the notion of being a sinful being and when "I AM GOOD" became my mantra.

SISTER I CALL YOU

Sometimes the droplets are all you have and need to get back to Source. When I called on Mary Magdalene for help to write this chapter, I was staring at the blank page and trusting that the message would show itself to me. And she came in drop by drop, revealing herself patiently until I connected all my droplets so this chapter for the Magdalene Codes could be written. Now I know why I have written it.
So I could strip deep layers of conditioning and, in the process, realize myself on an even deeper level. And to inspire you to connect your dots for whatever it is you need to connect them for.
Sister Mary Magdalene is calling you to re-remember that you have the access to her.

Drop inside and you will find your MAGDALENE.

Drop deep to acknowledge Magdalene in you...drop by drop, one intuitive impulse at a time. I don't care how fast or slow you will move. I care that you commit to yourself and keep moving forward grounded in self-connection to realize your true nature. If you find yourself in need, don't hesitate to reach out. I would be honored to use my God/Goddess-given gifts to help you guide you back to your True Self.

With Unconditional Love,

Agnieszka

ABOUT THE AUTHOR

AGNIESZKA GOLASIK

Agnieszka Golasik is a 2x international bestselling author, self-connection whisperer, creativity catalyst, intuitive artist muti-passionista, and joy and freedom messenger. She describes herself as a guide to go inside and an immersive experience leader on a mission to raise and expend collective consciousness by helping individuals increase self-awareness, catalyze reconnection to inner wisdom, and embrace creative powers.

Inner-wisdom focused, Agnieszka invites you to step on the path of liberation from the bondages of the conditioned mind. She calls you to embrace the power of contemplative self-inquiry, creative art's healing power, and nature's restorative power.

Passionate about various healing and therapeutic modalities, she weaves together contemplative meditation, intuitive artistic expression, prayer, journaling, nature immersion, and more. She takes those seeking clarity and change on personalized, transformational, soulful journeys where one's inner knowledge and creative powers take a driver's seat. Guided to connect with the still small voice, her clients find the answers within themselves while traveling the path of self-discovery.

Agnieszka works with people privately and in small intimate group settings. She hosts in-person immersions, circles, and online gatherings.

Privately, a proud mama of two exceptional preteen girls and a nature lover. Originally from Poland, she lives in northern New Jersey.

Schedule your complimentary "Let's Connect" discovery call with Agnieszka and claim your surprise gift here: https://calendly.com/agnieszkagolasik/let-s-connect

Connect with Agnieszka at: agnieszka.golasik@gmail.com

Find out more at: www.agnieszkagolasik.weebly.com

Photo credit: Lisa Guillard Photography

FINDING THE WAY HOME

ALLIE MARIE

THE PATH THAT LEADS US HOME IS USUALLY thought of as a well-lit walkway with beautiful flowers on a cozy winding river through a forest covered in beautiful ivy. A home straight out of a Victorian-era romance novel where a handsome, swoon-worthy hero is there to carry us up the walkway and across the threshold.

At least, that is what I always thought was the perfect home. Somewhere that I could rest easy knowing that in the middle of the night when all was peaceful and quiet, there he was, right downstairs in his study enjoying a glass of whiskey just before coming upstairs to bed to me.

Oh, how I remember being devastated when this turned out not to be the case. The road home was not cute, quaint, or even picturesque. At first...

I had to crawl through the mud, avoiding low-hanging

barbed wire. The skies had opened and suddenly it was raining, cold frigid rain washed over me, washing all over the cuts and bruises I received while fighting for my life in the mud, while being cut by the barbed wire.

Then one day, the clouds parted and the sun came out. Dazzling bright white light that poured into my soul. Warming up every part of me from head to toe. It was a beacon of warm motherly light calling to me, walking with me, showing me the way home.

The female energy was so tender yet so fierce, loving, yet demanding, soothing mixed with a little bit of scolding. The mothering felt good to my battered soul. The light shining was pure salvation like a drink of water after walking through the long desert, a breath of fresh air filling my lungs.

No longer was I the maiden in need of saving. No longer was I awaiting my dark knight riding up to catch me on his white horse. Now I was the mother, who herself lives in a beautiful cottage just on the side of the cozy brook, as it is babbling happily singing the song to my soul.

I am no longer lonely being alone, I am no longer sad in my happiness. My soul once trapped and yearning for more, is now fulfilled, I can look out the window of my soul and see what needs to be seen with love and appreciation.

No longer can we look back, for now, that is the past. That is what is behind us and we can no longer go back to that place. Why would we want to? We are no longer that same person. The one who was walking the singular walk with no company except our own misery. There was a final and complete ending, as we have started a wondrous new beginning. We are no longer yearning for something that we can no longer have, we have moved forward, into the future.

WALKING IN THE LIGHT OF THE MOON

The sun is burning bright, and the rainy days are as glorious as a wonderful moonlit walk beside the silent lake as the moon caresses her with its love. The timelines of loneliness, aching, and yearning are no longer a part of this new timeline of infinite love. We have taken that leap of faith and have surrendered, and now all is love, all is peace, and we are walking side by side with Mary Magdalene.

They say that the eyes are the windows to our soul. So what do we see when we look into someone's eyes? We see a little twinkle of something magical. Mischief maybe? Happiness that we can no longer contain so it dances out of our eyes. Hope, love, peace, excitement? We are ourselves, our souls, our holy immaculate temples, and we are made of stardust. That is what that little twinkle in our eye is, that is the magic that we hold so deep down inside of ourselves.

We must find this place of inner magic. It is there, bubbling just beneath the surface. It is waiting to come out to the surface. It is waiting for us to wake up and realize that it has been a part of us all along. To discover our souls so fully and so completely, that we can never be what we left behind ever again.

For this we must turn inward. To walk in the light of beauty and grace with not just ourselves, but also with our fellow man. Here in this divine vessel that we keep, this wonderful Shekinah where we hold the temple of the White Rose is where we will find answers. We will seek solace, silence, and listen to all that is. Here we will find the God mother of life.

She wants to walk with us on our soul's journey, on this wonderful path we are being guided on and learning from every day. We must listen to the trees and hear their sacred ancient knowledge. For they are wise and carry grandfather medicine from generations past. Return to the Earth and listen to her heartbeat. It will carry us, soothe our souls, and transform our lives into something wonderful.

Once we come into divine union with the being of our souls, we can learn to speak and hear the language of the other side. We will come into perfect communication with all that is. We are ready for purification and unity as it drifts all around us just below the surface and ready and waiting to permeate through to the deepest part of who we are.

SACRED FEMININE ENERGY RADIATES AMONG US

This energy is slow, sacred, and utterly feminine. It is sensual, it is sexual, and it is strong, playful, and exuberant. The energy stream is purposeful and languid in its intention. It seeks to call all women forth to love, to worship, and to be worshiped. Just as if we are sitting in the sacred temples as divine priestesses, robed in virginal clothing ready for service.

We are here to carry this energy like the sacred white beacon that it is, to flow as the sacred waters wash over our divine nakedness in the lakes, rivers, and streams of undulated adoration. This is the sacred sisterhood of Mary Magdalene as she appears to me. We are here to carry each other, to spread love, unity, and the sacred ways of women that have baffled men for eons.

My soul yearns for days long ago when the wild women would wander barefoot over sleepy meadows, foraging for herbs yielded from the soft womb of Mother Gaia as she blessed us with all we needed. So that we could take it home to where the fires burned hot to make medicines, teas, and salves.

Times when ancient wisdom was passed down from mother to daughter and carried in the ancient feminine ways that have long since been forgotten. We are to sit in sacred ceremony with other women and share what knowledge we have, to pass this to our own daughters so they may pass it to theirs. In the energy of sacred womanhood, we are here to nurture each other, to show and share in the love of community, and to walk this path together.

As we walk on this new path of enlightenment, love, and beingness we must also shield against the negative energies and darkness that also walk beside us. Protect your thoughts from negative energy. We are now the priestesses that walk in the light of love.

THE BIRTHING OF A SOMETHING NEW

This is the new creation and the dawn that has risen in the east. The energy of the crystal magic that we have called upon for healing within ourselves is all around us. The Earth is filled with these crystals, we have only to look and find them.

These crystals have been here on Earth since the beginning, so too must we go back to the beginning, something more simple, something easier than the rat race we have been stuck in. No longer are we stuck in "keeping up with the Joneses." We are here to look out for our sisters, to embrace them, and to step up when one has struck their knee on a boulder in their path.

These are the bonds of sisterhood that we are being called to embrace. A newer, higher energy is fast approaching us. There is beauty, grace, love and elegance in even the smallest

28

faery as she flies as fast as her little wings can carry her to keep up with the bigger, stronger faeries that have forged the path before her.

In this new shift, this new paradigm, no one is left out in the cold, and we are to return to the old dance of community. We are to meet the Gatekeeper of this new shift and meet her in the spot of all that is. There has been something happening with time, everyone feels different, and no longer the same.

There has been talk that all timelines are happening at once. Somehow, I can feel this shift, this sacred dance with what is. I can see myself in 1700s Scotland, waulking wool and singing the old songs as the men sit by the fire, cooking the meat, drinking their wine, and telling tales as tall as the ancient redwoods.

This was a simpler time, maybe not a peaceful time, with towns being raided and such. However, simple it was and simple we need to be once more. We as humans are craving human touch. We are so connected technologically, yet we couldn't feel farther apart.

There is an initiation, an invitation to become whole again. To feel the connection between us as a people and to exchange energy once again. We are at a time when we are the fool, giddy with anxious energy. Standing on that precipice, waiting, wondering, listening intently. For a sign, for anything that tells us to move.

For about the last year, I was held in this sacred liminal space. I held silent. I was listening, waiting, and feeling. I was using my intuition to maneuver my way through the darkness I was leaving behind. Coming into my soul, my purpose, and loving myself all the more while I sat in this incubation period.

There were shifts happening all around me, magic, I could see it. That magic was not for me at that time. I felt I was missing out. What were the possibilities if any that I held back from myself? "Not yet," came the whisper. "It isn't your time to make a big move. Watch, learn, soak it all in."

SEEKING THE DOORWAY TO FREEDOM

Then suddenly, as I leveled up through the game I have been playing, I stepped through that doorway. The energetic doorway that propels us into the future that we want but are not yet ready to achieve. I wanted it all. I sat in sacred ceremony. I was guided by my angels, by Mary Magdalene, Mother Mary, Ganesha, Jesus, and Kali.

I was not alone. I felt their presence, I heard their song, and in my mind, I could see them all around me. Helping me, taking my athame and cutting, slicing and peeling off the old cords that no longer served. I saw them fall, black in color, and like dead plant matter that is lying dormant in the forest of possibility.

Into the container they went. They were no longer mine to carry. The weight that was lifted off felt amazing. I felt lighter, physically, and I was called to physically purge and detox my body on a whole new level. This detox came to me naturally and easily. The residual sludge is now being purged from my body and lifting me ever higher into new realms of energetic alliance. After I let my guides and guardians assist me in this most holy purge, I knew the time was right. It was my time to take flight. No longer was I sitting in the background wondering what I could contribute, besides what I already had. I wanted to get in the ring, I wanted to take off my gloves and get my hands dirty.

I first had to wait for the right moment. I had to put away

30

my Taurus energy–my bull in a china shop headlong rush…into what? I don't know. Anything, everything. This is what my journey has taught me. To sit in the beautiful light of what is and to be ok with not knowing. I am ok with not knowing exactly what tomorrow holds. I am ok with not knowing what I have to do five minutes from now, or not knowing what will be for dinner, or any other number of mundane things.

I am held, safe in the knowledge that I am. That sacred knowingness that is uniquely and divinely feminine. Knowing that I have me on my best days, and if I don't have me on my worst days, then God has me on those days, along with my angels, my ancestors, and the guides and guardians.

"The Goddess doesn't enter us from outside; she emerges from deep within. She is not held back by what happened in the past. She is conceived in consciousness, born in love, and nurtured by higher thinking. She is integrity and value, created and sustained by the hard work of personal growth and the discipline of a life lived actively in hope."–Marianne Williamson

I have my own special place where I go to feel all the emotions. To know that I am ok, that you are ok, and that we are ok. I am ok knowing that I do not need all of the answers right now. This is the safe space, this is the simple life that just is.

Of course, there are those of us who are still asleep, unconscious and unaware of what is happening around them, and that is okay. Leave them there. That is where they are happy. That is where they are contented. I have learned from my own family that we cannot control what another person thinks, how they feel, or even what we want them to do. To even try is a gross waste of our time, our energy, and our effort.

We can use that energy towards other adventures. We do not need to bring others up with us when it is their time, or even if it isn't they will come up when they are called and most definitely when they are ready.

BECOMING THE GODDESS WITHIN

In the meantime, stand on the precipice of the ancient wishing well. Manifest into your reality all that it is that you want, let yourself have your soul growth, grow in wisdom, in respect, grow in the ancient ways of womanhood and connect with your guides, your guardians, and the ancient ancestors who have spent their eternity waiting for a connection to you.

This is the path that we are here to walk, we are here to tap into ancient ancestral magic, the ley lines that lie throughout the Earth. They say that we, as lightworkers, have been placed upon the Earth and have incarnated at this time in a strategic manner. Does it have something to do with the ley lines? Some think so. Some think we have incarnated here for a purpose, we all have a soul purpose, but what about that of a bigger purpose?

We are here to transcend our ego, to learn, to elevate our souls for that bigger purpose. As long as we are learning to tap into our sacred feminine, and balance her with our sacred masculine, our intuition will guide us along this path.

This is the ancient dance of our souls. We must balance the feminine and masculine within ourselves, and with our partners. We all have both within us. Men are seen as weak if they show their softer side, so they put on a mask and pretend they do not have this part of them. Women are considered too weak and needy if they show this softer side

32

of themselves. This is the work that needs to be done right now. It is a balancing act, and sometimes it is a struggle to learn the steps to this ancient rhythm.

We must learn the give and the take, the masculine, and the feminine. One gives to the other while the other is open to receive, and vice versa. This is the dance we must perform, even within ourselves. To really step forward and balance our yin and yang, we must first grow, we must mature to an even greater depth than before.

We must turn our attention inward. This is the hard work, the work that not a lot want to do. It is hard and difficult, but worth it. This is how we reach that emotional maturity deep in our souls, and this is how we rise. There is a deep respect for the way in which we must learn to live.

Reconnect. Reconnect with nature, grow plants in your home, grow plants outside of your home. Research herbs, ancient customs, and see what resonates with you. Reconnect with your soul, reconnect to your partner's soul. Let go of old hurts, old memories, and old ways of thinking and living.

Let your guides carve a new path for you, let them know that you are ready, and listen for the cue to take that first leap forward. Change is inevitable, so be the change that you want to see. Reclaim your secret, sacred, sensual feminine self and put one foot in front of the other.

Your guides are here with a gift, they are here to nurture you and help you along this path to untold pleasure. First, we must remember to slow down. Time is different in other realms, the Earth moves slower, she breathes, she grows. Just look at the forests, look at the Amazon, she is alive with possibility, because she is slow. She doesn't miss an opportunity that has been presented to her.

33

When we are moving at such a fast pace, we miss the little things, the doors that are being held open to us, the path that has suddenly been cleared. We miss the love that has been offered to us time and again. We have been trained to move so fast, but we must stop. See from the perspective of a snail. Slow, steady, quiet.

Detach yourself from old painful memories, detach yourself from bad situations, see it through a different lens, change it, mold it, and let it propel you forward. These are the gifts that we are being offered. The gift of taking an old situation, turning it around, and making use of what it was, giving thanks for what it is no longer, and moving forward with peace and gratitude.

This is what is meant by walking in beauty and grace. To live for beauty, physical beauty, sensual beauty, pleasure, daydreaming of all that you desire, manifesting it into your reality, and serving this world and those around you with unconditional love.

Namaste,

Allie Marie
XOXO

ABOUT THE AUTHOR

ALLIE MARIE

If you enjoyed my chapter, check out my links in my About the Author section and reach out to me, I would love to connect!!

Allie Marie is CEO and creatrix of Sacred Woman Healing, an International Best-Selling Author and a Holistic Healer, Reiki Master, Shamaness, a Priestess, and a certified Crystal Healer. Allie brings passion, enthusiasm and a wonder lust for learning to everything she does. Allie is passionate about helping women, who like herself, have been through abuse at the hands of their significant other.

Allie has a holistic and loving approach, where she heals the whole woman and not just the effects of the abuse. Allie empowers other women to heal themselves through energy work, building self-confidence, and reclaiming the power they know deep down is their birthright. Through powerful sacred ceremony, Allie creates a space of loving acceptance to heal what has been broken.

Allie has earned her associate degree in Human and Social Services from Bryant & Stratton College and is currently working on earning her Bachelor's in Sociology from Grand Canyon University.

Allie lives in Colorado with her children. They enjoy spending time with her grandparents, swimming and hiking through the Mountains of Colorado. She has a Great Pyrenees named Bailey, and a black cat named Gregor MacGregor, that she fondly nicknamed Mr. MacGregor and gave him his very own garden.

If you enjoyed my chapter and would like to connect, please reach out!

alliemarie@sacredwomanhealing.com

www.sacredwomanhealing.com

https://www.facebook.com/thesacredwomanhealing

https://www.instagram.com/spiritualgoddess101/

WHOLE WOMAN
LIVE A HEART-CENTERED LIFE

ANCA LAVINIA

IT ALL BEGAN WITH MY HEART

I WAS AROUND 10 WHEN I REMEMBER WAKING UP in the middle of the night to just talk to God. I was never taught how to pray and I did not have any religious education.

I just remember crying warm tears and having this fire in my heart while talking to God.

Later on, I kept looking for God in churches and different confessions, always thirsty to regain that feeling of union, peace, of Presence and warmth.

I did not find what I craved in church. Women almost did not have a place there. The rules seemed so awkward to me and they only made me drift away...

I wanted to *feel* divinity. Something inside me knew She/He was a part of me. I did not want long sermons about a God that I should fear, about punishment, restriction and sin.

That did not feel like home to me.

It took me many years to feel that sacred connection again, to live with God/ess again but in a totally different, almost heretical way.

I felt like an outsider all of my life.

At about 14 I started smoking, skipping school, then drinking and self-harming, had suicidal thoughts and wanted to run away from home. I felt alone, disconnected, unheard, unimportant, fat and unattractive.

I wanted boys to like me and I desperately started seeking their attention by becoming the perfect people pleaser, a good and fun pal for them.

Until I was 25, I managed to become almost alcoholic. I had slept with different men thinking I would be seen, appreciated, loved, but got dumped over and over again. I spent my nights in dark bars, at rock concerts and worked jobs that I did not like during the day.

I was a mess. Hurt. Had the lowest self-esteem, always on a diet, wanting to be invisible, always with a dark cloud above my head. The world seemed gray and nothing was going my way.

Until this one guy.

I was literally naked on top of him and I told him I wanted more. I needed more. I would not just give myself in flesh

38

and be the girl with benefits and no commitment. I had done this too many times. No more.

His words came like a sharp dagger: "I can't, I am not prepared for a relationship, not now."

My world sank, my heart broke one more time, tears flowed just out of nowhere, and I collapsed. Then and there but also for the next few days...in my room with the blinds lowered, in darkness, not sleeping, not eating, crying.

This was the story of my life! The nice, fun girl who was always friends with the boys, always falling in love and secretly craving their attention.

And by then I already had learnt that being good, feeling a lot, being sensitive and big-hearted was a bad thing. A weak and silly way to be. I had to be "strong, ambitious, rational" to be worthy, accepted, to fit in.

I was in darkness. I was living the "hell" part of my life.

Days later a friend came and long story short I got to the psychotherapist's office. Head down, eyes lost somewhere far away, ripped jeans and black nails, wearing a gun as a necklace. I remember I said, "I am here because of my relationships with men and my mother. I can't seem to make them work." I was soooo sad. And embarrassed. And confused. Angry, too.

One year later, I enrolled in the University of Psychology (my long lost passion since high school, forgotten between bottles of vodka and beer).

During the process of becoming a psychologist I had another meltdown. This time with tears of joy, overwhelmed in the best sense, gratitude...and THAT feeling: *home.*

This happened when I came across books about angels, angel cards, and energy work.

I felt like this was what I had been looking for my entire life and did not know it. Freedom to know, explore, have a personal relationship with Divinity. My WAY. Through my experience.

I avidly started on this path and went to every course you can think of, read every book, practiced meditation and used incense all day, channeled, sang mantras, the textbook spiritual person. I was discovering my gifts and in love with my new path. Quit my job. Trusted my SOUL, my JOY, and not long after I opened my OWN practice.

I was so proud, but also I soon noticed that *I was struggling* with my actual human life, my finances, my relationship, my body, my self-esteem.

And this question arose: "What does it mean to be a woman?"

Looking back, I can see now I was completely living on clouds drunken with light and angels, away from my body, my emotions, my wounds, my own shadows. I had no idea who I was. And I kept lying to myself that I was okay.

I had no idea what it meant to be a *Woman.* To live as a woman. To feel as a woman. I was just a child that had a big heart and discovered mantras, zen states of being which became my drug.

I needed to take my dose every day so that I would supposedly be love and light.

I became aware that I was behaving, speaking, doing, living like a MAN, that I was so into doing, chasing, so focused on the "next thing to do" to demonstrate I am worthy, I am valid. All the doing came from my smart mind so well-read and knowing sooo much information, so many concepts.

I did not know how to live in my body, in my emotions, in acceptance with myself, my wounds, my past. I was completely disconnected.

This is how I plunged into Shadow Work. Into my wounding. Into my Humanity.

After almost two years of deep inner work, I met my husband. THE MAN. The one I was desiring so much. I chose to trust he would appear at the right time and in the exact form it is best for me. I consecrated this man and future relationship to Divinity. And trusted. And he did appear. Unexpectedly. But with sooo much peace, quiet, flow.

I had never experienced anything like this before. But this story is for another book.

We got married after one year. I realised that alongside him I would learn how to be a *Woman*. What that meant. How that felt (and I still do).

I was still feeling like a 15-year-old having no idea how to love, how to behave, what to do or say....and I was 30. The journey to myself was just beginning.

A NEW PATH

The Path opened for me to descend into myself soon enough. I discovered womb awakening, sacred and conscious menstruation, womb practices, heart practices. I

41

was surprised by how deep I could go inside.

I discovered Mother Earth and her calling, and I started letting out the grief, the pain, the anger that I had accumulated for lifetimes, stuck in my body, in my cells.

I started the journey back into my body.

Back into Myself. Into my Humanity. And this is when I came across Mary Magdalene and Jesus, their story, their codes and initiations that I intimately received through visions, meditations, sacred places and sometimes just in simple day-to-day ways.

I discovered quietness, resting, slowing down, my rhythm, my cyclical nature. I was now really feeling everything I was denying for years, lifetimes.

I also discovered all of me that I had rejected, was ashamed of, thought unworthy and bad. And I still learn to accept all these me's, integrating all of my shadows and alchemizing them into real light.

The more you walk the dark valleys inside, the more you integrate what you run from and this way you hold the truest Light within, the truest Self.

I discovered my mission – to open pathways, to lead women back HOME Inside their hearts, wombs, bodies. Lead women to discover their magic, their beauty and power. To live as Whole Women, free, creating the Life to FIT *Them* and not having to fit in an old, limited, patriarchal culture. To know that it is okay to FEEL a lot and LEAD with your heart.

I discovered that I am a vessel between sky and earth, that I am all my emotions, my lost parts, my big dreams, my wisdom, my shadow and my light. And I am not broken. I am not less.

All I did my entire life was to forge my path struggling to be seen, accepted, to occupy my place in the world not as they want me to be but how I really am: weird, magic, idealistic, "too" good and open-hearted.

The other day I had this image of me in a black pit clawing with my nails to get out and I was not helped by anyone. I was flawed, broken, too weird for them. I was denied my essence, my purity.

Now I take steps to let all of me out there to be seen, and to stop fighting for freedom that is mine.

I keep learning that my vulnerability and my sensitivity are my strengths.

I discover God, Goddess in me and in the mundane life every single day through the purity of my heart. I bring sacredness to little everyday actions and situations. Because now I Feel Divinity everywhere. Not up there. Not in books or in buildings.

EMBODYING DIVINITY

I don't like to just talk about concepts like love, sacredness, and divinity, I WANT TO FEEL AND LIVE IT, embody it. To let earth, air, fire, water, ether, the moon and the sun flow and weave life through me, awaken and activate me further.

I choose to be HUMAN first. To bring all concepts and all the spiritual talk into practical things, into the body, into feeling and changing step by step from the inside. I value honesty, transparency and being real in a world built on false power, false values and pretending.

My beacon, my loving Divine Masculine I go to for healing and true, pure love is Jesus. Not the church one. The Man, the Avatar, the Message, the energy–the Love, the Call Back Home.

Now I know him differently, personally. Now he is my friend, my inspiration, my guide, my mentor. In a personal, deep way. I was afraid for so long to tell this story. I was afraid I would be judged and labeled because I am a sinner or a crazy woman...but now I choose to let the world know that Jesus, Mary Magdalene, God, Divinity are here, within, in my heart, leading me, inspiring me, opening me up. Every day.

So that you know you can also have this intimate, deep, heartfelt relationship with Him/Her. Your OWN relationship beyond any imposed rules.

As a bonus to this process, silence became vital for me. It is that space where I can talk to HIM or to HER and when my heart bursts open with sincere love, gratitude, bliss. Even if it is for an hour or a minute or a day sometimes.

As a woman I discovered that it is essential to STOP. To *feel* everything. To let yourself cry, mourn, get angry, to let yourself say NO and sit under the covers as long as you need. I learnt that I am complex and utterly MAGICAL, paradoxical and mysterious. And CHAOS that births life itself.

I learnt that the WAY BACK HOME is through the BODY and the HEART.

Through getting to slow down and creating space for you. So that you can see all the masks, the roles, the fears that drive you every day. Unmask them. See the TRUTH, that truth that it is hard to sit with. Because this is the only way BACK HOME TO WHO YOU ARE: the Creatrix of WORLDS, the Healer, the Priestess, the Lover, the QUEEN, the mother, the leader.

Reading all there is and going to every course to get your ZEN dose will not change anything if you do not slow down, practice the little practices, create the little moments to really, actually connect with yourself.

Being exhausted and always checking tasks is NOT a badge of honor. It keeps you away from your Soul, your true desires, your feelings, your Inner Sanctum. It keeps you disconnected.

My Invitation to You

Slow down. Become aware. Breathe deeply. Feel yourself.

Sit in your home or down on the earth and allow yourself this space and time just for you. Start nurturing yourself.

Start seeing all that you ran away from all your life.

Start naming your emotions and wounds.

Start holding yourself in a gentle embrace throughout this journey.
Start saying NO and having boundaries.

Start seeing, recognizing all the MASKS and ROLES you wear every day just to keep the appearance, to be liked–secretly, desperately longing for love, appreciation, and validation that you did not get as a child.

You need to accept to be HUMAN first, to go through your

45

own wounding, dark places, scary feelings and moments to FIND GOD, to find the true LIGHT and INTEGRATE it in a healthy long-lasting way. For life.

Once you really, sincerely come back inside in TRUTH your world will change. You will never go back to being miserable. Everything shifts. It did for me.

I do not want to live by some outside standard of who I should be to be happy, successful or accepted. I want to live by MY HEART being deep, serious, silly sometimes, too emotional or intense, firm and kind at the same time.

I understand now that I am a disruptor. I am a leader for a New way of Living. It is big, it is scary, it is magical, it is humbling and also takes a lot of courage. I can't pretend I am not all that and go back to "sleep."

The journey is a spiral. I get down in the dark sometimes as a WOMAN does...naturally...I allow my shame to die a little bit more, my guilt to drain out from my womb a little bit more, my arrogance to dim a little...

Every time I go into the DARK FERTILE INNER SOIL I let parts of me die, images that I held up for so long die .... I let old wounds leave my veins.

And I get up again with MORE REAL LIGHT integrated.

With MORE trust, peace, with my SPINE straighter, with a lot more confidence in the MAGIC that I AM and the WISDOM I came here to be and gift the world with.

Dear Woman, life is about experiencing, letting go of control and rekindling a real, intimate relationship with the Divine and with the Earth but primarily with you, your body, your heart, your truth.

Being Human IS divine. There is no separating human stuff from divine stuff. Life becomes sacred with every small ritual, intention, with you being present in your actions, choices.

Your Body is Sacred. Money is Sacred. Sex is Sacred. Eating, Dancing, and Working are Sacred.

Take a moment, take a breath. Long, deep. Put a hand on your heart/womb. WHAT is REAL now inside of you?

If it hurts it's ok, let it hurt.
If you feel like you want to scream, just do it.
If you just feel irritated or confused it's totally okay.
If you feel like crying, cry.

You are not weak. You are STRONG. Strong is feeling, experiencing, letting all come and flow through you. Strong is saying, "I feel hurt now, I feel sad now and that's fine. Or, "I need help now, I can't do this alone."

We were taught to not feel, to not show our true selves, to not expose ourselves as we would get hurt. We were taught to shut up and listen. To stay small because we do not matter and we need to conform.

A new World is being born now.

The WOMAN as a VESSEL for Divine Truth, wisdom, magic, love, gentleness is being revived in each of us.

We remember step by step, through accepting ourselves, liberating ourselves from cages, that we do MATTER and we are here with a MISSION beyond all others: to anchor and give birth to the New Child, the New Earth and repair the *big* wound of separation, disconnection.

Jeshua and Magdalen left their sacred love imprint on this Earth. We are now reactivating it through our own inner processes. Raw and honest processes. Through learning how to make the most of being a WOMAN, learning how to forgive the masculine and all its wounds, the feminine and all its wounds....and create inner union. Rediscover that we are gifted and that we thrive when we sing, dance, weep, hug, when we do rituals under the moonlight and talk to the underworlds, when we collect our blood and give it back to the Earth.

We thrive when we slow down, get out of our heads, start to tear down the walls around our hearts, when we see and let go of the conditioning, the abuse, the rejection, the humiliation we suffered...and still open our Hearts to Life. We still dare. We still dream.

But we do it all not from chasing or demonstrating, not from the mind motivated by competition or fear, but we do it from our HEARTS, from our INNER SANCTUM because we feel it soooo deep inside that it needs to be let out...naturally pouring into this world like the healing balm on a wound.

We do it slowly, giving all projects, dreams, ideas time to grow and get their essence from the DEEP inner truth.

That is why we need to take this step first, to slow down. To breathe. To start to feel again, start to really tell ourselves the truth. Recognize the wounds, the needs, the wants, the fears, the aspirations and all in between.

IT IS TIME FOR YOU TO LEAD AS A WHOLE WOMAN

48

LOVE is not a concept or a spiritual idea. Love is here now, in you when you listen to the wind, the bees, when you feel the sun or the water on your skin, when you taste fresh fruit or good chocolate, when you really look into the eyes of another and let tears come out naturally...tears of connection, recognition.

It is time for Love.

Not the word love, but feeling love. The love that is kind, gentle, firm and truthful even if it doesn't feel all fuzzy all the time.

Real love takes courage and a lot of responsibility.

It is time to let the old die and build a new World but based on our Hearts, our truest desires–and forget about competition, chasing, demonstrating, knowing it all but applying nothing.

It is time for you to UNlearn all you were taught and come back to your natural way of being in tune with the moon, the seasons, the earth, the womb, the SACREDNESS. To Live as a WHOLE WOMAN.

I call upon You, Magic Woman, Vessel of the Divine, rooted deep in the Darkness of the Earth! Rise and remember! Dare to Shine, Dare to Lead, Dare to tell the Truth!

You have millions of ancestors supporting you to Grow and to Remember. You are made of fire, water, earth, air and Magic. Honor that.

You are the Portal between Worlds and the Mother of all that Is.

I call upon you Sister! Rise and take the road that leads back HOME, in your Heart, your Womb, your Feelings, your Wisdom, your Body!

Once you walk the deep dark path with courage you will be born all over again, and again .... holding more precious LIGHT, TRUTH, LOVE, Wisdom. And this is how we bring forth a new paradigm. A new Humanity!

I honor you.
I bless you.
I leave the doors open for you....as I have already paved a path with sacred codes. It is time for you to remember. (MM)

ABOUT THE AUTHOR

ANCA LAVINIA

Anca Lavinia is an energetic and emotional alchemist, birther of sacred, transformative spaces for women and the founder of Authentic Feminine Online Community.

After 10 years on this path, she offers down-to-earth magical practices and rituals to integrate in your daily Life. Find your Center, awaken the Magician in you, the woman, the leader and bring forth her Gifts and soft power.

You will thrive following the guidance of your inner wisdom, embracing all of who you are without shame and inner separation. Feeling WHOLE and equipped to easily deal with all life's valleys and peaks, in harmony with your natural feminine energy and aligned with your Soul is the life you will manifest.

Having held hundreds of individual and group processes, ceremonies and journeys, Anca Lavinia has created "Whole

Woman"–the Journey that brings forth a Heart-Centered living instead of a mind-doing-agitated life. A life in union of your humanity and divinity.

Living in the Sacred Mountains of Romania with her beloved, they are now creating their paradise away from the busy city to live in communion with nature, surrounded by children, animals and like-hearted Souls.

If you are tired of living an agitated, exhausting, fear-led life, enroll now for the most transformative, tailored to your specific needs Journey you ever taken:

Work with me: www.ancalavinia.ro/en/workwithme
Facebook   page:
www.facebook.com/AutenticFeminincuAncaLavinia
Instagram: www.instagram.com/anca.lavinia
Youtube: www.youtube.com/AncaLavinia

FROM BETRAYAL TO BADASS BITCH

ANGELA ROSENOW

THE DOOR OPENED AS I CAME DOWN THE STAIRS, and I looked up to catch a glimpse of a friend's new boyfriend. Thirty-five years later I can still clearly remember what filtered through my mind… "Why did she have to meet him first?"

I had no way of knowing he would ultimately become my husband, my love, the father of my children. Or that he would cause me more pain and heartache than an innocent fifteen-year-old girl could possibly fathom.

THE BETRAYAL

I remember the day my marriage imploded like it was yesterday. Coming home to find him sitting on the front step, refusing to come inside. The resolve on his face tried to mask his obvious uncertainty. I didn't realize he had already moved out, had already made the colossal decision on our behalf, ripping our life to pieces.

What I thought would destroy me turned out to be a catalyst for the woman I was destined to become.

This isn't a story of divorce, it's a story of my revolution and rising from the ashes. Of turning my darkness into my superpower and reclaiming my inner badass bitch.

Something shattered in me that day that would remain buried for a decade. A betrayal so deep, a mourning for what would never be, a loss of trust that would haunt my life.

It's taken me fifteen years to fully emerge from that darkness where I let fear rule my thoughts and the deep inner sorrow control my mind.

I woke up the day after he left with conviction – I wasn't going to let this bring me down. I had spent a good portion of the night crying, releasing all the anger, fear, frustration, and doubt (or at least so I thought). The truth was, subconsciously I chose to bury them that night. I was too naïve to understand the harm this would cause years later. My focus was on survival. Of showing the world I've got this.

You see, as a child I had been taught to put on a brave face and keep going, never showing my pain.

As a child when I cried, I was told to stop, the more I cried the angrier my father would get. I was called a spoiled brat by a cousin when I was too excited to enjoy all the rides and games at the annual Stampede (having never been and being unaware of the expense). I craved attention, but not to be the center of it, I just wanted to be seen. To feel like I mattered.

A good portion of my childhood was spent disappearing into books and dreaming of how different things could be. Visualizing how I wish my family was. From the outside it looked like we had the perfect life, but behind the walls we were just existing together. The turmoil was never known by anyone but those inside.

This carried on into my adult life, living but not really living. Existing. Completely unaware of the masks I was wearing, the façade I was still trying to hold onto.

I think I saw my ex as my savior, my escape, the one that was going to make my dreams come true. He seemed like the perfect man, and I was in awe that he chose me. I couldn't see how worthy I was, how divine I was, how lucky HE was to be in my energy. The only thing that mattered was I was the chosen one and I wouldn't have to be alone anymore.

All I wanted was the perfect life I had envisioned.

And for a while it was – marriage and three beautiful babies, from the outside it looked like we were living the perfect life. But underneath the darkness was brewing in both of us. Two unhealed people desperately trying to be happy, avoiding the wounds that were festering deep inside.

I would have done anything for him, to make him happy, to hold on to our life. My deepest, darkest fear was of him leaving. Of not being good enough, not being able to make him happy, and of him finding someone worthier of him.

When the subject of an open marriage was brought up, all my insecurities screamed NO FUCKING WAY. He wanted new and different...I immediately thought "because I'm old and boring." Always the master manipulator, he enticed me with a man he knew I wouldn't say no to, and the unspoken threat of *get on board or else* hung between us.

Our first venture into the lifestyle was with friends of ours desiring to explore the life too. They were supposed to be a safe way to dip our toes in, with people we could trust. The fun was quickly extinguished when I discovered the lies, the going behind my back, the betrayal of our promise to each other. Two partners blindsided by the people they loved.

An end before it really began, but his desire for more hung between us.

And then, in the middle of trying to regroup after betrayal, a beautiful opportunity for a new adventure fell in our laps. A huge career advancement for him, a move to the US for our family, a fresh start.

But in truth, we never leave the baggage behind.

The Olympia years hold some of my favourite memories, but also some of my worst. Our little family thrived as we explored, made new friends, and reconnected with each other. And as we emerged from the cloud of betrayal, I agreed to give the open marriage another try, only this time it was on my terms, and no matter how hard it was at times, I could never regret the choice as it's part of the woman I have become, and this woman gives me chills.

THE BETRAYAL

As I blossomed, he faltered. As I explored my sexuality, he felt lost. As my confidence grew, his unworthiness did. Everything he had imagined about an open marriage came true for me and not for him. He believed it would "fix" him, boost his confidence, and heal the wounds that he refused to face. But instead, they cut deeper, and he lost his way.

56

When he was diagnosed with severe depression, medication wasn't enough and he spent nine months in weekly therapy, forced to face his wounds. I saw the light at the end of the tunnel for us, but he could not; fearing for his health, I had to make the hard decision to move our family back home to Canada to save him from the downward spiral he couldn't pull himself out of.

But the return home brought new challenges. We explored the open marriage to new extremes and our community grew. Weekly hot tub parties became the norm (much to our neighbours' unhappiness!). Friends were always coming over, and I thrived on having their energy around to break up the mundane of living with a deeply unhappy person.

I became involved with a man who would one day be my husband. On our first date he made me dinner and stayed up till seven am talking and discovering the deep connection between us. And as this grew, the flaws in my relationship became more obvious. Yet my loyalty was still to the man whose name I shared, and I almost ended it out of fear of losing my husband.

I was crying out for his attention, to rebuild what I could feel slipping away. He was supposed to be my forever and couldn't imagine a life without him. But my demands for time together went unmet again and again…

"I don't want to spend time with you, I just like knowing you are here," he would say. *Like, what?!?* The audacity of him to think those words, let alone vocalize them. My soul wept as I felt the fracture between us expand. But still I clung to the belief it was repairable.

And then everything changed forever.

When Lady D walked into his life (well really, I introduced them) it would lead to our undoing. He fell hard and fast, again. At first it felt cathartic to see him come alive again after the endless days of depression, and it allowed me to seek my own adventures without guilt. But it didn't last.

His obsession with her took over everything, he had finally found what he was searching for and she became his everything. Suddenly he was encouraging me to go to my lovers so he could be alone with her. I was no longer wanted in my own home as Lady D was uncomfortable sharing him with me, her jealousy not built for the poly lifestyle. And when she ended it, he came undone.

It took only five days for him to leave me. To walk away from over thirteen years of marriage and three kids to be with someone who would ultimately destroy him. Five days to destroy our family and all my dreams.

The next decade would become a blur as I held myself together for my children. I needed to be the mature parent, the one they could always count on, the one who put them first no matter what. I harboured huge guilt about not keeping our family intact, my inner child screaming that it was my fault and that all along I hadn't been good enough.

CHALLENGING MYSELF TO KEEP GOING EVEN WHEN IT FELT ICKY

I clung to the memory of what my life was. The anger of losing it, the sadness over our lost future, my identity no longer certain. I had put being his wife up on a pedestal and losing that title left me feeling naked and raw. Who was I without him?

He became the metric of my success. Proving to him, more

than to myself that I could make it. Or maybe it was all about showing him what he lost out on? It owned my thoughts no matter how hard I tried to move on.

One month after my divorce was finalized, my lover became my husband. We drove to Las Vegas and eloped in a cheesy little chapel on a hot August afternoon. He had been in my life for the last year of the open marriage and was everything my ex wasn't. Most importantly, he saw me... like, REALLY saw me.

My soul screamed, "Please see me, I'm still a badass woman who can do anything!"

He could see deep into my soul, and I felt parts of myself slowly rejuvenate. He would cook me romantic dinners, surprise me with rose petals and a hot bubble bath and made it his mission to make me feel good. It felt like a dream come true and, as we settled into our new life together, I buried the heartbreak and pain that was still festering in my soul.

Did we rush into marriage too fast? Absolutely! Once again, two unhealed people trying desperately to be happy.

THE PRESSURE VALVE COULDN'T HOLD

I craved being seen like never before, needed that external validation that I was still desirable, worthy, exciting, all the feelings the open marriage had bestowed on me. And at first, my husband fulfilled this need, but it was never enough. There was a fire burning inside me begging for fuel.

Our differences that excited us at first slowly became the issues we fought over. The romance was replaced by drunken nights with friends and an obsession with guns and the world ending. This was not what I signed up for! The eruption happened at a Christmas party followed by a silent drive home, angry words thrown, and his walking out the door.

This time instead of the shame of another marriage ending, I felt empowered. And by the time I heard from him two days later my response was, "Don't come home."

On my own I navigated a bad car accident, selling my house, buying a new one, and moving. I found my footing again. I looked fear in the eyes and said, "Not this time, fucker!" The badass bitch energy arose in me again, and I felt more alive than ever.

As the badass bitch took over, the sexual diva from my open marriage days awakened and came out to play...and play we did. For the first time in over twenty years, I was single, and I wasn't going to sit at home and wallow in my pain, fuck that – it was my time. Our sexual energy can bring the wounded parts of ourselves back to life, and I was awakening again.

More importantly, I began to truly see myself. Standing naked in front of a mirror and taking in every glorious cell of my body. I saw the goddess inside me and invited her to awaken. I connected with my younger self and gave her the love she needed so desperately. And as I healed myself, my eyes opened to what I had let go of in my marriages.

I had been so busy pointing out their flaws that I hadn't owned mine.

A phone call asking if he can come see our puppies led to us talking about our time apart and admitting we missed one another. And no matter how hard we tried to move on, we found our way back to one another. Two opposites that together just make sense, beauty and her beast. This time as true partners, forever entwined.

LOSING MY FOOTING AGAIN

But of course, every time one thinks she has life figured out, the universe throws her a curveball.

A legal battle with my first husband, though ultimately won, was the catalyst in the rapid decline of my health. The stress of this fight combined with pressure from my corporate job would be my undoing. Years of unexplained health issues seemed to worsen overnight, and I lost myself.

As the days progressed, I found myself struggling to finish each day, ending up in tears on the bathroom floor more times than I can count. Barely able to function yet refusing to give in. Until I pushed too far and ended up on medical leave. The days became a blur of binge-watching Netflix and building Lego, anything else would incite panic attacks. Overnight I went from being the caregiver to the cared for.

I had pushed myself too hard and for too long, my body couldn't keep up anymore. The universe bitch-slapped me with the message I had been trying to ignore...I needed to stop. Everything. And rest.

I wasn't ready to surrender, I didn't trust... I was so used to holding on so tight that I didn't know how to let go.

I went into my leave with the mindset that I would be back at work in a month. And when it turned into two, and then four, and then nine months...well, I was still fighting it the whole way. Is it any wonder I wasn't making any progress? And even when I was handed a severance package instead of returning to work, I was unaware of how tightly I was still hanging on.

Until one day it just clicked, I was the problem. I was blocking my progress out of fear, clinging to the old me like a security blanket. After a decade my job had become a part of my identity, and I no longer knew who I was without it.

But the message that came through was clear. It was time to surrender.

I thought surrender meant giving up, but in reality, it means letting go. That included listening to my body, setting boundaries, and learning to say no to what didn't feel in alignment with my journey. And most of all, forgiving myself for failing.

With the guidance of coaches and mentors, I shed the weight of this pain and began to release the deep breath I had been holding for far too long.

A NEW ERA

I didn't know how much my life would shift over the next few years as my divine feminine showed herself. As I explored holistic nutrition and my spirituality, my psychic abilities began to emerge, and I realized that I had always known I had the gift.

My story is still the same, yet the telling of it is through a different, uncorrupted lens. I now own my part in it and am no longer afraid to share my truth, to be audacious, to own all the exquisite parts of me.

Forgiveness. This was the missing piece all along.

I had to forgive my ex for betraying me, for leaving me, for not being the husband he promised to be, for abandoning his children, for being incapable of loving me the way I deserved. And I had to forgive myself for letting him have that power over me. For turning my back on who I was to make everyone else happy. For not loving myself as I desired to be loved.

I had to forgive my parents for not being who I needed them to be. And forgive the younger me for being too afraid to be big energy, for allowing myself to be silenced.

And I had to forgive my husband for not knowing how to be a better husband in the early days. He didn't have healthy role models to teach him how to be a man. And yet now, he is the strongest man I know with the biggest heart. He has truly stepped into the role of husband and stepfather with so much love.

With it came my unquenchable desire for more knowledge. I re-listened to old coaching calls I had never given myself 100% to, I was drawn to new mentors that rocked my world, and I dove into my own spirituality with absolute trust in myself and the universe.

This beautiful journey was the one I had chosen long before I arrived on this planet and, like most of us, I had forgotten. It has only been as I awakened the goddess inside me that I was able to see clearly why I had to go through the pain and heartbreak. This is part of the evolution of my soul.

I know who I am. I know what I am here for. I am meant for so much more than I had ever dreamed of. And I know my story needs to be told so that my sisters know it is safe to tell theirs.

I am here to guide women through their own awakenings,

their own journeys of death and rebirth. My mission is simple, I don't want a single woman to feel the way that I felt for the past two decades. It all became so clear. I am a healer, an oracle, an activator, a priestess, a witch, a divine goddess of light.

The women I attract into my life are all on similar paths...some ahead of me and some following. We are all connected through our sisterhood. No matter where you are on your journey, you are never alone.

So why am I sharing all of this with you?

I want you to see there is a light at the end of your tunnel, you CAN make it through, you ARE strong enough, and yes...whatever your heart's desire is, whatever you're dreaming of – it is meant for you. Reach for it and trust that the universe will hold you, my love.

Xo

Angela

ABOUT THE AUTHOR

ANGELA ROSENOW

Angela Rosenow is a Self Love Oracle, Feminine Power Activator, and the creator of her signature membership The Badass Bitch: Fearless Pussy Magic Uncensored.

Her journey through the darkness of divorce, health struggles, and working in the masculine corporate world unleashed a passion in her to never want another woman to feel the way she did.

She guides her clients to shed old paradigm beliefs, heal their childhood and sister wounds, and own their voices.

She empowers women to embrace their inner wild woman, rise into their integrated darkness and light, and rebirth themselves as she did.

A decade-long search to heal herself led to becoming a Holistic Nutritionist and discovering the connection between holistic health and energy work so she could be a body of hope for women who, like her, felt powerless in their own bodies.

Angela is married to her best friend, mom to three beautiful adult children and three fur babies in the serene Rocky Mountains of Calgary, Alberta.

For the feisty women ready to let their bad girl out to play... The Badass Bitch: Fearless Pussy Magic Uncensored is calling your name.

Click the links below if you dare:

My monthly membership:

The Badass Bitch: Fearless Pussy Magic *Uncensored
https://angelarosenow.com/the-badass-bitch-fearless-pussy-magic-uncensored

Ready to unleash your inner goddess? Through intimate 1:1 mentorship we will discover her:
https://angelarosenow.com/private-coaching

Website: https://angelarosenow.com/

Badass Women's Club free Facebook Group:
https://www.facebook.com/groups/angelarosenow

Email: hello@angelarosenow.com

I AM NOT THROWING AWAY MY SHOT:
BEING A FOUNDING MOTHER OF NEW EARTH

CARYN TERRES

"Hey yo, I'm just like my country
I'm young, scrappy, and hungry
And I am not throwing away my shot"
- "My Shot," *Hamilton the Musical*, written by Lin Manuel
Miranda, 2015

IT IS 2016 AND I AM HAPPILY CLEANING MY HOUSE in the suburbs of Salt Lake City when I hear these words for the first time: "I am not throwing away my shot," followed by an amazing group of very talented performers rapping about what sounds like The United States Revolutionary War.

I run to my phone to see what extraordinary musical this song must be from and read the words "*Hamilton –The Musical.*"

I IMMEDIATELY start the album at the beginning.

Within two minutes my entire body is filled with an electric fire as I hear the words in the opening song *Alexander Hamilton.*

"My name is Alexander Hamilton—and there's a million things I haven't done, but just you wait."

For the next two and a half hours, I am transported to 18th century America, listening to the life story of one of the Founding Fathers that never got a whole lot of attention in any of my history classes–except that he died in a duel, and his face is on the nickel.

That fiery electricity continued to grow and grow as I prepared for the birth of my daughter. Each time I listened to *Hamilton* I connected deeper back to the political activist I had always been.

I dreamed of the future that our Founding Fathers may have thought of. The future that Susan B. Anthony formed the Suffrage Movement for. The future that Dr. Martin Luther King, Jr. spoke of this during his famous "I Have a Dream*" speech.* The future I saw portrayed in Star Trek. A planet where we are all truly free. Where medical care is a given right to all. Where poverty, famine, and disease do not exist. Where there is true world peace, and we are connected with other sovereign beings from planets far away.

Where was that world? And what was I going to do to make sure my daughter and her brothers lived in it?

"Don't be shocked when your history books mention me, I will lay down my life if it sets us free, eventually you'll see my ascendancy." -Hamilton, "My Shot," *Hamilton*

Before I go into the events that would ultimately lead me to audaciously proclaim, for the past several years, that I will be

President of the United States; let's rewind to where my political career began.

Beginning in 2001, with the attack on the World Trade Center, the following major political movements/historical events of the early 2000s shaped who I am today as a divine feminine leader. Why for me paving the way for others to take seats in public office, lobby legislation, and create global movements for the Heaven on Earth paradigm isn't just the way I make a living, it is what I was *born to do*.

Like most of us, my eighth grade English teacher had us all write a letter recording the events of September 11, 2001. When I go back and read that letter, I can feel the fear in my 13-year-old self. The confusion, the true sense of terror, and a new felt sense of patriotism that I had never before experienced.

Within a couple of months, I would find myself singing a whole other tune, as I watched in absolute horror as the word "patriot" slowly began to mean giving up our freedom for security or suffering the pain of ostracization.

By April 2002, I was on the other side of the aisle from most of my classmates. While they stood proudly wearing t-shirts from Abercrombie & Fitch sporting the American Flag, I would be inside the principal's office, fighting for my right to choose NOT to participate in the Pledge of Allegiance each morning.

Over those months, I had felt this fire beginning to burn inside me as I listened to President George W. Bush's assertions that Saddam Hussein's weapons programs were still actively building weapons and that large stockpiles of weapons of mass destruction (WMDs) were hidden in Iraq.

So, in retaliation, President Bush declared a "War on Terror."

It was all fucking bullshit! How do you declare war on a concept?

Even at 13, I knew my Constitution.

The US Constitution grants Congress the sole power to declare war. The last formal Congressional declaration was World War II; meaning EVERY SINGLE WAR since 1941 has been illegal and unconstitutional, including this so-called "War on Terror."

Here would begin my lifetime commitment to defending the US Constitution to the fullest extent of my abilities.

"This is not a moment, it's a movement, where are the hungriest brothers with something to prove went .... are we a nation of states? What's the state of our nation?"
                                    –Hamilton, "My Shot," *Hamilton*

Luckily, while most of the teenagers in my city were battling with the patriarchal control of the Mormon Church, I was a part of a Unitarian Universalist congregation. Within those four walls, I was learning an entirely different way of life.

The Unitarian Universalist Association is based on very basic principles:

-The inherent worth and dignity of every person.
-Justice equity and compassion in human relations.
-Acceptance of one another and encouragement to individual spiritual growth.
-A free and responsible search for truth and meaning.

70

-The right to the democratic process.
-A goal of a world community with peace, liberty, and justice for all.
-Respect for the interdependent web of life of which we are all apart.

These are the base morals that I have clung to since I was eight years old. Where I had first learned the names Abigail Adams, Susan B. Anthony, Frances Harper, and Elizabeth Cady Stanton–all Unitarians or Universalists of their times, and women disrupting the system to give a voice to the beliefs in their hearts.

To add to this, the minister of my church at this time was a transgendered male (married to another trans male). My Sunday school teacher was a lesbian. While most of my classmates were only dealing with their hormones and which boy/girl they should date or how they could "stay in the closet," I was confronted with the entire alphabet soup of options and COMPLETELY SUPPORTED in whatever choice I may make.

When I was 15 years old, I came out as bisexual. Today I proudly stand as a pansexual androgynous BE-ing who practices ethical-slutdom (polyamory) and whose pronouns are she/her.

I have stood on the steps of my State Capitol in protest of the inhumane way our government treats those in the LGBTQIA+ community on so many occasions I cannot even recount them all. But I know in my heart that a world where Love truly is Love is a world worth nurturing.

I took part in many different activism movements with my UU congregation, but one story comes to the forefront of my mind. A fellow teenage congregant was arrested for "being

71

black at the wrong place, at the wrong time."

It was 2003. Although it had been 40 years since the famous "I Have a Dream" speech was given by Dr. King, it would be another 10 years before anyone ever uttered the words "Black Lives Matter."

As a young, middle-class, white female that Sunday morning, I felt the fire that had started a few years prior RAGE inside me like nothing I had ever experienced before.

A few weeks later I would find myself speaking in front of my State Capitol building–for the first time, but not the last. I spoke on the topic of Racial Injustice. I will never forget that day, it was that moment that I decided one day I would be a politician, so I could create laws that protected our citizens, instead of enslaving them.

But I was too alone in this fight. Sure, there were those in Model United Nations or the Junior States of America or the occasional friend who would want to go to the latest popular rally. But nothing stuck. No one was willing to sit there and be a cohort in my plan for world domination, as a means of giving the planet back to the people.

As a result, the fire slowly began to fizzle out as I finished high school. Battling a constant slew of anxiety, depression, suicidal thoughts, and a general dread that because I didn't fit in anywhere, I belonged nowhere.

That was until The Great Recession began. My oldest son, Leonardo, was born the literal day the Lehman Brothers filed bankruptcy in 2008. I remember holding a one-day-old baby in absolute shock as I watched for the second time in my life people jumping out of buildings in New York City. Over the next few months, I rallied the cries of my other millennial cohorts. I even have photos of me, my son's dad, and a five-month-old Leo protesting with Occupy Wall Street.

President Barack Obama came with his own set of issues. But I was so lost in my world of being a young mom, and new wife, living with my parents during a recession, with only a massage degree, an autoimmune diagnosis, and on most days barely hanging on to my will to live that I had no will to fight for any greater cause.

Yes, I would become outraged at the continued abuse of Black Americans after the murder of Trayvon Martin. Yes, I was torn as school shootings continued to plague the nation. Yes, I was livid that after 10 years our troops were still in the Middle East, and our veterans were not being taken care of after their tours of duty.

But like most of us, life fucking happens, and eventually, the constant stream of death and mayhem became too much; so I unplugged from the news and attempted to plug into the life of a suburban housewife.

Utah State's legalization of medical cannabis would be the next time I truly felt that deep-burning desire to be politically active again. Cannabis had been the only thing I had found to help with the constant pain of fibromyalgia, and I had been using it illegally for nearly a decade.

During this time, I became heavily political again, serving as Secretary of the Libertarian Party of Utah and helping with Gary Johnson's presidential campaign.

Then in November 2016 the most unbelievable thing I could ever imagine occurred–Donald J. Trump would be elected the 45th President of the United States of America.

I could feel Alexander Hamilton rolling in his grave as I saw the election results.

"God help and forgive me
I wanna build something that's gonna outlive me...
If you stand for nothing then what'll you fall for?"
–Hamilton, "The Room Where It Happens," *Hamilton*

It was in the wake of President Trump's election that the final blow to my facade that I was born to do anything except BE the President would happen; the #metoo movement would sweep the planet and this time I had my daughter to protect.

Let's bring it back to 2017.

At this point, *Hamilton* was a staple in my house. My oldest could rap the hardest part, sung by LaFayette in "Guns and Ships'" and my middle son had learned how to spell his name from hearing "I am the A-L-E-X-A-N-D-E-R we are meant to be..." as I blasted "My Shot" over and over in the car.

That summer Xena, my Warrior Princess, my daughter came earthside during an unplanned unassisted home birth, and her umbilical cord had snapped as she entered the earth plane. She didn't take one single breath with any energetic cables attached to her. One thing I knew for sure during those few months postpartum–this country, no this planet, was simply not fucking good enough for her.

While I had gotten my degree in Political Science and had been involved in many grassroots movements, that fire that once blazed inside me had now dwindled to a tiny pile of embers.

With Xenavieve's birth, it had been stoked. And this time, I knew it wasn't ever going out again.

"Raise a glass to Freedom something they can never take away" –Laurens, "The Story of Tonight," *Hamilton*

Each one of those events, or any of the events that have happened in the first two decades of the 21st century, has had an impact on your psyche in one way or another. At one moment in time, even if just for a moment, you had a SPARK, a FIRE that was lit under your ass that said, "Fuck this! No! Not Happening! I cannot believe the world is this fucked up! What do we need to do to change it? And NOW!!!!"

Okay, you got it? Are you remembering that inner activist that existed at one point or another?

It was in the Fall of 2017 that I read my first personal development book *Get Your Sh*t Together* by Sarah Knight. From there I fell down the proverbial rabbit hole of author after author, all teaching various forms of the Law of Attraction, Mindfulness Practices, and New Age Prophecies of a Golden Era.

Then I read *Braving the Wilderness* by Brene Brown. While I had never heard of her before, she TOOK MY BREATH AWAY! Within the first couple of chapters, I was inextricably connected with this woman from across the country, whom I had never met, but who GOT ME!

If you haven't read the book, seriously, go do so. It was written during the aftermath of President Trump's election; when the USA was more divided than ever before and anyone who didn't fit the white, cisgender, straight male paradigm was terrified of what might happen next.

The entire book is based on this idea of "true belonging", from an old interview with Bill Moyers and Maya Angelou. I am including a bit of that interview below because this is what relit that fire under my ass and broke the OFF SWITCH to who I am and continue to BE as I move forward in my soul's Earth mission as a global gladiator.

BILL MOYERS: "…You've really been a mobile, nomadic, free person. What price have you paid for that freedom?

MAYA ANGELOU: Well, at some point—you only are free when you realize you belong no place—you belong every place—no place at all. The price is high. The reward is great….

BILL MOYERS: Do you belong anywhere?

MAYA ANGELOU: I haven't yet.

BILL MOYERS: Do you belong to anyone?

MAYA ANGELOU: More and more. I mean, I belong to myself. I'm very proud of that. I am very concerned about how I look at Maya. I like Maya very much. I like the humor and the courage very much. And—when I find myself acting in a way that isn't, that doesn't please me, then I have to deal with that…."

BILL MOYERS JOURNAL: ORIGINAL SERIES
A Conversation with Maya Angelou
November 21, 1973

CRACK!!
BANG!!!
CRASH!!!

Everything I thought I knew about who I was, what I was, and how I served, was imploded in a myriad of fireworks, gunpowder, and dragon fire, with the music of *Hamilton* ringing in the background.

"I've got to be in the room where it happens"
–Burr, "The Room Where It Happens," *Hamilton*

Right there, in 2017, in the living room of the house that I had lived in since I was 3 ½ years old, I DECIDED that one day, I would be President of the United States. I mean, come on… Donald Trump had set an entirely new precedent for what it took to become President, right?

If he could do it, I could too!

Now I know what you're thinking…Caryn, didn't you just say it was the autumn after you had given birth to your third kid?

Yup!!

I was 29, a middle-class, white, suburban housewife and mom of three. I had no fucking clue how or when, but I knew with every fiber of my body, mind, and soul that the reason I was put on this planet was to become the U.S. President and help lead the world into a Golden Age of Miracles.

The plan is pretty simple:

Create and nurture a world where every human being has access to healthy food, clean water, safe shelter, open-source education, and all medicines from East to West.

I'm here to turn the world upside down & see leaders who gave a fuck about their citizens be BRAVE & BOLD & BRIGHT!

I am sick and tired of the same old politicians.

I am sick and tired of the constituents who act like they don't matter. Who pretend that they don't have a voice, so they don't vote, they don't lobby, and they don't even know their rights.

I am sick and tired of who is continuing to stay asleep during this time in Earth Game by committing to their role as a Non-Player Computer (NPC)

But more than either of those groups, I cannot believe the response of my fellow alchemists, healers, and purpose-driven feminine entrepreneurs when I start talking politics.

Cue the eye-rolls, please.

Seriously, most of my colleagues would rather go on and on about how politics aren't their thing. They harp that anyone who gets into government ends up corrupt. They are more interested in building a luxury brand and creating massive wealth to live off-grid than in understanding their basic civic rights and duties.

These are the same women who make INSANE amounts of money ($30,000+ monthly average) as badass CEOs led by a soul mission, or God's call, to make the planet better for future generations.

Yet, they don't give a flying fuck about who is sheriff, how a law is passed, or the mid-term elections- because "they don't do politics".

This mindset is why it is so important we stop throwing away our shots at creating MORE IMPACT FASTER by getting out of our niches and getting into office NOW!

"When you got skin in the game, you stay in the game
But you don't get a win unless you play in the game
Oh, you get love for it
You get hate for it
But you get nothing if you
Wait for it, wait for it....!"
–Hamilton, "The Room Where It Happens," *Hamilton*

The fact that you have made it to the end of this chapter tells me that you are cut from a different cloth.

Something in these pages resonated within the fathomless cavern of your core. There is a fire that is burning from deep within your belly, climbing to the back of your throat.

The Dragon's Fire.
The Sacred Rage.
An unconditional love that is wise, resolute, devout, and also wrathful.

The systems built on fear cannot exist on a planet where LOVE reigns supreme.

This chapter has been my offering as the beginning activation of your heart womb, the super chakra that is created when you combine all the chakras of your CORE and truly embody the BE-ing you were born to Be.

A Golden Dragon Teacher. A Heart Womb Leader. A Global Gladiator. A Founding Mother of New Earth.

Someone whose name will be written in the history books. Someone who, for better or worse, will be the ultimate reason why a child in the future decides they are not throwing away their shot to Be Something Great!

"We are outgunned, outmanned, outnumbered, out planned, we're gonna need to take an all-out stand!"
–Washington, "Right Hand Man," *Hamilton*

It doesn't matter to me whether you are fighting for the rights of BIPOC, LGBTQIA+, women, the homeless, veterans, climate change, universal healthcare, poverty, education–or any of the other hundreds of minority groups that don't have a voice in public office that deserve to be heard with the same honor and respect as the lobbyists from Pfizer, Monsanto, and American Airlines receive.

Just. Take. A. Stand.

Be fucking loud!

Take the risk that your bottom line may be affected when you put that lawn sign out, but God has got your back.

Take the chance to find out exactly how the government works in your country, from the smallest level to the largest–and see how the pieces fit together.

Make the choice–that you are far better off being bold and brave and taking a front-line position in this Revolution of Love than sitting on the sidelines, just waiting for it all to play out.

You are not an NPC.
You are not asleep.

You are dreaming with your eyes *wide fucking open.*
You know Heaven on Earth is here, *right fucking now!*

It's time to *lean the fuck into* the edges of what is possible.
It's time to hold steady to the vision of Unity

Consciousness.

Because we are the ones we have been waiting for, we shall wait no longer!

Watch out world, here we come–and we are not throwing away our shots!

ABOUT THE AUTHOR

CARYN TERRES

Caryn Terres, The Dragon Doula, is a multi-dimensional entrepreneur, political activist, and internationally known author/speaker.

She is the Creatrix of The Freedom Frequency Shift, which attunes you to the true energetic frequency of your Soul Mission, allowing you to activate your heart womb chakra so you can be the superconscious leader you were born to be.

Caryn is the Founder & CEO of Heartwomb Leadership, a global company empowering high-achieving purpose-driven entrepreneurs, healers, and innovators to run for office & lobby legislature that will truly change the world. Her revolutionary ways of bridging the metaphysical with the geopolitical allow you to BE the Dragon and take positions in government so you can RADIATE that Freedom Frequency & enact real global change, NOW!

When she isn't on stage, with clients, or working on her 2032

Presidential Campaign; Caryn enjoys hiking the Wasatch Front with her dog Shadow, playing with her kids, relaxing with friends and being art as often as possible by modeling, singing, and dancing. Caryn lives as a newly single mom of 3 in Salt Lake City, Utah

If you have been LIT UP by anything in this chapter then make sure you check out her Global Gladiators 13-Month Group Mastermind. Use coupon code MAGDALENE for 10% off registration.

Global Gladiators: www.heartwombleadership.com/GG
Follow on Instagram: www.instagram.com/carynterres
Follow on Facebook: www.facebook.com/thedragondoula

THE JOURNEY OF INNER SPIRITUAL AUTHORITY

CASSANDRA FINCH

WHEN WE INCARNATE ON THIS PLANET, WE ARE born into a family its own energetic resonance, which we learn many things from, whether it's healthy or not. These are our first "authority figures" in our life, where they are meant to guide us step by step into our potential of who we can be, based on what our inspiration is.

Unfortunately, what has happened with many, is there are projections of who you should be, how you should act–who you trust, who you don't, and how situations are dealt with according to these projections. Up until recently, though, there weren't many resources available, which has given me much compassion for certain situations I endured at a young age.

Although it was a lesson to trust myself that my parents tried to incorporate, many situations left me in this place of fear of who do I trust? The "programming" of certain people close to our family and certain family members was of keeping silent through trauma. Not only did this come from pride, but it also came from fear of how others would perceive you–in the family, as well as where you stood in the Spiritual hierarchy of the church.

Growing up, we were introduced to different forms of Christianity. My parents were not overly religious, but other members of the family were. Even at a young age, I was questioning many things I was taught and gripped by fear of being taught about Revelations at age six.

It was at this young age that I started to identify with a spiritual authority outside of myself, whether it was considered family, a priest, a group leader, or God itself. I felt that I had to live a life of atonement, I had to work extra hard to be rewarded by a God who looked at every second of my life to achieve any sort of enlightenment, any potential to get into a "heaven," despite in my teenage years rebelling against the escapism teachings that I had learned. I always knew that this felt outdated, as an indigo child who didn't fit into the normalized structures that seemed to lack efficiency and harmony for me.

I always knew that I was different from many others around me–I learned to keep many things to myself, such as seeing spirits and different kinds of elemental energies, seeing people's spirits before they passed, dreaming of certain natural disasters…because this was still under the mid 90's stigma of being labeled as "crazy" or needing professional help. I bought into that thought form as well, I thought there was something wrong with me up until my early 20s. All I wanted was to shut this part of me off. I prayed, I begged with the Universe to take it from me, but it stayed.

QUESTIONING EXTERNAL AUTHORITY AND ENMESHMENT

Many events occurred that made me question authority. As I mentioned, in childhood I was very trusting because I trust those that looked like my family trusted. I also trusted certain members of the family because you're taught that family is everything. Usually, this meant you looked the other way, forgave anything, or risked the drama that could cause a major falling out. It was enmeshment. I learned quickly through traumatic experiences with a group leader at our church, who was almost ten years older than me, that many would choose to believe him. It was then that I saw that image and acceptance in the church were far more important to them than acknowledging what was really going on. I now realize that they gave up their own sense of free will unconsciously, following the lead of others, fearing their own exile and perceived connection to community.

It led me to believe there was something deeply wrong with me, that it was my fault for the experience that happened, and even more so with similar experiences that continued to happen as I got older. I froze, I let them happen over and over while telling no one. My body, my voice, nothing felt like my own, I was completely disconnected from the person I wanted to be.

The theme for me was to allow abuse toward me, to stay silent and protect the abusers—which did not end until my early adulthood.

When I had intuitive feelings about certain people, I felt as if I didn't have a voice. This didn't come from anything my parents had taught or said to me – it was because it was those closest to us, and I was afraid I would either not be believed or that I would get in trouble or get others into trouble. As a child, I just wanted everything to be okay and to be in harmony. This does not create harmony, it creates self-abandonment, especially on a soul level.

I began to deeply mistrust my gut feelings, my instincts, and experienced the consequence of that. There was a time when we lived in a townhouse complex – there was a resident manager who took care of the property and dealt with complaints. One day, he asked me and a couple of other young kids to go get ice cream with him. He told us our parents said it was okay. I knew my parents would never give consent without letting me know, but again, another authority figure abusing his power and using manipulation. The moment I got in the van, and he began to drive away, I knew I had made the wrong decision. My heart sank, my stomach felt sick, my inner authority was screaming to get out of the van…but I was frozen. Luckily the van was found, and we were taken back home. I don't remember all the details of that day; all I knew was that I was very lucky to have returned back   home.

CONDITIONING FROM AUTHORITY FIGURES

I had tried to shut off my intuitive side many times–I was told it was a connection to Satan, and it wasn't serving me to see Spirits, to see death, I couldn't do anything with that information–I often wondered why me? Why get these glimpses, why get these gut feelings when I couldn't explain with "logical reasons" why? Somewhere along the lines, I learned that I needed to justify my "no," that no *wasn't* good enough.

Believing these things were normal was much easier than accepting this was completely wrong and my intuition was right. It wasn't until recent years that I realized many situations were me being groomed by a trusted person, who would put me in online chatrooms to talk to older people at the age of twelve. The same person who intentionally guilted me about how much food costs and withheld food to the point that when I was staying there, I would sneak peanut butter and stale crackers in the middle of the night because I was so hungry. I was sixteen when I finally said I will have nothing to do with that person ever again, I will never stay or spend time with them, to much criticism and backlash because many didn't understand why. Although now, I know how I was treated because of how I felt, it was not okay, and it's most definitely how I would not treat my family. I would honor their decisions, I would never force any interaction, but make it known they are respected and loved.

Even though I did what was right for me, I remained silent as to why, still protecting the person who was being physically and emotionally abusive.

When I finally spoke up about that situation recently, I was shocked to find out that food was given to the person to take care of me during the day or two I was there; food that was never given to me, and I realized this was another repeating pattern of abuse for that person. I found out how deep that ran and how they treated others. I was one of the first to end that connection; it took almost ten years, but many followed suit.

I felt as if many of the experiences, and so many I do not have the space to write about, were a deep initiation into the underworld, as well as the polarity of the world; being prepared to meet the depths of darkness within myself and ending cycles so I could create a new life. As an adult, I had to realize and see the illusion of not having a choice for what it was–just a façade for control. I have compassion toward myself, as a child, for not knowing any different than the information   I   had   in   front   of   me.

88

SELF-SABOTAGE TURNED INTO SELF-AWARENESS

When I turned sixteen was when I wanted the freedom to make my own choices. I was pushing more boundaries. I was experiencing more with my intuition (although I could not 'control' it at will). I began a series of bad choices, ranging from drinking to sneaking out of friends' houses with them to going to parties where everyone was on several drugs and drinking. I was lucky that nothing bad ever happened during those times–I would stay sober and drive my friends, but many times these parties were out of control.

I had become the person who pushed everyone away, who didn't care if I hurt someone, I would justify my actions. It was a defense mechanism to not allow myself to continue to be hurt, but it turns out, doing just that was hurting me more. I was hiding myself, hiding my potential, destroying friendships, being self-destructive because the world seemed so unfair. I felt the polarity inside of me–I wanted to break free and accept all parts of myself, but I also wanted to continue hiding and numbing myself.

By this time, I had already had intuitive feelings around death, I had intuitive feelings around car accidents we were in, as well as a stalker, but it all seemed too much for me to hold. Not only was I people-pleasing, protecting abusers, drinking, partying, working almost full time while attending high school, but I was bitter. I was angry. My body was inflamed. These were the precursors to my fibromyalgia and chronic fatigue. What I was looking for was a way to block out the messages and then block out the physical pain I was experiencing.

ARCHANGEL MICHAEL AND MARY MAGDALENE AS GUIDES

I had my first experience with Archangel Michael and Mary Magdalene when I was 21. The first message I ever received from Mary was: "To walk a life of healing, you must understand the depths of pain, not just to meet others there, but to be the space in which they can rise into the possibilities available to them. To hold compassion and love for all walks of life, to be present, but to also do your own inner work."

This message solidified I wanted to be an energy healer, as I was endlessly searching for what I was meant for. I made the decision that it had to involve my intuition, and I wanted to make an impact to guide others into their own healing. When you're bright-eyed, bushy-tailed, armored with so much experience at a young age, you think you can change the world instantaneously. I had to dive into a dark night of the soul, realize my negative patterns and my own toxic traits. I had to become self-aware and responsible for my part, learned by the abusive situations, because this is how I coped to survive, in order to be in service to others.

Archangel Michael was the first Angel to really show me the power of intention. It was late at night, I was trying to sleep, but there were multiple entities in my room, all black, surrounding me in bed. A spark of light came through me. Up until now, I didn't believe much in angels, I disconnected from any religious words, but I called out to Michael to protect me and clear the room of these souls.

Within seconds, there was a bright flash, and he stood almost as high as my ceiling, as an energy of white light and gold. The entities were gone in that flash. My heart expanded, and I felt tears run down my face as I felt the power of asking for support. My boyfriend at the time witnessed it all. He wasn't spiritual or religious and this whole scenario shook him to the core.

The message I received from Archangel Michael during that time was that our intention, coupled with action, is far more powerful and—in time, knowing that I'm already in control of my energy and am divinely protected—is more than enough to clear these energies out.

He has given me many messages over the years, one a few years back at Lake Louise. He reminded me that the path I am on only needs to make sense to me. Not everyone chooses or wants to work in the shadow realms, and that is okay. I do not need to explain that world to them, I can just assist and guide souls as well as people into healing, transitions, and it is a gift of mine to bridge the physical world, death and the etheric world.

THE PAST LIFE REGRESSION THAT CHANGED MY PERSPECTIVE

I experienced my first past life regression in my early 20s. I knew I had to break any contract with certain people in my life that stemmed from outside this life. Although I had glimpses of Mary, and small interactions up until now, she was my guide through remembering that life.

The first thing I smelled was humidity and dirt, as I opened my eyes in that life. I felt the cold stone, the dampness on my skin, in what looked like an underground cell.

I felt sorrow and anger in my chest, as I lay on the floor. Mary sat beside me, and she told me that living a life of Divinity hasn't been easy, it has been traumatic and has come with certain consequences, but those who continue to act from Love and their inner Divinity are what has been changing the world. It has seemed like a slow process, but it has created more safety for the Golden Age to come.

She smiled, her eyes pierced through my agony, and she asked me if I would like to see what happened in this lifetime. I eagerly said yes, as she took my hand. She told me to not be afraid, no one could hurt me or see me. "We are just observing."

I saw myself in a nun uniform, with two other Sisters walking down the hall, whispering about the day's events. We discussed how we would be trying to get the babies out of what looked like a church. Any time someone would walk by we would be silent, keeping our distance from each other, trying not to arouse suspicion.

The other two sisters kept on their way as "I" carried water and cloth, then I opened a door to a room full of women, dimly lit, on small beds that had some sort of cloth and what looked like hay. These women were in labor, scared, and asking me if they were going to be okay, if the babies would be okay. It seemed as if I had a telepathic connection to this incarnation, as I watched from the corner with Mary, I just knew that the babies would be taken and killed, or forced into adoption, while the mothers would be told they had died of infection.

I took the supplies to the other women assisting the births, and as I left the room, I saw a man with a wheelbarrow that had infants who had passed. Our eyes met, and immediately I knew the connection in this lifetime as my stalker.

I watched myself send a silent signal with a hand gesture to another Sister, who was walking down the hall, and that's when everything began.

I watched myself check in all the rooms filled with women about to give birth. Every so often, when it was safe, they shuffled out infants from the mothers who didn't make it through childbirth or the days to come of them not making it through infection, to protect the babies from an almost certain death. Mothers were being separated from their children, forced to give them up while others profited, or dying of infections.

Other times, they shuffled the mothers and babies out to other homes who would have them and take care of them, as well as women who were being abused.

The small group of Sisters wanted them to have a better life, to protect the mothers and children, so they helped many escape.

Eventually, the trifecta was found out from the man tending to the graves who then gave up the Sisters for more power, and the Sisters were punished for going against their orders and vows. My incarnation ended up in that cell where I first landed into that regression, and I watched as I resisted any attempt to ask for forgiveness.

My heart knew that what was happening wasn't fair or just. We did what we could in that lifetime to make a difference, no matter how small. We swore an oath to protect and do what was right, even at the cost of our lives.

Even if it was rogue leaders who tried to instill their authority, it was that life that I saw that we all have free will, despite any illusion of intimidation, fear, trauma, or manipulation tactics. It is up to us to stand in the Truth of who we are, to assert ourselves and remove ourselves from situations that are not right.

I watched the execution of the three, and as I came back to this life, I had a greater understanding and compassion of how unsafe the world once was, how many were unable to truly take a stand for their Truth for fear of death. To be spiritually powerful was to risk everything. How being victimized can traumatize you into believing you are not powerful, you are always in danger, and not having the tools to regulate will lead to more suffering from the fallout.

MY OWN HEALING AND BECOMING A SOUL GUIDE

Shortly after this past-life insight with Mary, I continued my studies in energy healing and made the choice to move to another city to begin my career.

A pivotal moment was the first week of my new career at a clinic. It was sunny, I saw a sundog for the first time, my ears rang with a high-pitched frequency, and I heard, "Welcome to the New Earth." This was 2012, I didn't understand, but ten years later, I see the quantum leap in consciousness all around. We have truly awakened a time where for so many, there is the choice to be powerful in all ways, to create a life through love and make the impact of guiding others to the same possibilities.

I had to meet myself in the shadows, I had to reclaim all parts of my soul, I had to regain control of my own energy and call back my power. I knew I had to stop acting from a place of fear, helplessness, and trauma – it was a long road of healing for which 10 years after the start, I only began to understand the level of positive choice available. I then began to fully break out of my shell and allow myself to be seen.

This is also an ever-evolving process, it will never be fully done, as we continuously change and meet ourselves in our new versions.

Too often in this life, we are taught to give up our freedom, our energy, our time, to an authority outside of ourselves – to not trust ourselves because someone else knows the way, or we have no control over our fate. It is not often we are taught to connect with our own divinity within – our connection to God-source is THROUGH our own heart space, not another person. There is no middleman to our own Divine Connection.

You are your authority. Whether they're family, bosses, spiritual authorities, mentors, coaches will show you, what healthy leaders will show you is the way to walk on your own. How you can connect with your innermost self, to take action congruent with YOU while also having a community of support and love. Notice the spaces where interdependence is celebrated, your potential and your actions most aligned for you and those who will lovingly call you forward when you go against yourself.

Do not give up authenticity and surrender your responsibility for creating a life congruent to you because of fear or false promises. This is your permission slip to fully embody your own inner trust, inner authority, your inner architect. You have the power to take positive action and create a new future. All it takes is courage to act from your inner Truth.

ABOUT THE AUTHOR

CASSANDRA FINCH

Cassandra Finch is the CEO/Founder of the Phoenix Mystery School for Soul Guidance and Transformational Healing. She is the Creatrix of "Ignite Your Soul Gifts & Embody Your Soul Wisdom" program that connects you to your powerful abilities and who you are at the core, so you can truly see yourself and your potential while transforming the past into wisdom. She will guide you into self-trust, confidence, and clarity so you can create a positive impact as you evolve and make decisions in congruence to who you are at soul level. She stands for empowerment, self-responsibility, compassion and grace.

Cassandra is a BodyTalk Practitioner/Instructor, a Reiki Master Instructor and Soul Realignment Practitioner. Cassandra lives on beautiful Vancouver Island, Canada, with her young daughter, where they enjoy being active in nature.

Find her online: www.phoenixmysteryschool.ca and www.facebook.com/cassandra.finch28

Book a consult: https://phoenixmysteryschool.as.me/

WE'RE ALL FULL OF SHIT. OWN IT.

CATHY HO

I JUST WANT TO REMIND YOU THAT YOU ARE FULL of shit. I am full of shit, we're all full of shit. I wish I had a whole book for my shit, because one chapter just ain't enough for everything I've done and been through. You really can't make this shit up.

Did you get triggered by the first paragraph? If so, this was written specifically for you. Why? Because I was, still am at times when I'm not conscious, a person that could get triggered about a lot of things. That sounds like fun to be around, doesn't it? With that volatile, unconscious attitude, people around me naturally started to peel away–who wants to be around a ticking time bomb? Not realizing that this was my own shit, having people fall away from me found me in a victim mentality. It was everyone else's fault that we had a falling out. Knowing what I know now, I recognize that triggers are signs that we have unresolved trauma—they invite us to go inward. So I did that—went inward after many mistakes, or I mean lessons.

Looking back, I was triggered a lot of the time because I had a lot of healing to do. I was full of shit. Shit from my childhood and upbringing; shit from getting bullied as a child; shit from ex-boyfriends that cheated on me and physically abused me. Because of my inner wounds, I attracted people into my life and they showed me just how unhealed I was. Yeah, I was that person. They say hindsight is 20/20 though. Everything that happens in our lives, if we're conscious enough to recognize it, are moments for us to reflect on what needs to be changed—healed—so that we can become our best selves. This isn't a sob story or playing victim or minimizing how I've hurt people, this is my story.

If you get too triggered by what I wrote, that shit's on you, not me. If this is the case, I politely invite you to dig within yourself, because how ridiculous does this sound? You don't know me and what I wrote pissed you off. You feel me? If you got triggered, good. I'm glad it did, because we are mirrors for each other to shine light on the shit we need to work on. So for now, you're welcome.

How my shit began: trigger warning—I was molested when I was three years old by another young boy. The adult I told at the time did nothing about it. I knew and they knew it was wrong, but nothing came of it. Fear and confusion clouded my young brain. Why was this kid not getting in trouble? I can remember the whole thing as if it were yesterday; From the smell of the room to the feel of carpet beneath my little feet, and all the clutter that surrounded the room where we were playing hide and seek. That was my first of many traumatic experiences as a child.

Who did I become after this experience? I became that kid that never felt good or worthy enough—the one who felt unheard and unseen, which led me to earning a master's degree in people pleasing. Do you ever feel this way? If you do, it's a good opportunity to reflect back on your life and what happened to you as a child. Do you recall any moments that stick out for you? Oftentimes, you'll see where some of your adult shit comes from. What we experience as children, good or bad, can shape who we are as adults. Most of us don't know or recognize this because it's not taught in schools or in our homes—at least not in my home. My parents weren't taught this, so how could they teach me? My parents gave us everything they could to give us a better life. With eight mouths to feed, clothe and house, survival mode was the only mode we knew growing up. I mostly remember chaos, so as I became an adult, I attracted a lot of that same chaos and drama into my life. These are the lessons I had to learn to get to where I am today. It meant getting bullied in school, and to cope with that pain, I became the funny girl, because no one really ever picks on the funny girl. I ended up becoming the bully too and became quite good at it. I wanted to make sure that getting bullied would never happen again. The ridicule and pain were unbearable. I attracted boys and friendships into my life that kept me feeling unworthy. When I felt these kinds of emotions, I would chase for their love and attention to fill that void inside. Constantly looking for external validation. Super cringeworthy when I think about it now, but I also can't really say I'd change a single thing. It taught me so much that I'm able to share openly with you today.

It all changed five years ago, after becoming a mother. I became angrier and angrier. It was getting more and more noticeable to those around me. I was becoming a total bitch. One day, my sister pulled me aside after one of my anger spouts and planted the seed for me to look into postpartum depression and anxiety. I heard her loud and clear. I became more curious about the topic. I looked long and hard at myself and slowly I started to see things. I started to own my shit a little bit at a time.

That was the beginning of my healing journey—sniffing out all my shit and flushing it. Fast forward five years and I'm still working on it. This healing business is never-ending. There are always areas in our lives where we can improve. I'm becoming a person who speaks her truth, hoping to inspire all of you to do the same. Keep in mind to be kind to yourself and those around you, because my truth may not be true for you—and your truth isn't the truth for me. It's about owning our own shit to the point where someone else's perspective doesn't phase you—it invites healthy disagreement and discussion.

We all go through shit and for most of us, society didn't teach us how to deal with it. Our parents didn't have the tools to teach us either. So, before you continue projecting and dumping your shit on those around you—like I did—I'm here to remind you to go inward and sniff that shit out. It's not fair to cut those who never made you bleed. I love that saying. I don't remember who wrote it, but it's a good one. Look, we're all full of shit to think we're not full of shit. Everyone has shit to deal with. The difference is, who is ready to go inward with it? That's the big question. Most people are too afraid to look inward, because we're too egotistical to think there's anything wrong with us. I said what I said.

Trauma…it can be a big, scary word for a lot of people and it looks different for everyone, and some don't even recognize they've experienced it. This is why there are a lot of unhealed children impersonating adults. I was one of them and still am sometimes. My mother left my twin and me on our first day of school, not knowing when she would be back for us after being with her every single day for the first five years of our life. Needless to say, I cried for the whole day

101

and continued until we got home. Another time, I froze and couldn't sing at my first Christmas concert in kindergarten and was told when I got home how stupid I looked-I was taught to take this type of criticism as tough love. A way for me to do better next time. I know this will resonate with a lot of you, tough love, but that requires a whole new chapter. I can go on and on with these traumatizing events—there are too many to count. However, trauma is trauma. This shit gets stored in our bodies, so when we get triggered, it's usually these old stored emotions that are coming up. We must not turn a blind eye to them and start releasing them. Trauma has a different meaning and feeling for each of us and when I spoke about these stories openly, people would say things like, "I didn't have those things happen to me". So, this makes it difficult for some of us to even recognize that we have any trauma at all. How are we supposed to own our shit if we can't recognize we even have it?

I used to be so ashamed of my past and all that I've gone through because of family conditioning. I grew up in a traditional Asian household where we had to maintain perfection. We could never let anyone see the dysfunctions of our family dynamics. The image we needed to uphold was we're perfect, happy kids and we're all going to university to become dentists, doctors and lawyers. I grew up in a place where expectations were high and nothing was ever good enough. This was my parents' way of trying to motivate us to do better for ourselves—negative reinforcement. Because of this conditioning, I became a parent pleaser, and parent pleasers become people pleasers. Don't get me wrong, there were benefits to this negative programming. I became that overachiever–which is great—but the adverse effect of this was that I got addicted to external validation. If I did x/y/z, I would be loved and validated, instead of being loved as I am. Isn't that sad? Because I am Asian, I can say that this happens a lot in our community. We were taught to be ashamed of things that didn't go along with societal norms. I can play victim all day long, and I did for a very long time but I'm not here to do that. It doesn't serve me or the people around me well to be a victim. Are you playing the victim?

Today, I can accept it all, because I can recognize and acknowledge my shit. Well, not all of it—I'm human and still make mistakes. I'm a work in progress—cliché as it is, I would not be who I am today if all that shit never happened. I can see why all of it happened to me and I'm lucky enough to have found the strength to share it openly so that you, too, can do the same.

Here's something to think about: Isn't it ridiculous to get pissed off at another driver on the road that you don't even know? What if that person cut you off because they were rushing to the hospital to see their dying loved one for the last time? Or to get mad at the grocery clerk because they bagged your groceries in a way that you wouldn't have? Or get mad at your spouse because they left their socks beside the hamper instead of putting them directly inside? There are bigger problems in the world than these trivial things, yet, we allow them to bother us so much because we are carrying shit that we may not be aware of and they trigger these responses in us. I feel lucky now for these triggers, because it was a way to show much shit I needed to work on.

Can we see how ridiculous it is when we slow down and take a hard look at our triggers? and how upset we allow ourselves to get over them? I'm pretty sure when our spouse is putting their socks beside the hamper, they're not thinking, "I'm going to put my socks beside the hamper because I know it will piss Cathy off". Sounds ridiculous, doesn't it? When we can re-evaluate what bothers us, we can acknowledge the useless shit we carry around with us. We can see that there is a lot of subconscious programming

103

running our lives behind the scenes, making us ready to pounce at any moment. That sounds like a super fun person to be around. I love walking on eggshells around those types of people.

Healing is a never-ending journey. I can see why it is difficult for people to look inward and do the healing because this path can be a very lonely one. This whole "owning our truth" business is not fucking easy by any means. However, it's so freeing when we consciously make the decision to work on it. What's even more freeing is when we can own our shit and not give a fuck what people think. That is taking our power back, which brings me to my next point: self-love. We are taught to be ashamed for the things we do or experience that go against society's norms—whatever the fuck those are. We are not our temporary emotions. We are not depressed—we go through periods of depression. We are not insecure—we go through insecurities because of our experiences. We are not angry people—emotions don't define who we are. Triggers are unresolved trigger responses that we were taught when we were kids. If you're telling yourself that you have no triggers after considering all this, you're probably full of shit.

Whatever we suffer from needs to be addressed once and for all. The first step is acknowledgement and then being open to getting the help you need. The rest will flow as long as you keep putting in the work. I didn't do this all on my own, of course, I had people in my corner who have gone through their own shit, which gave them the strength and wisdom to call out my bullshit. There's that saying that it takes a village and I strongly agree, because it doesn't just take a village to raise our children—it takes a village to keep the adults in check, so that we don't pass on our shit to our children. When we openly face our shit, we can receive authentic, genuine advice so that we can break the cycles that get subconsciously passed on from generation to generation.

It wasn't until October 2020, when my body started to shut down and I was bedridden for three weeks, that I took my healing more seriously. I knew in my heart it was a combination of not taking care of myself and constantly living in chaos and survival mode, constantly trying to figure out why I was feeling so shitty, emotionally and physically. Communication with my spouse at the time was most of the time argumentative because I spoke with a harsh tone of voice that was hard for him to receive. I was trying the best I knew how to hold it all together while trying to navigate being a mom and working hard to not be like my parents. The juggling act of life is real and no one talks about it. Everyone on social media made parenting look so perfect. I kept comparing my life with what I saw. I gave and gave until I had nothing left for myself. I completely lost who I was. Mothers—we are so used to giving to others from an empty cup.

As shitty as I felt at the time, this was the moment I knew I had to make a hard change. I opened my heart and prayed, "Please guide me. I surrender because I don't know what else to do. I need help." I started to see posts from a friend that resonated with me on Instagram. So, I reached out to her. That was when I was introduced to inner child work. From there it led me to understanding my childhood traumas, then to a bunch of different healers and healing modalities. I'm fortunate that I became more open-minded, because I'm in a way better place today. I'm proud to say that I didn't need to count on the typical pharmaceuticals—a whole other rabbit hole to go down.

I took a holistic approach to my healing, which included sound therapy, hypnotherapy, inner child and trauma work, meditation, yoga, exercise, heavy metal detoxes—you name it, I did it all. I was in desperation mode. One thing just led to the next and here I am today.

At the end of the day, everyone just wants to feel heard, acknowledged, and most importantly understood. I could go on and on, but the point is: own your shit because it stinks just as bad as anybodys. Owning it is a form of self-love. It's worth it to get brave and just flush it once and for all.

Don't know how to get started? The first step is to get radically curious about why you do the things you do. Here are some questions you can ask yourself:

Am I getting triggered?
What triggers me?
Why am I triggered?
Where do my triggers come from?
What trauma did I experience as a child?
How did I feel in my family dynamics (was I the rescuer, the parent, etc.), school, with friends? Is there a common theme/dynamic in these areas of my life?
What do I like, not like, and why?
What is inner child work?
What motivates me to do the things I do?
How well do I take feedback?

Own your story because the most important relationship you'll ever have is the relationship you have with yourself. Get honest, get vulnerable, go inward and get out of your comfort zone. Get brave and get the help you need. We don't know it all and we shouldn't pretend we do. That's a load of shit. Dig into your shit so you can be seen, understood and loved just as you are. Become the shit by owning it! It's much better than sitting around feeling like a piece of shit, don't you think?

ABOUT THE AUTHOR

CATHY HO

That Cathy Ho was born in Calgary, Alberta, and raised in Vancouver, British Columbia. She shares her experiences of childhood trauma and learning self-love through the trials of motherhood. She believes in building community by creating events and safe spaces for people to share their personal stories.

After her own experience with postpartum depression and anxiety, she saw the need to normalize these conversations around mental health and trauma. She educates and empowers mothers to come back to themselves through sharing her own story, group coaching, comedy, movement and sound healing. She adds lighthearted irreverence to the standard approaches to taboo subjects.

In her personal life, she's a budding integrative health and wellness professional and an aspiring comedic motivational speaker. She currently resides in Nicaragua with her son, where she offers Ayurvedic therapies, sound healing, creates community events, and works on her immaculate tan.

If you are a mother or planning to be one and you're ready to step into your shit, join her private Facebook group or email her to get into her free upcoming workshop where you can openly and safely shoot the shit with other women.

https://www.facebook.com/groups/464165312274165/?ref=share_group_link

E: thatcathyho@gmail.com

Instagram for some funny and motivational content
https://www.instagram.com/thatcathyho/

REGENERATE YOUR HEALTH

CHELSEA BOISSONNEAULT

I AM NOT A DOCTOR

I AM NOT CLAIMING TO BE A DOCTOR, SO IF YOU BELIEVE that doctors know best, please disregard what I am talking about. But if you are open to the idea that what I am writing about it here could be true, I encourage you to keep reading. I truly believe this is one of the most important topics to understand as western society is deeply controlled by the belief in the unfounded germ theory. Not only that but what they tell us is health is actually unhealthy, as they are trying to keep us sick. Sick people are much more controllable especially when you are also selling the "cure." Once you come to understand that health is from within you can't be controlled with fear which is particularly helpful during a pandemic.

HEALTH IS WEALTH

Without health other forms of wealth can't be fully enjoyed as much as they could be if you had great health. Contrary to what many believe, health cannot be bought with money. Yes, you can afford food that is healthier, but you can also grow your own food which is less expensive in the end and your best option for food. Yes, you can pay for services that help you heal yourself from disease, but you can also do this without money. Yes, you can afford to work less which often leads to less stress which brings about less disease, but you can also find work that brings you more joy. I'm not saying any of this is easy, I'm saying it is possible without money without denying that money can help in most cases.

What does it mean to regenerate your health? It means to bring the mind, body and spirit to their optimal state. We are not all born equal in terms of any of these aspects of our lives. Some are born into a family that has a lot of trauma, and those individuals have more work to do in their lifetime than those who were born into a family with less trauma. Don't get me wrong, I realize that we ALL have trauma and anyone who thinks they haven't experienced any trauma does not understand what trauma is. Some individuals are born with health issues that may be not resolvable and others are born perfectly healthy. Some individuals are born into families that are in tune with their spirituality and pass that on to their children. That being said, overcoming trauma can lead to huge breakthroughs and that growth is so healing. But it is not a race, we aren't meant to compare ourselves to others. In fact, this way of thinking can keep someone from regenerating their health to the best of their ability. We should encourage each other to all go at our own pace. Not only that but healing is not linear, it's a path of hills and valleys, loops, bumps. It is often two steps forward and one step back. The step back is often for one to be able to get a better picture if they are open to it and allow them to see their path more clearly and adjust.

Our souls in this lifetime chose this life path, this is

important to remember. With this realization one can blame others less for their misfortunes and understand that the setbacks are meant to happen so they can learn and grow from them. Nobody has a perfect life, and your soul would only sign you up for what you can handle in this lifetime.

THE PARADOX OF HEALTH

Often when someone thinks of the word health they associate it with physical health, which is part of your spectrum of health indeed. Mental health is something as a society that we are aware of these days but often one sees poor mental health as something that is uncommon. Spiritual health is something that many do not think is a factor to our overall well-being, but it is becoming talked about more and more in many parts of the world. Health is a combination of our physical, mental and spiritual aspects of our lives. Sometimes we will focus more so on one of these areas than others, and that is ok. Nobody is perfect, and striving to be perfect in all areas won't work. We need to have compassion for ourselves and our healing path. Perfectionism is actually something that works against us and does not allow us to take that step back and then see the path forward. If one resists the step back and has thoughts that are negative in nature about themselves, then they are not allowing the healing to follow its true path and slow it down.

Let's begin with physical health since this is often the commonly thought of aspect of our overall health. I will start with explaining that most of what western medicine says about health is incorrect and actually totally upside down.

Western medicine treats symptoms most of the time. Have a cough? Take medicine. Have a fever? Medicine. Have a rash? Medicine. They definitely stop the symptoms as they are meant to do, which leaves one feeling better so they think they are cured. But what caused the symptoms to appear? What are the symptoms doing and what is their purpose? Unfortunately, these are not questions that many ask. The doctor will hand you a prescription for some medicine and send you on your way to stop the symptoms and the patient feels like the doctor helped. Part of the issue is we as a society are taught not to question authority, and doctors of western medicine in their white coats are seen as god-like. They went to school forever, how can we even question them when we did not go to medical school? They must know more about our bodies in a 15-minute appointment than we do, they are the experts. This god-like complex has set us up for failure. When you are not allowed to question and try to understand the "why" behind your health then you are stuck at their mercy.

Once you start to question and keep going further back in time to when western medicine was truly created, you will see what happened and why. But that takes a lot of time to research, one has to be very curious and be able to look past all the social conditioning to understand why we have been told to treat symptoms and not the actual cause of disease. The truth is, that the reasons are really dark and hard to imagine that we have all been lied to for a long time. Why would they try to convince humanity that what is healthy is actually not? What do they have to gain by keeping us sick and not understanding the true meaning of health? The answers to these questions are not ones many are ready to face.

GERM THEORY FALSEHOOD

When germ theory was born, this is when western medicine was also born, so it is imperative that one understands the basics of what germ theory is, as well as what terrain theory is, which is the theory that was pushed to the side to posit

112

germ theory on us. To summarize germ theory: it was created by Louis Pasteur who was hired to figure out why wine was going bad. Louis found that the wine that was going bad had a high bacteria count, and he found a solution which was to boil the wine to kill off the bacteria. Now you know why the term of boiling milk (rendering it no longer healthy) is called Pasteurization. The bacteria was there for a reason, it was breaking down the cells that were dying, part of a natural process, it was not something the wine "caught" that needed a solution. Then the Rockefellers hired Louis to study bacteria, and he came to the conclusion that the bacteria came into the wine and was the cause of the problem. How did he prove this? He didn't. Then somehow Louis also came to the conclusion that viruses exist and that both bacteria and viruses were the cause of disease. Funny enough, Antoine Bechamp–who found that germ theory was actually false and touted terrain theory–said the opposite was true, that viruses and bacteria were not the cause of disease and that an unhealthy terrain was the cause of disease. Also, funny enough, Pasteur admitted on his deathbed that Bechamp was actually correct!

The Rockefellers then took Louis Pasteur's false science, called it the germ theory, and made it the basis for all western medicine. This was very worthwhile for the Rockefellers who owned 90% of the oil business and drugs are made with oil. They then paid Abraham Flexner to write the Flexner Report, which then they used to teach all doctors in medical schools across western societies, gifting money to the schools at the same time (bribery). It was taught as fact without proof, and if a doctor questioned the narrative they were in trouble, still to this day. Funny enough the same people who "invented" the germ theory also have a huge hand in the pharmaceutical world. You know, the one that has all the solutions to all the diseases caused by "germs"...? Weird!

113

So, if viruses are the apparent reason for many diseases then there must be proof of their existence and proof they cause disease right? But not a single virus has ever been truly isolated, not a one. Nor has any ever been proven to cause a disease; I mean, how could it if we haven't been able to isolate them. Yes, you can find many scientific articles that claim virus X, Y, or Z has been isolated but if you actually look at their methods you will see that in fact the virus has not been isolated. What they do is take dying tissue, they inject it with antibiotics (anti-life is the translation) and many other toxins. They see the tissue dying and say "must be due to a virus!" Seriously... it was already dying then they poisoned it. Also, they witness exosomes appear and call those the virus cells. But where did they come from if not from inside the cell? Thin air? Exosomes are one of the cleaners of the body, they bud out from cells when needed to take the garbage out of the body. They are the same size, shape and appearance when compared to the apparent virus cells.

Think of maggots... where do they come from? Put meat in a plastic bag, then open it up a week later and you'll find maggots. How did they get in? They didn't, they came out from inside the meat to do its job which is to break down the dying tissue, similar to exosomes. The human body is brilliant, and western medicine treats it like it needs pharmaceuticals to survive. If we didn't have vaccines, we'd all be dead right? That's so far from the truth and they know it, that is why they've never to date done a study of the vaccinated vs the unvaccinated. Others have done this study and the results are clear, the unvaccinated are healthier. People try to pressure you to inject yourself and your children and often use fear tactics. But once you know viruses haven't been proven to exist or cause any actual disease the choice is clear.

Along with the idea that nobody is allowed to question the narrative or you will appear to be a fool, is the loss of one's intuition when it comes to many things including your own body. You have to have someone to trust for answers, and if you aren't in touch with your intuition then you will have to place your trust on an external source, which is often doctors. Those that have lost their intuition over time (partially due to fluoride) often get offended by anyone going against the narrative and it's terrifying to them to not be able to trust the experts as they don't trust themselves.

MENTAL HEALTH

Mental health is another component of our overall health that we cannot ignore. Mental health issues and diseases are often caused in part (or in full) by the body being overloaded with toxins. If a client of mine has any mental health issues such as depression, for example, I would have them physically detoxify first for a while, and in every case their mental health would improve significantly due to the physical removal of toxicity in the body. Depression wouldn't be a symptom typically due to simply the presence of toxins in the body, but the toxins amplify a mental health issue. The reason this person became depressed needs to be addressed and the reason is always an unhealed trauma, and often one we have either chosen not to deal with or more often do not realize (yet) that we have a trauma or that what we think is normal is actually a trauma. Once the trauma is realized, then the healing can begin along with the physical healing to treat the mental health issue.

SPIRITUAL HEALTH

There is also spiritual health, which often gets lumped in with mental health, but it has its own merits and is not the same. Mental health deals with unhealed trauma as does spiritual health, but spiritual health also takes into consideration how one views themselves and humanity in the giant picture of things as well. Oneness is an important aspect of this, if we see ourselves as separate from others or nature, then we experience more fear and division and less love. To have good spiritual health one has to have begun the path to healing their traumas and be open to receiving and giving love. Meditation is a tool for this—it is not the be-all and end-all, but it is where I recommend one starts and continues to work on their spiritual health.

WHAT REALLY IS DISEASE?

What would you say if I told you there is only one single disease of humanity? That every symptom of every disease is just a different symptom of that disease? This disease is toxemia which means the body is overburdened by toxins. We like to categorize the symptoms of detoxing, we group them and name them so we feel we have control over them. But we mess it up, as we then "treat" the so-called disease by treating the symptoms. All the symptoms are trying to do is rid the body of toxins, so by stopping this process the toxins stay inside the body and create more dis-ease including cancer. Notice that diseases can't seem to find a cure no matter how many billions of dollars have gone into research? Or those "cures" that work are vilified and made to seem crazy? The ones that "cure" the disease are the ones that simply help the person detoxify and therefore remove the physical cause.

The presence of toxins in our world today is rampant, from GMO foods, pesticides, herbicides, food colouring in foods, chemtrails in the sky, toxic cleaning products, fake foods, our cosmetics, shampoos, creams…and the list goes on. Not to mention the toxic thoughts put out in the media these days. And the very worst offender is the pHARMaceuticals including vaccines, all of which are pure poison.

Our bodies are either at-ease or in dis-ease state, and that depends on the level of toxicity your body is holding onto. Our brilliant bodies are great at letting us know when they are overburdened. We tend to be tired, which is our body telling us to rest, or we lose our appetite and sense of taste and/or smell, which is our body telling us to fast. Our bodies are brilliant!

CANCER – ANOTHER LIE?

Did you know that once upon a time they tried to convince humanity that cancer was contagious? Fortunately for humanity that did not work, so they could not develop a vaccine for it either, as most would have taken that one for sure since cancer is so feared. So, what is cancer? According to my research, what I understand it to be is once again the opposite of what we are told it is. We are told that yes, it's brought on in part by lifestyle choices and habits, but we are also told that in large part it is genetic and therefore out of our control to a degree. But the biggest misconception is that cancer cells are the enemy and we have to kill the cancer and fight a war–which most of the time western medicine says needs to be done with chemotherapy, radiation and/or surgery.

But what if cancer is actually the cure? I believe that cancer is there to protect us. If we are too toxic, we die, but cancer cells appear and trap the toxins inside them. Of course, if we end up with too many cancer cells then we can have growths of clusters of them that can negatively affect our health and even kill us by suffocating an organ or area of the body. But if we choose to view cancer as the cure, we can take the route of detoxifying to remove the cancer and it works! We do not need billions of dollars a year to research a cure for cancer, it

117

is not that complicated, but they do not want you to know this and they censor anyone who says otherwise. The cancer treatment business is even more lucrative than the vaccine business, and yet another way for them to control us and keep us sick sadly enough.

As you detoxify the body the cancer cells will shrink and even disappear. With this view of cancer, you can see why the western medicine ways to treat cancer do not work. Chemotherapy is simply poisoning the body further; it kills cancer cells but also poisons the entire body and the rate of recovery is very low. Radiation is similar. Surgically removing the cancer cells can be effective if they are able to get all the cancer cells, and the person changes their lifestyle and heals themselves so the reason they appeared in the first place is no longer a factor. When they perform surgery though they poison the body somewhat as well with antibiotics and other pharmaceuticals. Not to mention surgery is a trauma to the body so one must heal the effects of this as well. But it is very difficult to get all the cancer cells intact out of the body, most often they cut some of them open which releases toxins into the body, toxins the cancer cells were trapping to help. This is part of the reason that cancer spreads after this type of treatment all too often.

SUPPLEMENTS – ARE THEY BETTER FOR US THAN MEDICINE?

Contrary to most natural healers, I do not believe that anybody needs to take pills or potions, regardless if they are made from foods or natural ingredients. Most of the time when these are prescribed, they are done so to treat a symptom, which again traps the toxins in the body. Sometimes they are prescribed to support detoxification, which is the right idea, but from my research anything that isn't a natural food we are meant to eat is seen to the body as

118

a toxin and treated as such. Why the need to take healthy food and make it in a pill form, apart from making money off the consumer? The argument often is that the food today has much less nutritional value than it used to. That may be so, but to take a food and make it into a powder to put it in a pill or shake isn't the answer–the food now is so processed it's no longer good for you anyhow and now toxic to the body as it can't be processed properly. The answer to lower nutrition in our foods is to fix the soil, since modern-day mono-crop agriculture is one of the reasons our soils are degrading (permaculture on the other hand is the answer).

END THE FEAR

I encourage you to dive deeper into all that I have talked about here, because the result of feeling in control of your health is so very worth it. Remove the fear of germs and contagion and you will be able to focus on healing and living life to its fullest potential instead of focusing on made-up problems. Grow your own food if you can, meditate, move your body and work on healing your traumas. It may sound like a lot to do, but one step at a time...remember, it is not a race.

ABOUT THE AUTHOR

CHELSEA BOISSONNEAULT

Chelsea is a Regenerative Health Guide where she helps people naturally heal through nutrition, exercise, mindfulness and shamanism. Chelsea helps her Regenerative Health Guide clients take a deep dive into all areas in their lives that affect their overall health such as nutrition, fitness, mindfulness, trauma and more.

Chelsea brings together her expertise in all these areas having been a personal trainer and nutrition consultant for over 15 years. Chelsea also brings her knowledge of mindfulness to her clients which she previously shared with her meditation studio called The Peace Room.

Shamanism training entered Chelsea's life in 2020, learning many tools to help clients heal trauma. This training was a continuation of Chelsea's ongoing learning and research into how to heal and become as healthy as possible.

Chelsea is 42 years old and was born in Canada. She now resides in Nicaragua since May 2021 with her daughter. Chelsea spends her free time riding horses and learning how to homestead.

Chelsea is offering a 15-minute consult for $25 to see if her services are the right fit for you, her program that looks at all areas of your health including nutrition, fitness, mindfulness and includes an energy healing session.

LINKS
Book a Consult https://calendly.com/chelseaboiss
Instagram https://www.instagram.com/chelsboiss/
Facebook https://www.facebook.com/cboissonneault

WOMB WEALTH WISDOM RECLAMATION

COLLEEN M COYNE

DIS•TILL, AND KNOW THAT YOU ARE A GOD/DESS!

It is time for us to RISE, to till our inner soil, to tell a new story for ourselves and humanity, and anchor Heaven on Earth *now* through our embodiment of the codes of Mary Magdalene and our own inner sacred union.

She has woven her golden thread throughout my many lifetimes in such exquisite ways. Every day I am learning more about how to weave and embody her codes of fierce unconditional love, our Erotic Innocence, Womb Magic, and Divine Sacred Union withIN, as an Ascended Master.

Her story has been hidden, fragmented, distorted, and misconstrued for far too long. Her story is *our story*.

Her codes have directed me to align with my deepest Truth, reclaim my power, walking in love and *as love* and to end the separation and suffering timelines once and for all. To restore harmony on this planet by restoring harmony within myself and integrating and loving all aspects of myself that have ever felt shame, guilt or doubt, especially with regard to my past. Our innate divine sexual nature and our innate worthiness to not just survive, but to truly THRIVE, is the fullest embodiment of sovereignty, abundance and freedom as our birthrights.

We are all being called forth to pay homage, deep honor, respect and reverence for all those who have walked the Magdalene path before us. To our sisters who have been persecuted, raped, oppressed, murdered, mistreated, and abused for following their truth and innate divine blueprint. To all those who have kept the Feminine Mysteries alive. To feed the sacred flame of Truth through transmitting and imprinting our unique story codes in our lifetime into this 3D matrix — every single one of our voices *matter* here!

As Clarissa Pinkola Estés so wisely shares in her famous book *Women Who Run with the Wolves*, "If a story is seed, then we are its soil" (p. 387). When our unique golden story thread is woven into the tapestry, we leave sacred breadcrumbs for the generations to come. Our legacy.

We are here to free the ghosts and "skeletons in the closet" of our past, both individually and collectively, and integrate, heal, and unveil our Soul Truth. In doing so, we break free from the spell that the Collective has been under and re•member our innate power to *choose* sovereignty, love, abundance, joy and freedom in each Now Moment.

Magdalene is literally BEing resurrected through each and every one of us as we choose to embody her consciousness in mind, body and soul in each Now Moment…how we walk with love guiding our way.

Though it's vulnerable sharing the following stories, Magdalene has summoned me. May these codes be the rocket fuel and inspiration for you to free your voice and reclaim your womb wisdom and aligned wealth to live a life of choice and freedom—Heal One, Heal All!

REMEMBERING OUR EROTIC INNOCENCE

For six years prior to the global shift in March of 2020, I was an exotic dancer. I had been called to this after working in social services for five years and having my big awakening in 2012 amidst my Saturn Return, knowing that the world was rapidly changing, and my soul needed to spread her wings on a mission! I sold almost everything I owned and flew on a one-way ticket to Mexico for the end of the Mayan calendar, traveling much of 2013 and reconnecting with soul family during that time.

When 2014 rolled around, I was tired from traveling and knew I needed to ground and integrate from so much movement during the past year. I knew a few amazing sisters that worked in the industry whom I deeply respected, so I decided to put my own inner judgments aside and follow my curiosity.

Although I felt super awkward when I started, there was a deep part of me that felt liberated walking on that stage and being witnessed in my radiance without any stories or judgments attached to who I was. My playful spirit felt safe to be fully expressed and shine as bright as I desired, unlike in the outside world. Naked and free.

What began as an innocent exploration of awakening and embracing my full confidence, sacred sensuality and sexuality and power while making good money within a couple of years morphed into the dark underworld of heavy alcohol and drug abuse, unworthiness, lack of confidence, depression, self-imprisonment and so much more.

124

What happened? Where did I go?

By the end, I felt like a shell. Literally stripped of my sense of self.

During that time, I did experience really beautiful healing moments, but I also witnessed and experienced a lot of imbalanced manipulation and toxic energy as well. It was full spectrum!

I was warned. I entered in with the idea that I would bring light to this dark industry and contribute to transforming it to empower both men and women in embodying healthy sensuality and sexuality with a playful spirit. And I know that in many ways I did.

No matter how strong and powerful a woman you are entering into that space and with the best of intentions—after a time, it gets to you.

I know deep down that my soul *chose* to dive into these depths so I could serve in a greater capacity of understanding and compassion during this Great Collective Purge and Spiritual Awakening.

I now know that I do not have to *choose* timelines of suffering any longer to learn these lessons.

These past few years, I've been gathering back all the parts of myself that fragmented throughout the years. Acknowledging deep roots of trauma. Not only mine, but what was passed down through my ancestral lineage and our collective programming.

What we've done is placed our sexuality in a box, in the dark, dingy, shadowy corners of society…aka strip clubs—

which are essentially a playground for our repressed sensual and sexual traumas. Mostly run by men. With so much manipulation and control going both ways between men and women, both waving the carrot on the stick to persuade the other to obtain what they wanted. All of this perpetuates our root wound of separation.

Albeit it's not ALL like that—there are a lot of these trauma wounds playing out though, and it needs to be acknowledged and cleared.

This is the same distorted energy that plays out in the modeling industry, in Hollywood, the music industry—in almost *all* performance industries. This is the same distorted energy that has literally poisoned the world, our sacred waters, and the minds of the majority of the people on our precious planet.

We simply cannot continue to work under the umbrella and within the structures that were built under the exploitation, manipulation, and oppression of women's innate sexual power. Under physical, mental, emotional and spiritual slavery. Under the oppression of literally thousands of innocent children and souls all across the planet because this is also a largely unacknowledged shadowed undercurrent in these industries as well.

It's time to dismantle these distorted programs withIN ourselves, CELL'ves, and our SOUL'ves and release the tendrils *once and for all*.

I know we have been summoned here to REWRITE THIS WHOLE WORLD SCRIPT RIGHT NOW ToGetHer… for ourselves and for our future generations, backward and forward through all space and time.

The past does not define us, it's here to remind us of our power to *choose* our highest timeline, to wake from our collective slumber and take full OWN•OUR•SHIP of our agency!

Deep down, I believe every woman has an erotic dancer withIN, whether she actually has realized this or not! These are the inner Magdalene and Priestess codes being asked to awaken across the planet right now.

It is up to us to pull ourselves out of the dark corners and to shine our sacred sensual light in the world as embodied Priestesses. And to create sacred temple spaces and containers curated by women to honor and revere the Goddess and her erotic innocence and unique expression through each of us!

I'm deeply grateful for the time I experienced dancing, and I also am deeply grateful for the past few years that forced me to stop enough to Re•Member who I am and why I came here.

WE ARE THE CHAIN BREAKERS

Prior to the first lockdowns in March of 2020, I was swirled up in the throes of alcohol and drug abuse. A common side effect of working in the entertainment industry. Heavily smoking, rolling tobacco all day long. Cocaine binges. I was lying to myself—I told myself I was okay. I put on the facade that I was alright on the outside, though I was praying for some drastic change.

I made misaligned decisions that rippled through past traumas in the echo chamber of my mind as I drank myself into oblivion most nights of the week. My partner would wake up at 9 am to find me still up drinking, blacked out in the backyard on many occasions. I drank myself sick often, toward the end. I felt helpless, hopeless, stuck, constricted, anxious and depressed. I was checking out of my body and out of this planet.

In many ways, I felt it was too late. The voices in my head told me, "I'm too broken" and "I'm too far down the hole." I just couldn't do it anymore. Either I was going to drink myself to death, or I was going to rise like the Phoenix and make shifts to realign on my soul's path and reclaim my power.

As alcoholism has affected many of my family members and grandparents—I knew it was time to heal this.

The lockdown was the greatest opportunity for healing that I could've ever asked for. I was more afraid of what would become of me if I continued on this path of self-destruction than I was of honestly facing all of the distortions and distractions that were keeping me bound to a power outside of myself that felt so incredibly dark and all-consuming at times.

My inner light felt so dim.

A little after a month into the first lockdown, I made a powerful decision. I knew it was time. I dove deep. I layered therapy in with women's online groups, learning healing techniques that supported me in clearing energetic parasites and entities, cleaning up all my energy bodies.

I also courageously chose to quit drinking and doing hard drugs. And a few months after I quit smoking for good. I journeyed through a couple of deep cleanses to detox my body from years of extensive alcohol and drug abuse, sloughing off the layers that had hardened my heart, mind, body and soul. I deeply desired to embody my most true and authentic soul essence...not who I thought society, my family, or anyone else wanted me to be.

So I laid it all out on the table to take a radically honest look at everything—I saw all of the ways I was checking out because the world just felt too much. I felt like I was just too much. I could hear the voices in my head telling me that it wouldn't really matter if I was here anymore or not. My throat and voice felt muffled and restricted.

I felt an even stronger sense of the strength of my spirit to persevere and witness my human experience from a place of love, deep self-compassion and full acceptance, allowing my higher self to take the reins.

After all, what better time to do this than when the world was being shown we needed to make some big changes and heal anyway?!

Deep down, I knew that this was my soul mission in this incarnation. To be the embodiment of transformation and infuse deep Courage Codes into every WOMB•an on this planet to rise into her power, share Her Story and to re•Member Her Innate Worthiness to receive aligned wealth flowing into her life without compromising any aspect of herself—to create whatever she so desires and to release any constrictions or resistances to embody her deepest soul essence and womb wisdom.

When we peel back the layers, we're not as different from each other as we may think, and we carry many of the same root traumas asking to be transmuted Now—one of these being deep shame.

OUR WOMB CARRIES ALL THE KEYS

I remember the depth of guilt and shame I felt and carried in my teenage years and well into my 20s about the burden of being born into a woman's body.

I spent these years doing everything I could to minimize the intensity of my period cramps by taking birth control pills starting at the age of 16, prescribed extra-strength ibuprofen (which led to debilitating stomach and digestive issues) and eventually a Mirena IUD to halt bleeding altogether for two years straight, treating my womb as if it were something I needed to fix rather than the source of all of creation and the very natural expression of the infinite abundance flow that it truly represents.

The first time I was shown just how much of an alchemist my womb really is, was in the summer of 2014 during Illumination Fire Alchemy Circle, a powerful gathering with well over 100 beautiful souls to intentionally transmute our energetic lead into gold over the course of three nights through dancing, singing, drumming, playing, and praying around a sacred fire circle resembling the solar system, with the fire representing the sun.

On the first night, I called in releasing all energetic cords being stored within my womb from past sexual partners. Within 18 hours, I began bleeding more heavily than I ever have in my entire life. The bleeding continued for the following three-and-a-half weeks, ultimately resulting in an ultrasound and a diagnosis of a ruptured cyst that had been around my right ovary (the Masculine side of the body).

You can imagine what an initiation this was for me! I felt like many parts of myself were dying. It was the death of the lovers that could not meet me in all the ways I most desired to be met. Those who were misaligned and who had taken energetic residence in my most precious womb temple.

130

Nothing is a coincidence. Just like our nervous system and our fascial tissue, our womb remembers. There is a direct connection between our relationship with our womb, our self-worth, our magic and our relationship with money and wealth, or as I like to say, WELL•th.

And in this instance, it's not about the money per se, but the energy behind it. It's about our ability to *receive*, integrate, assimilate and digest our life experiences and embody our innate abundance and natural flow of life in alignment with our unique soul codes and blueprint—just like our womb.

The more we cultivate and deepen our relationship with our womb and untangle and unravel past traumas, the distorted frequencies of lack mentality and limiting belief patterns, all of the personal, familial and collective guilt, shame and blame we have carried—and any ideas that we came here to "struggle" and to merely "survive"—the more consciously we awaken the Magdalene Priestess Codes to move and dance, to pray and play through us, as us.

We release any stagnant, fragmented, rigid energy held within our womb that would cause dis•ease and open up our receptivity, creativity and fluidity channels, allowing wealth and abundance to *flow* to us and through us.

"Since Wild Woman is the Río Abajo Río, the river beneath the river, when she flows into us, we flow. If the aperture from her to us is blocked, we are blocked," says Clarissa Pinkola Estes in her wisdom book *Women Who Run with the Wolves* (pg 299).

By raising our consciousness and bringing our awareness to this surging river beneath the river within our wombs, we reclaim our power as Conscious Creators. We clear the toxic blocks of the old matrix templates that have poisoned our inner well within not only our physical bodies, but our minds and souls— personally and collectively.

Creating from this space clarifies our blood, lineage, DNA and sacred womb waters and restores harmony and balance once and for all. As below, as above. As within, so without.
No matter where we come from, what decisions we've made, who we "think" we are—we are perfect, whole, enough, and oh so worthy RIGHT NOW.

It is in our own inner Divine Sacred Union embodiment and personal reSOULution that we break the illusive chains of separation. It is then that we can move onto the bigger missions we came here to bring through!

What a time to be alive and lift this veil to see the truth of our power!

RISE, SISTER, RISE!

Once we see, we cannot unsee. It then becomes our sacred response•ability. To reclaim our sacred womb seeds. To IN•body our unique keys. And unlock the great My•Story–Herstory.

To forge the paths of truth by telling our stories and unapologetically getting paid to embody ourselves.

This is what we came here for. We know how to do this, sisters!

All of our stories are like spokes of a wheel and threads of a spider web— when we share the wisdom from these stories with deep self-compassion and meet this whole life, and especially our past decisions, with curiosity instead of judgment, we strengthen our connection to the whole wheel and web…

When we leave these stories unexpressed and unprocessed, there becomes a fragment from the MOTHER WOMB MATRIX (the Latin Roots for the word Matrix is Womb, Mother, Uterus).

We are here to integrate and *assimilate the matrix*, not exit the matrix.

It is easier than ever to ripple our codes both on and offline, to weave our story threads so we may remember who we truly are, and to get paid abundantly for doing so and co-creating a healthy wealth matrix that is deeply rooted in integrity for the regeneration of ourselves, Mother Earth and all sentient BEings! I believe we have been gifted this beautiful crystalline technology aka the Inner•Net from God/dess to imprint our FREEquency and help shift the collective consciousness.

There are particular women who need to hear your story and, through sharing, it becomes the integration (INTO•GREAT•ION) and the accountability to dedicate to your soul mission *while* creating massive impact, income and inspiration.

Embodied *devotion in motion.*

The world is ready for you to share and *shine* your light and fractals of our Collective My•Story—we are all each other's missing puzzle pieces!

It is how we heal our relationship with our wombs, our Sisterhood, what and how we create in this life, our voices, our choices, our money flow, our self-worth, our time, our energy, and our innate wisdom. To remember our sacred

133

assignment and take action with deep alignment!

We are here. We are safe. We are home.

We Now reclaim that which has always been ours—the innate Wild Womb WELL•th Wisdom that flows from our sacred chalice, the HOLY GRAIL.

May we show up in loving devotion, in playful co•creative curiosity with our womb. May we tend and mend the relationship with ourself *as* Mary Magdalene, an ascended Master in form. May we remember that the Kingdom and Queendom of Heaven on Earth is withIN.

Heaven IN Earth.

She is weaving her stories, her songs, her dance, her threads of love and peace through every waking moment reminding us to trust, cultivate patience, remember faith, invoke clarity, embody alignment, reconcile reSOULution withIN, anoint ourselves with remembrance, ATONE our past regrets and mistakes, dance and weave GRACE to life in every dimension, and infuse our actions with COMPLETION as we are ALREADY liberated souls and there is not one task or thing to DO that will make us more complete —we are WHOLE RIGHT NOW!

I remember from the future that when every woman on this precious planet Earth embodies herself as The Goddess in form and reclaims her womb, body and blood as sacred, the world shifts into more expanded states of consciousness and we collectively calibrate into higher frequencies, enabling us to hold more light within our body temples and restoring harmony once and for all.

It is here and Now we grid the New Earth Matrix and bring

all systems back online, weaving Ancient Future codes in full alignment with our precious human self and the Divine, the bridge between Spirit and matter, the seen and unseen—as the New Earth Priestesses and Oracles. Our inner Divine Feminine and Masculine as ONE.

We are the future ancestors. Bridging past, present and future here Now.

DISTILL, AND KNOW THAT YOU ARE GOD/DESS!

References:

Estés, C.P. (1995). Women Who Run with the Wolves: Myths and Stories of the Wild Woman Archetype. Ballantine Books.

ABOUT THE AUTHOR

COLLEEN M COYNE

Colleen M Coyne is a Wealth Activator, New Earth Frequency Leader & the founder of the Global Womb Wealth Wisdom Reclamation Movement.

She guides deep women & New Earth Priestesses on their journey to tap into an aligned & conscious high profit wealth stream & automated business platform by sharing their Truth codes & building an authentic personal brand online.

It is her soul mission to empower women to reclaim their womb wisdom, FREE their souls & voices, move beyond limitation and embody their most LIT AS FUCK frequency — all while unlocking aligned wealth flow for the regeneration of ourselves and of Mother Earth.

She currently lives in the lush Pacific Northwest in Portland, Oregon with her partner and their two cats. She loves communing with nature, nurturing her body temple and honoring life as a continuous ritual.

If you're ready to create an aligned high profit & high impact WEALTH ECOSYSTEM that allows you to live a life of freedom & choice with an amazing commUNITY of soul sisters, CLICK BELOW *to join* the Womb Wealth Wisdom Reclamation Movement Portal for New Earth Priestesses FB group to code swap and learn how this New Earth business vehicle works!

New Earth will be built ToGetHer sister!!

LINKS:

FB Group: https://bit.ly/wombwealthwisdomFBgroup
Website: https://www.colleenmcoyne.org
Milkshake: https://msha.ke/colleenmcoyne/
Instagram: https://www.instagram.com/colleenmcoyne/

FEARLESS DIVINE FEMININE DISRUPTOR

CRYSTAL LYNN PRIVETT

IT IS WITH AUTHENTIC COMPASSION THAT I IMPLORE you to activate your greatness within by embracing the truth that we do not have to be perfect to be amazing.

In fact, the sovereign gifts within you are all you need to answer all the questions you seek in the depths of your soul. It is not learning or earning your greatness–indeed quite the opposite, as you were created with the perfection of self-divinity to co-create your best life.

It is my great hope that you will feel a deep sense of peace and connectedness wash over your soul like a warm shower...cleansing all negativity on your healing journey. Embodying comfort despite our circumstances and embracing the knowledge that you will **always** be a holy being.

Unconditionally... and with great reverence.

You will sense many pleasant and perhaps some uncomfortable feelings, as you activate Magdalene Codes within yourself. Restoring, aligning and rebuilding your spirit as you continue to read this chapter. It may indeed leave you encouraged, re-energized, and with a newfound zest for your quest by absorbing the codes within this story.

Please be advised...if you are reading this chapter, it is no accident...the time is NOW to reclaim your boundaries, boldly speak your truth, take up space, and be offensively optimistic!

We must continue to break down stigmas and reclaim OUR HOLINESS despite generations of social conditioning. Just like the journey of the Magdalene, trailblazing the way for our future generations to come, so we can one day live in the harmony of the delicate balance of the divine feminine and divine masculine ecosystem.

We Can Do It and the Time Is Now!!!!!!!

STRENGTH OF THE SUPPRESSED SOVEREIGN

Luke 8:1-3 "Soon afterwards he went on through cities and villages, proclaiming and bringing the good news of the kingdom of God. And the twelve of them were with him, and also some women who had been healed of evil spirits and infirmities: Mary called Magdalene, from whom seven demons had gone out, and Joanna, the wife of Chuza, Herod's household manager, and Susanna, and many others, who provided for them out of their means."

It can be perceived that even the best of us carry around demons that we need to expel and Jesus in all of his sovereignty made a connection to this intrepid female and held her in great reverence. There were three that always

139

walked with the Lord: Mary his mother, and his sister, and his companion. His sister and his mother and his companion were each a Mary, as told in the Gospel of Philip 36. Not only was Mary his dear friend, but he clearly confided in her in a way that made even his twelve disciples envious. He freed her from her demons and in return she devoted her life to supporting him in a multitude of ways. Providing financial, mental, physical, emotional and spiritual support to a King on Earth. Even staying with his mother and helping maintain his family home while on long spiritual pilgrimages. Doing her great works with supreme humility yet with all the reverence, poise and strength of a queen. Her volition came internally which proved her dedication in such a way that seemed both clandestine and otherworldly. Precisely why this gnostic goddess is one of my favorite female embodiments that I aspire to honor on a deep and meaningful quantum level by proliferating her holiness.

Lady Magdalene has an effervescent and resilient quality about her that I can't help but admire. Her tenacity and loyalty were unwavering as she was one of the few witnesses of the burial and crucifixion of Jesus and was famously the first person to see him after resurrection. This showed a deep level of connection between the two and leads me to believe she also had something very special within her. Jesus clearly saw something and early Christian literature indicates that she had a leading position and often demonstrated spiritual insight greater than that of the apostles. When asked, "Why do you love her more than all of us?" by the disciples, Jesus replied "Why do I not love you like her? When a blind man and one who sees are both in darkness, they are no different from one another. When light comes, then he who is blind will remain in darkness."

There is this same deep beauty, power, and light within us. Most of us learn to be grateful for our gifts, especially as we

140

remember what we already know; that these gifts then become awareness and the slight shifting of our perception to something that was unequivocally already there. We begin to awaken to the truth that we already embody our highest form of consciousness." As I wrote in my previous book Magdalene Rising you can sense a deep reverence for this critical individual that supported the Son of a King with humble servitude and allowed Him to find strength in union with Her. Teaching us that we are truly better when we can work together with those we love with common passion.

CODE: HOLY LIBERATION OF MIND

How long must we allow the Ego to run rampant amongst humanity?

When will our females get the credit and acknowledgment that they deserve for all the sacrifices we make for others? We can still be full of love while we smash the patriarchy and use our feminine creativity to design a mosaic masterpiece of harmonious splendor and beauty. This power IS already within us.

Driven by compassion and empathy we are naturally programmed to put the needs of others before our own. A gentle reminder that this program does have its time and place... like when a baby wants food when we are tired, we sacrifice convenience for care. On the other hand, our attentiveness can often lead to enabling, codependency and lost sense of self...beware of this trap!

Just as there is no growth in victimhood...

We must take serious caution people-pleasing, as this pattern is a natural trauma response. Without holding firm boundaries, you may continue to attract narcissistic partners

141

and our sovereign subconscious knows we are much holier than that!

It took me the last five years of my 15-year marriage to admit that my putting the needs of others before mine would not actually allow me to attain the happiness I desired and embrace my life's purpose. I was torn, as I found a deep joy in providing for and protecting my family in a more traditional role where I took care of the home and schooling, and allowed for him to focus on work and finances. Unbeknownst to me at the time, I had not done a good enough job holding space for my needs and had deferred my personal pleasure and passion for so long that it felt as if parts of my soul were dying off from atrophy. Playing small was not serving my spirit or those around me, and allowing hurtful behavior chipped away at my boundaries until I found myself completely exposed with a partner that lacked any compassion or equality within the relationship. I was in emotional pain, but I deserved an Oscar for faking my happiness, yet the lack of authenticity was debilitating my spirit. Was I going to be a better mother by acknowledging and addressing my needs? Something surely had to change, and I began to own my truth that I deserved to be adored and respected like other wives.

No longer judging the years it took to acknowledge my truth and learning to unconditionally love myself enough to say a healthy NO when needed and practicing the joy of saying YES to me! I could not see it yet but just like you...I had always been exactly where I was supposed to be and learned all the painful lessons that will vibrantly alchemize into great internal power.

For if you no longer give your power away...
who then could ever take it from you?

CODE: BECOMING THE BODY OF LIFE

"The world is a dangerous place not because of those who do evil, but because of those who look on and do nothing." – Albert Einstein

No longer will we look on as injustices to our divinity take place...we must speak up for our sovereign sisters and brothers in order to claim our sacred authority. Embrace your faith over your fears and stand boldly for the desires of your heart. We all share our own unique expression of life, and it is in our diversity and collective wisdom that we can access the gifts of the heavens within our souls. The more facets we have, the more brilliantly we sparkle. We were given a plethora of talents and skills that can serve ourselves and humanity...but only if we take action.

"You cannot get through a single day without having an impact on the world around you. What you do makes a difference, you just have to decide which difference you want to make." – Jane Goodall

So what difference DO YOU want to make in this world?

Take a moment to check in with your soul.
Make a list of five things you need to accomplish in this lifetime...
in order for your soul to feel complete.
Grab a pencil and paper.
Write three things you must accomplish...
and two dreams that are non-negotiable for your spirit to embrace its purpose.
Let's clarify our passions to our subconscious minds.
This exercise will support your truth and awareness.

Make a self-love wish list:

I Must Accomplish _____ to live my purpose.
I Must Accomplish _____ to live my purpose.
I Must Accomplish _____ to live my purpose.
I Am Worthy Of Achieving My Dream Of _____.
I Am Worthy Of Achieving My Dream Of _____

Now what actions can you take to support these goals?

It's easier to set healthy boundaries from people, situations and energies that do not serve us when we clarify our intentions to our subconscious mind and the Universe. Bringing awareness to what will help us or hinder us along our journey, so we can rally for our own rights. Considering the subconscious mind is one million times more powerful than the conscious mind, we can benefit dramatically by upgrading our mental programs for supreme success.

CODE: ENCHANTED SOUL OF PASSION

When we don't stand firmly in our truth or temporarily lose our footing, our highest self can use people, places and situations to get our attention, because our subconscious mind does not utilize verbal communication. We are meant to be thriving and living our passions for all to see. In my case, I recently had a series of negative manifestations that were trying to redirect my trajectory.

I share this with great vulnerability and because I hope the lives of those we have lost do not go in vain.

Upon reading some of my precious books, you will have noticed I had written about some adventures in Jaguar Medicine, with my bestie Paris, as we narrowly escaped an Istanbul nightclub with our lives after being drugged and targeted for sex trafficking most likely. This is one of those unique friendships where you can truly be yourself and open up to a fun and authentic connection. Traveling the world, we learned quickly to guard and protect one another. The thing about life is she doesn't always give us the warning and guidance we need until we seek it out. We have had many men accosting us for our beauty, yet we still decided not to play small for the sake of others. And took radical action to hold the men accountable…even having one man kicked out of Hilton for life, after chasing us and accosting us for his desires. It's harder to stand up for one another when our soul suffers in silence. Embracing our passion means standing up for those who can't stand up for themselves…and sometimes that includes ourselves.

As a single mom, I had so much pride that I had just purchased a new Lexus RF 450 Hybrid Sport. I was so happy that I could have a safe vehicle to allow my oldest son, Landon, to begin driving with, as he was just turning 16.

Meanwhile my youngest son, Luke, was in middle school and I had been actively contributing to his Valley Middle School PTA, along with running my business Mindset Service, writing multiple books, training businesses, taking care of kiddos and my two adorable pups, finalizing a divorce, and lots of business networking, so my plate was awfully full. I was in the throes of spirit wear sales at school registration and was nearing the victory line with our sales goals being decimated. I love being an active part of my children's community and find great joy in the happiness of the little ones.

Little did I know that soon there would be much more decimation to follow.

On the second out of the three registration days things began to take a nose dive into negativity without my consent.

I received a call from my friend Paris telling me that our mutual friend Kelly had just been broken up with by her long-term boyfriend and kicked to the curb. This young woman was drop-dead gorgeous and deserved to be treated much better than this by someone who claimed to care for her. This was the second time a rich man dumped her for another lady. WTF? On what she expected to be her engagement, this jerk literally broke up with her with plans to visit Club 33 in Disneyland. She proceeded to go anyway and try to enjoy herself, but her mental health drastically deteriorated.

What is about to follow is quite graphic and that is why I will continue to push myself to share the horrific results of our mental health being compromised. This beautiful young lady believed she should have been farther along in life and had hoped to have a family instead of a series of heartbreaks.

She had decided to return to San Diego from Disneyland the same day, but all her hope was lost... and her following actions were as incredibly painful as the emotions she had been experiencing.

This man had just broken up with her and he already had a replacement for her, and the devastation was too much for her heart to handle. She thought she was going to begin her life with this man and he had just pulled her dreams from underneath her feet with no remorse.

She proceeded to drive to his work office... pour gasoline all over her body... and she lit herself on fire and took her last breath in despair. This news was so tragic it set off ripples of negativity that were like a super volcano perilously destroying everything in its path. The next day I tried to muster some strength to complete my tasks at hand.

First, I was being inducted to the Rancho Santa Fe Business

Professional Women's group, which I was excited to be a part of. They forgot to announce my induction into the group, but I am a patient person so I said no worries, and headed off to the school to serve the kiddos.

Without any notice... BANG... CRASH... Oh no... am I dead?

I see, hear and feel the violent crashing of metal and glass as my life quickly flashes before me. My vehicle called 911 as I had just been struck head-on by a Range Rover heading down a steep grade and hauling ass around a blind turn. Airbags smashed into my face and body, the impact violently struck me so hard, my engine was on the ground spraying liquids and smoking as onlookers pulled me from the vehicle so I could breathe amongst the airbag debris.

I had just narrowly escaped with my life... oh my God!

Seriously...did that just happen? I had been working four jobs for the last two years and this vehicle had been the first thing I had invested in...and how grateful I was that my vehicle had taken the brunt of the blow leaving me with a concussion, soft tissue damage, deep bruising and blistering on my legs and arms, but the pain reminded me I was alive.

This deep devastation at the time made it hard to embrace passion in some regards, but the fact that I could live to see another day, when a fallen sister was not so lucky, made me embrace an attitude of gratitude. Horrible things happen to good people and several additional injustices and injuries ensued including a rape, hospitalization, and trauma all within days. I knew I had homework assignments to utilize the science-based process I facilitate and train others to use to remove triggers, traumas, and stressors from my mind and those of my friends. We needed the pain and negativity to cease. We saw firsthand the devastating effects of a disempowered mindset. We had to do it for ourselves, for Kelly, and our brothers and sisters suffering in silence.

PTSD is real and the cellular response to negative situations only takes 17 seconds to alter the chemicals in your body and 68 seconds to literally change your body at a cellular level. Meaning...all of the negativity was attracting more negativity and it needed to be contained and alchemized, because we were falling down a cellular rabbit hole. This trauma needed to be converted to triumph. Lessons and blocked, trapped subconscious emotions were ready to be purged, and when we choose to learn from hardships treasures of the soul will be revealed through the muck and mire.

No mud... no lotus... no judgment... only love.

COLLECTIVE QUANTUM QUEEN EMBODIMENT

Do you remember the precaution we hear each time we take an airplane flight?
What do they say about our oxygen mask?

That is right...we are instructed to secure our own safety, so we can continue to be a resource for others. It's our right and responsibility to engage in radical self-love and the power of healthy boundaries that serve to protect our unique breath of life. You are greater than the sum of your past mistakes and the same God that created the Universe also created you and in divine creation there are no mistakes. That means you do not have to be perfect to be incredible.

It's my great passion and pleasure to guide others to reclaim their holiness and divinity with authenticity. Finding lessons in the failures, embracing unconditional grace for yourself and others and taking action towards the desires of your heart, are all possible.

Just like a hot air balloon rising in the crisp morning sky...it can only rise as the attachments holding it back are slowly released. This is why I created the online program Crystal Clear Mindset to help you upgrade and track your progress in 12 fundamental aspects of life that comprise The Cycle Of Consciousness. Reach out today to reprogram your subconscious mind to think, feel, act and react in a more positive way with a science-based process that allows you to grow your brain with your mind. We are told we cannot solve all our problems with the same thinking that created them. Act today to shift your perspective and nourish yourself with the healing process of the future.

If you are worthy and deserving of accomplishing your dreams... then why have they not all come to fruition? Let me share the secrets of divine feminine holiness as we collectively collaborate to enlighten the mind, body and souls of humanity and usher in a new era of peace and sustainable joy.

Please let this story be a reminder that being selfish is a healthy quality in moderation–and standing up for your well-being is a necessity.

Consider this your official permission to live your best life.

You have worked so hard to get here...

What if there was an infinite well of knowledge and wisdom we could tap into to live our purpose daily like Lady Mary Magdalene?

There is, my love...and I am here to shout it from the

rooftops that your mental health is a priority and I am here to guide you to supreme success.

MAGDALENE CODE MANIFESTATION:

Take a deep breath
Close your eyes after repeating each code for 30 seconds.
Really feel the intention and envision your new life,
as if the desires of your heart have already come true.
These codes will activate the subconscious agreement that it is you who claims your divinity and it is time to live this new life henceforth and forevermore.

I am a fearless divine feminine disrupter.
I convert suppression to sovereign strength.
I embrace my divine and unique body of life.
My enchanted soul of passion thrives and drives me daily.
It's fun to embody the wisdom of past, present and future female leaders.
I am worthy of this new life.
I am deserving of this new life.

• SO IT IS. •

All My Love...
Crystal Lynn Privett

Master Your Mind & Conquer The World!

ABOUT THE AUTHOR

CRYSTAL LYNN PRIVETT

Crystal Lynn - CEO of *Mindset Service,* is absolutely enthralled to share her sincere passion for mental health as a renowned energy psychologist.

Your ability to reprogram the subconscious mind is validated by some of the most credible neurological scientists around…the possibilities are endless. We can all let go of the past and embrace a new future with only the best possibilities, so we can achieve sustainable joy.

Imagine improving your health, enhancing your relationships, removing your annoying triggers, and helping your business get to the next level all in one session!

It's possible!

4 X Best Selling Author

- *Magdalene Rising,*
- *Jaguar Medicine,*
- *Sovereign,*
- *Isis - Mother of Magic*

San Diego Power Woman 2021 & 2022
Mrs. United Kingdom 2021
First Runner-Up Mrs. Europe Global
Role Model of the Year 2022

United Nations Association Women's Leadership Award
BNI Escondido - Education Coordinator

Proud single mom of two remarkable boys Luke and Landon.

She created an innovative online course, **Crystal Clear Mindset**, to help others achieve supreme success by gaining insight into and enhancing 12 fundamental aspects of consciousness that balance your life.

Crystal is making an impact in her community and would also like to make an impact in your life.

www.MindsetService.com

SURRENDERING TO MY INNER GUIDANCE HEALED ME

DAINA GARDINER

IT'S BEEN OVER 11 YEARS SINCE I WENT TO A doctor.

And, year after year, I've only been feeling more energized, balanced, lighter, and happier.

Wanna know my secret?

I ended my relationship with fear of diseases and health problems and experienced the most beautiful, massive, powerful awakening.

I took back control of my own mind, body and health.

I embraced my inner wisdom, creativity and intuitive guidance from the Divine Feminine.

And I got serious about learning how to heal my body naturally.

But, most importantly, I awakened my problem-solving skills into an expertise of understanding that symptoms tell a story. And this story is the foundational, fundamental, root cause that, when addressed, initiates lifelong healing.

WHAT'S A LIFE WITHOUT PLEASURE?

I was 15 when a doctor finally took my bone-crushing exhaustion seriously.

For three years, every medical professional brushed me off as lazy or depressed.

My brain literally hurt to think. Any type of exertion took days to recover from. A flight of stairs had me gasping for air, desperately trying to slow my racing heart.

When that doctor took my fatigue seriously and diagnosed me with Chronic Fatigue Syndrome, I was excited! I had a diagnosis which meant, from all the traditional medical knowledge I'd been taught, that there must be a fix.

Phew…Massive sigh of relief.

Imagine my devastation when he and every other medical expert told me there was nothing anyone could do to help me. That I'd have to learn to "cope" with my debilitating exhaustion.

Exhaustion that had forced me to quit everything that made life fun–figure skating, gymnastics, volleyball. Attending sleepovers and gravel pit parties.

I felt powerless. A weight of frustration, exhaustion and utter hopelessness kept pressing me further into a state of hatred for my life. And the unfairness of my health situation led me to become a victim. I felt worthless yet I wanted pity from everyone around me–professors, parents, colleagues, and friends.

For years, I surrendered to my fatigue and the situation I'd been dealt. I made a pact with myself that if I hadn't found a cure by the time I was 30, I would end my life. Simply because I felt like I was just wasting mine away.

Honestly, I never felt depressed. I just had zero motivation, and my life was devoid of excitement, joy, fun or happiness. This is the life of the chronically fatigued; your energy is nonexistent and your emotions just fade away.

WILD, FREE AND SCARED TO BE ME

As a child, I had a wild imagination.

Growing up on a farm in rural Manitoba, Canada, I had many opportunities to embrace my inner creativity.

Our backyard and the surrounding trees served as my own personal Labyrinth. I raced around the paths in an oversized light, flowy skirt, getting closer to the Goblin King as I had adventures with Hoggle (my dog) and the talking door knobs (just tree knots).

My dad laid out our round hay bales in these wonderful lines that afforded me corridors and hidden hay caves to play Ewoks. And our trampoline was the perfect gazebo to re-enact that infamous scene from The Sound of the Music.

I loved my life, I was proud of my crazy imagination, and I

felt so connected to myself.

No one else's opinions of me mattered.

Until the name-calling, exclusion and avoidance began.

It started slowly in my second year of school and progressed to a place where I became a pariah for everyone to treat like shit. The worst part of being bullied was that I never understood why.
It just came to be, and as I was called a "bitch," "slut," and other derogatory names, I was deeply hurt and confused, down to my core.

My spirit started to fade away.

And I began to hide.

To avoid saying or doing anything in case the wrath of the bullies came down upon me.

For over 15 years, I did anything and everything I could to not "rock the boat". Even in my IT career, if I knew the correct solution to a problem, I wouldn't speak up. I let others take credit for my ideas. I asked my colleagues indirectly to hold a confrontational conversation on my behalf.

I lived in fear of being ridiculed, judged and outcast.

"...those of us who color outside of the lines get called
sluts. And that word is meant to keep us in line." Jaclyn
Friedman

I'd always had a bit of a rebellious streak in me, and I wonder if I just began to show up too loudly and proudly with my individualism as a kid.

I dressed differently on purpose–because I wore what I loved. I was smart and good in school; I was easily bored so teachers advanced me in any way they could. Plus, I loved to push limits.

The year before I became the target of the bullying, I'd broken community tradition and joined the woodworking 4-H class (4H is a community organization that helps youth learn new skills by doing them-cooking, babysitting, raising farm animals, public speaking, and leadership). My parents had to informally petition for me to enroll. It had always only ever been boys who took it.

Who was I to NOT want to join the girls in the traditionally female-centric classes of crafts, sewing or cooking? Oh, the scandal!

By standing up for what I wanted and embracing my love of new learning, I may have put myself right in the bull's eye for ridicule.

As a 12-year-old, I wasn't yet strong enough to hold my power.

My fatigue got worse, and I completely lost any will to stand up for what I wanted or needed. I gave up trying–trying to feel healthier, trying to enjoy life, and trying to aim for the stars.

IF EVERYONE ELSE IS DOING IT, IT MUST BE RIGHT…RIGHT?

Almost 10 years ago, I did the unachievable. I put my chronic fatigue syndrome into remission.

Western medicine can't do this–search Google and you'll

157

find that, even today, mainstream medicine and science says it's impossible to cure CFS. The medical community still only focuses on treating it, wrongly, with medications or low-dose, incomplete nutraceuticals.

Western medicine has lost its ability to truly reverse health conditions because people are no longer treated as individuals. They're treated as part of a playbook, and everyone gets the same treatment. Solely focused on symptoms, not the root cause.

And, as a result of this weird acceptance and trust in the medical field, women have lost touch with their feminine energy, their intuitive guidance on what feels best and right for their bodies.

My own battle with chronic fatigue continued for over 15 years because I kept "doing" the treatments and following the advice that I was told by the "experts" in health.

Following a strict "one-size-fits-all" diet plan.
Checking off the daily exercise box.
Scheduling in self-care practices even when it didn't fit.
And, worst of all, following the advice and prescriptions I received from doctors, peers, and online health bloggers without considering the consequences.
Or realizing how shitty they were making me feel about myself.

I was following the crowd, taking direction and not asking questions. Trying but not really…

Following the crowd, conforming to tradition, is why I stayed stuck for over 15 years.

I had lost my inner fire and surrendered to the wrong parts

of me, specifically my masculine energy that kept me focused on logistics and direction I received from others. To always follow what I was told to do. Even if it wasn't working.

Your health isn't something to trust in the hands of anyone else wholeheartedly. Only you know your body best.

And that means surrendering to your inner guidance, to the messages and signs your body is sending. This is how you successfully restore your health.

LIBERATED AT LAST – SURRENDERING TO FREEDOM

Freedom. This is the ultimate outcome with health that we all crave.

When I opened my heart and mind to the power of surrendering to my inner divine guidance, that's when my whole world changed!

However, yes, asking for help was a stretchy and scary first step!

I'm fiercely independent and always want to do everything on my own. Like research the hell out of my fatigue and figure out how to fix it!

Yet it was surrendering to the programming within me that allowed me to find hope, energy and my inner power.

Asking for help freed me from anxiety, frustration and lack of confidence in myself.

It allowed me to let go of fear, sit in peace against the media health propaganda that always seems to want us to cower.

Surrendering to my intuitive guidance liberated me from the time I was wasting feeling so exhausted.

As women, we need to take back control over our own bodies and health. We need to embrace our inner wisdom, our connection with ancient healing modalities, and our creativity.

We've been brushed off, called hysterical, treated with the wrong medications, put in asylums, and told to "cope" or that it's "normal" to feel so shitty. For far too long.

We women need to stand up and say NO MORE to the masculinized medical field with their one-size-fits-all protocols. Protocols that were tested on men; men without our unique, beautiful hormones; men without our glorious biological makeup; men without the full power of our inner goddess.

To surrender to the power of natural health and ask for help, to achieve success through personalized, female-centric health counseling and protocols:

This is to live without fear.
To be free.
To feel liberated and in your own power.

EMPOWERED RESISTANCE

"How much less dangerously can one live if one runs with the herd and aligns oneself thoughtlessly with old tradition, instead of swimming against the current for one's conviction and bearing all consequences as an 'outcast'." - Constanze Hallgarten (a note written during exile, Germany, 1939/40)

I'm fascinated by the ancestral load and DNA imprints that we all bring down with us. As a holistic energy recovery coach, I remind my clients that their stress load is not just their own, but the load of at least seven previous generations, all of which have impacted how resilient their adrenals and nervous system are to the stress they experience.

For women, this ancestral load often stems from the persecution of the female in history. *Because a strong woman is a woman to be afraid of, right? A woman with an opinion and a conviction is a woman who should be controlled, of course.* (Obviously, this is sarcasm.)

I've always been drawn to stories about past lives, the witch trials centuries ago, and, closest to my heart, the women of the resistance during WWII.

Sophie Scholl. Mildred Harnack. Nancy Wake.

These women are my heroines, the women I feel compelled to embody in my daily life and my work. To stand up for what's right regardless of consequences, because the health, safety and sovereignty of the people is at stake.

Which is why my mission is to guide and inspire tens of thousands of women worldwide to stand up for their own health, not just to fix their fatigue, but to take back control. To achieve and stand for body autonomy. To fully embody "my body, my choice" on all levels, so that more and more women are inspired and compelled to live their best, most liberated lives.

I SURRENDER TO DIVINE GUIDANCE, AND I LIVE HARMONIOUSLY

My own intuition has led me to make the most aligned

decisions for myself. My Mom was right–my intuition is very strong and I should listen to it.

I honor my intuition and listen to her often.

This intuitive guidance, along with the inner fire to create my own path in life, is my connection to Mary Magdalene. A woman who was powerful, who forged her own journey, and who embodies intuition, femininity and the Divine.

Trusting my body was a turning point in my health and energy. Trusting my passion was pivotal in my career, from proud IT geek to holistic nutrition.

My ancestors survived on natural healing long before the introduction of pharmaceuticals and chemical toxins. Food has always been considered a form of medicine–just look at Hippocrates. After all, he is famous for stating, *"Let food be thy medicine, and medicine be thy food."*

Much of my success is due to tuning into my personal hormonal cycles. Something most Western medical studies and protocols ignore when fatigue is the main complaint.

As a woman whose entire journey from exhausted to energized has been laser focused on her own hormones, I know you can rebalance them thoroughly and improve your health and monthly cycles year after year. Yes! As you get older, you CAN create happier hormone harmony within you. And this harmony is a key factor in your overall health, radiance and energy.

Nothing balances out if your hormones are a hot mess. Yet most mainstream health, wellness and medical advice wrecks our delicate female hormones. Women are powerful, strong and vibrant when they are in tune with their natural cycles.

This connection with the Divine, the feminine energy inside me, has been the turning point for my own health. Not a prescription drug or medical procedure, not a symptom-focused natural treatment either.

My feminine energy thrives when my hormones are harmonious. My intuition excels when my hormones are happy. My energy is out of this world when my hormones are balanced, naturally fed, and resilient against the stress in life.

OUTCOMES MANIFEST FROM THE DEVOTION TO OUR INNER POWER

I'd love to tell you that there was one inspiring event that completely changed my life and restored my energy. I'd love to clearly point you to the one thing you need to do to restore your health fully and naturally.

But that's not how natural health and healing work. It takes time, patience, commitment and surrender. When it's done right, it lasts a lifetime.

In my field, I hear stories from hundreds of women who continue to stay stuck battling long-term, bone-crushing fatigue. And it's not because they're lazy or have no desire to change. It's because they've become manipulated by mainstream health and wellness.

If a woman fails to reach her health goals, it's because she hasn't yet grasped the importance of surrendering to her divine feminine energy guidance. If we don't trust her, we stay stuck in a fog. A fog of confusion, never knowing which direction to take, worried we'll make the wrong choice.

And this fog only lifts when she stops wanting the outcome

before taking the action. When she surrenders to the process and asks for help.

Because asking for help is a divinely sacred choice that the most successful, healthiest, and abundantly free women make.

Surrender doesn't mean giving up your power; it doesn't mean failure.

To surrender means empowerment, choosing to love yourself and your soul in the name of health, happiness, peace, abundance and anything else you deeply desire.

YOU HEAL BY LISTENING TO YOUR INNER GUIDANCE

A common misconception is that healthy eating equates to a healthy body.

Yet that's an oversimplified mindset, because not all healthy food is healing for all people. Many healthy foods are harmful to women's hormones–they add stress and inflammation to her body, and they continue to dysregulate her nervous system.

This makes it difficult for her to connect into her own inner goddess. Her brain is infused with toxins and inflammation, and her mind becomes too foggy to create clear direction and connection. She loses motivation and falls back on the stress-inducing mainstream advice and suggestions.

You have the power within you to create your own healing journey. All it takes is tapping into your inner guidance and really listening to the intuitive hits and downloads. Not every piece of advice out there is right for you–your power comes from your creativity, your experimentation and the messages your body, mind and soul send to you.

It's time we surrendered to the process of listening, allowing divine guidance, and embracing more flow and ease into our lives.

Ditch the diets. Say goodbye to the exercise challenges. Roll your eyes at "just eat healthy and move more." And, by all means, end the cycle of "manage your stress better" because, girl, as exhausted, busy, ambitious women, this is one of the most stressful, exhausting things we can hear!

You've gotta listen to YOU. You've gotta stand up for what feels aligned for YOU. You've gotta embrace, embody and empower yourself with the divine feminine energies circulating and permeating your every cell.

This is how you heal and live your best, most vibrant life ever!

YOU'RE INVITED TO UNLOCK YOUR FEMININE POWER TO BECOME YOUR VIBRANT, ENERGIZED, AMAZING SELF

If I could create anything in the world and no one could stop me, I would eliminate all unnecessary medical protocols and prescriptions. I would stop the removal of organs that doctors have decided women just don't "need."

And I would teach every female out there, starting from a very young age, how to tune into her own feminine energy and signaling.

We're kinda awesome, really.

Because the best, easiest way to begin this connection with your internal health signals and stories is through your natural menstrual cycle.

Stop masking it and start paying attention. It's the single most important tool a woman has to start identifying her health imbalances, nutrient deficiencies, hormonal issues, and so much more.

Always ask "why."

Why are you so exhausted? Why is stress exhausting you? Why do you keep feeling run down with a viral infection? Why is your period so heavy? Why does your head hurt? Why can't you eat beans?

Why... This is your power question because it'll lead you to the root causes.

With root causes at your fingertips, you not only find simple, clear direction and answers...

You also unlock your inner feminine wisdom, power, flow and radiance.

Your health complaints, as a woman with all you've got going on, are NOT normal. Don't let anyone else ever tell you this again.

You deserve to feel your absolute best. You deserve happiness all throughout your days. You deserve to enjoy high energy and clear thinking at all times. You get to feel important, powerful and fierce.

It's your birthright to get to feel sexy. Intelligent. Successful. Healthy. Embrace your inner goddess and worship your divine energy.

Now, doesn't that sound liberating?

ABOUT THE AUTHOR

DAINA GARDINER

Daina Gardiner is a Certified Holistic Nutrition Consultant, an Epstein Barr Virus/Chronic Fatigue Syndrome warrior, and owner of Mind Body Healthy Holistic Nutrition.

She is wildly passionate about dissolving the mainstream "symptom- or organ-focused" treatment mentality and creating a world where women become intuitively guided to choose the best natural options for their personal long-term health. She understands the damages done by mainstream health, wellness and medicine and is fierce about changing the way women view their own bodies and healing potential.

Her Energy & Hormonal Rebalance System coaches women

to discover the magic of food and divine intuitive guidance as personalized medicine. Having spent years living with chronic fatigue and many other confusing symptoms and eliminating her health problems naturally, Daina is devoted to rebalancing and restoring the health of each client's whole body so that they can live freely, energized and excited for life. Daina supports her clients in rebalancing the entire body-physically, mentally, emotionally and spiritually.

Her philosophy is to identify the true root cause of a diagnosis or symptom, and to develop a protocol that is unique to each client's hormone and health status. She treats each client as an individual, ensuring that they are heard, supported and loved.

Daina lives with her husband and two cats in Nicaragua, on their journey of discovery. She hopes to travel the world and embrace many new experiences before settling down in her perfect long-term home.

Links:
The Energy Rejuvenation VIP Experience:
https://mindbodyhealthy.ca/ehrs/

Free Holistic Nutrition Resources for Chronic Fatigue Recovery & Energy Healing:
https://mindbodyhealthy.ca/free/

Other ways you can find Daina:
Instagram: @the.energized.woman
www.mindbodyhealthy.ca
Facebook: https://www.facebook.com/mindbodyhealthy
Email: daina.gardiner@mindbodyhealthy.ca

MAGDALENE MOMENTS: DRAGON TALES OF A KALEIDOSCOPIC PRISMATIC SOUL OR HOW I DECOLONIZED A RAINBOW

DHYĀNA KLUTH

PART 1

THE MAGDALENE ESSENCE PULSES IN AND OUT OF this dimension, leaving a trail of connections across generations. Rivers of menstrual blood, placenta, and stem cells. Rites of passage incarnate with their stories and transmissions shining light out into the dim places of cognition. Her voice, a powerful beacon, announces the return of life, the sacred and the union, an immersive light that activates the heart and descends into matter borne of the womb.

A mosaic of timeless moments illuminates embodied codes; a sentient light revealing the sensual and shadow, taboo and nature, calling forth that primal essence that was repeatedly persecuted and banished.

All that follows and comes before is a love letter to that sovereign essence of love, to exalt that radiant light of love inside myself as I continue to embody the feminine mysteries to liberate joy and weave radical passions into a harmonious way of life. May the words and re-membering transmitted here be received as a gentle, loving invitation to celebrate what your soul knows.

WANTON RAINBOW BLISS AND THE SUBTLE POWER OF SOVEREIGN RADIANCE

The lusty maiden seduced and invited every young man called friend to be straddled by her passion before her twentieth year. As one childhood schoolmate left home for college, he confided his vulnerability, seeking from her a balm to soothe his virginal concern. How beautiful a blessing, she felt it was, to receive in the giving; an act of honor to be of sexual service, to awaken that sensual dragon, and a gift to embrace such a blooming masculine member! In those wanton acts of immersive union was the truth of a sacred seed, a fully embodied prismatic brilliance.

She relished the holy joy of that sexual ecstasy. The sensation of being penetrated. The salacious feeling of that juicy wetness. Of a firmness closely enveloped by her strong, young, muscular flesh. Her holy channel, that portal entrance, her womb temple gateway.

She walked toward the sun along deserted streets and noticed the young men and the large knife too late to become invisible. The only option she saw was to become invincible. Calculating the timelines and their outcomes, she weighed her options. Cross the street and have them magnetized to follow and cut her off at the pass? Turn, run, and pray she makes it around the corner and help is waiting? She had their eyes already but in what action would their attention result? Without flinching or pausing her stride, she rooted every step into the asphalt sidewalk and channeled strength from unseen realms. Ignited from within her core, her eyes ablaze, she strides toward them in a straight line, uncompromising (as if they were innocent children holding a lollipop rather than that big dangerous knife). Parting seas, she walks right through the center of the six men stunned into silence and inaction by her sovereign action, and the fortitude of the Magdalene within her. She was 15.

In the years that followed, her wild life became a more harrowing journey. In the process she finds a way to disintegrate that cloak of oppressive puritanism controlling the modern world, but for a time the memory of orgasmic relationship atrophies within her. She Who Loves Making Love and the essence of Magdalena Priestesses cannot be long contained by colonizing ancestors' programs of survival and societal etiquette. The fire of transformation continues to alchemize outdated programming and defense structures, in their loops and repetitive phrases digging their embedded trenches into labyrinths of unconscious psyche. The Magdalene descends her vision into the depths of the earth.

DEATH

Our sultry lass navigates places of shadows some dare not tread in this lamentable world. An endless well of grief stored deep in her heart, she perceives with knowing memory unwritten codes whispered from spirit to spirit over generations. Evidence. She has grown to understand these revelations at a soul level in a way she did not realize fully so young and tender. For a time, our young maiden is lost along an uncertain personal path, yet she catches glimpses of awareness in the kaleidoscope. Enfleshed burdens, the hidden weight of timelines of apocalyptic atrocities.

Trauma resurrects trauma. Ancestral shadows make themselves known to be released from generations of imprisoned grief. Years before remembering her name is Ceridwen and her womb a cauldron of holy song, she endures insidious fear, judgment and shame penetrating intricate layers of her psychic boundaries. Reverberating tar-like residue desecrates the holy rivers of her sensual body, creating a nightmare of separation-consciousness from wounded ancestors' distorted perceptions.

Oppression pressing into her bones, she dreams a terrible patriarchal vision: an unholy seductive feminine, a scarlet aberration of her innate bliss instinct, pressed its monstrous self upon the pristine innocent consciousness and petrified the sensual rainbow radiance that had once flowed so assuredly, shamelessly, through her being. She felt the shift of perception aligning with the inquisitors. Succumbing to the subjugation of a colonizing puritan mind-control, her organic nature becoming so debased, she eventually believes the reflection she sees of herself in that mirror of archaic "civilized" western rationality, which has effectively self-perpetuated cycles of persecution for generations like a well-honed marketing plan.

Mission accomplished, she let herself be led by an authority outside herself. Lacking vision, as separated from consciousness as she became, without access to her guides, she numbed her pain by perpetuating an abuse of sacred medicines.

How else can She Who is Wanton and Wild live and thrive in this controlling world?

Resurrect the archaic wanton to play and frolic!

The subversive programming of doubt and lack were seeded beneath the undying blueprint of generative, Christed, sovereign life, and tendril-like synthetic root-threads accessed her once fertile mainframe networks until they shut down all feral sexual systems but her dreamtime whispers. But the knowledge inside her remained intact, a spark of innocent, ecstatic, pure potential successfully kept safe. How well hidden she had kept her light from the inquisitors. Safe? No, not safe, but hidden from their timelines until the right time, until now, when the awakened ones accept the torch-lit responsibility.

PART II

REBIRTH IN WASTELANDS OF THE UNDERWORLD

Throughout the Spring and Summer of my life, I descended into dark nights of my soul and journeyed through the abyss of that inferno to get here. It is the Magdalene womb that initiates me in those spiritual depths of darkness and "not knowing." Organic menstrual cycles shed the pain-body, clearing histories of the mind. I resurrected myself through the darkness in rituals of renewal. My intention to uncover the red threads and pattern of Magdalene moments is to illustrate the revelations of rebirth that she catalyzes.

Many children are tasked with achievement of perfection, a repetition of which amounts to feelings of imperfection (a perfectly imperfect human). The love I received felt conditional and so, longing to be wanted and loved, I centered myself in experience. I was educated to seek connection by being shiny and to hide well the parts of self that were repeatedly condemned. Revealing my vulnerability came to feel like tipping myself into annihilation. I could not bear the pain of looking into that abyss each time an imperfection or vulnerability was threatened to be revealed.

174

I built a fortress and hid my Magdalene underground for safe-keeping.

Connecting with that wounded depth of humanity reveals the collective experience of trauma that has been perpetuated so long that the energy of it becomes archetypical and mythic, living in my body, alchemizing currents of evolutionary experience. A personal and collective menstruation of the indoctrination received at school—especially, and most traumatically devastating, the genocide of indigenous peoples of this earth. Navigating childhood sexual trauma, personally and collectively, I attune my senses toward this looming archetypal energy of The Abandoned/Conditionally Loved/Unwanted/Unloved/Sexualized/Abused Child and feel it reaching its zenith.

By collective I mean that accumulation of ways of being which we are transforming, transmuting. Counterbalancing what has come before with an embrace of the spiritual experience and the recognition that we materialize because we are Embodying Divinity, and that Divinity is not separate. We are manifest energy, of matter formed from spirit.

We are rebuilding the sacred temples within our consciousness, where our dragon-phoenix rebirths and soars unchained, released from her prison, greening the collective landscapes of pleasure.

Beyond the dreaded precipice of our fortress walls, our world-work has been healing the trauma. The fatherless child, the betrayed Christ, the patriarchal God-the-Father, and all the parents who, even when present in children's lives, carry such trauma as to be overwhelmed and disembodied, perpetuating that feeling of abandonment the child experiences. So that in those moments of feeling the child is

175

"too much," they face that abominable abyss. The experience of that too-muchness, too-loudness, too whiny, too upset, too angry–is tied to the trauma of the conditionally loved child. The unloved, abandoned, fatherless child.

The Divine reveals tremendous healing keys to work with this potent archetypical medicine. The holy feminine may have been exalted by Catholicism to be that pristine, righteous, pure, virginal state of perfection in Divine Mother Mary, Mother of Christ, but it is the feral essence of Mary Magdalene, She Who Nurtures the Destitute, that is at work within the heart-womb of saints such as Mother Teresa. Pulsating her liminal red threads, the fierce Magdalene weaves a connection of radiant light within Moses, too, set adrift in a basket upon a river, illuminating a divine relatedness with all the children left in baskets and on doorsteps throughout time, and with that imprint of being abandoned, unwanted, and then being raised and loved by some miracle. I feel in my womb that revolutionary alchemy of metamorphosis.

Experiencing that essence of love in the world transforms the history of lack into a powerful movement for liberation and social justice, transmuting our personal birth trauma and origin story into an evolutionary fire for collective sovereignty and the well-being of all life. This catalyzing flow is the Magdalene fire at play. The Burning Bush of Magdala is essential for our r/evolution.

The history of unwanted children in the collective global storylines—of infanticide, abuse, and the missing and murdered indigenous maidens and stolen children—is the archetypal mythic thread of trauma that has been woven into the fabric of the world's ancestral human body. It is the trauma that facilitates the strangling of a crying child.

Our inability to face our own broken hearts within the experience of our children is the epigenetic trauma perpetuating itself. The inability to remain present with that annihilating feeling, and just wanting to stop experiencing the pain of our ancestors being mirrored by our children, continues the cycle until we choose to do it differently.

Our relationships mirror this reflection of ourselves and our pain, our longing, our need—all our unmet needs. What is required then is the igniting of that catalyzing creative current of holy fire to clear the channel and guide us home, to be a keeper of the flame of our generative essence, and return to our sovereign power to act in the name of the lost and missing, the betrayed and trafficked.

And yes, to harmonize with that blazing holy fire, I will weep over the world and centuries and ongoing timelines of injustice, racism, abuse, genocide, and the trafficking of sovereign bodies. The weeping of precious tears is an unraveling of mystery. The act is a sacred menstruation, a clearing, a pristine medicine. My tears carry the codes and memory, absorbed by the earth and ether. Carrying with it codes of tenderness, of my soft power to be vulnerable. This is the sacred union alchemy of merging masculine and feminine principles which our planet greatly requires.

All my teachers have taught me to discern which elemental medicine is needed for equanimity, to feel so present in this life as to be able to take action in the world and welcome the sensual experience of my existence. These Magdalene tears respond in dialogue with my environment, tending the space to birth beauty and joy in my body and the world around me. It is a sacred dance, this ritual release, to shed tears for my joy in exchange for my sorrow and grief. The grieving knows no bounds. I release grief for the feminine who has lost her way—the maiden, the mother, and wise queen. I witness the

177

grief and outrage of mothers, for all the world's children. I witness the sacred masculine, his descent and resurrection.

I weep for the rebirth of life on earth with these salted waters and remember. The mirth of our birth within the original earth-womb garden of creation, within which our mermaid ancestors continue to undulate in graceful currents. The power of grief rituals, and feeling the outrage, transmutes my holy tears into connection, and nurtures that which has been torn, alchemizing the energy into a mended cloth of radiant light.

WEAVING WITH WOMB WISDOM

The bleeding Magdalene dances upon my womb making me pregnant with my sacred, untamed nature, teaching me to accept myself unbound, in an expansive wave of embodied bein-enoughness. These red Magdalene rivers that flow in the second spring of my life are mycelial networks connecting spirit and place and ether, and the elemental beings, and nature's magic within my body.

It is the clearing release of these descending flows of red rivers that continue to fertilize my nature, reignite my spirit in the wild ways of earthen Magdalenes, original mermaids and sea dragonesses; the earth-womb and lava-blood of Pachamama; and the celestial realms from which I am formed, I emerge, merging with comprehensive acceptance, dancing wildly in a harmonious crescendo of ecstatic waves of gushing, birthing. Fertile life perpetually blooming myself, again and again, I disown that puritan task of attaining the impossible perfection and embrace the sacred codes of wild sovereignty that makes me whole.

Within that untamed ferocity, in vulnerable and messy moments of divine imperfection, I revisit places of trauma and wounding with a loving heart. Having embodied the

178

unconditionally loving Mother Goddess to myself, I begin now to embrace my role as Spiritual Grandmother, guiding myself to rewild the landscapes again as I sway my hips into the Autumnal gardens of my life.

Her energy, her tears, her laughter, her love—all of these qualities have been reparative and regenerative, transmuting the distorted illusion of separation to love myself unconditionally. Becoming the Magdalene, aligned with my truest self, my sovereign soul, I end the epigenetic curse perpetuating the infinity mirror of trauma and injustice of conditional love.

Visuals of nature's beauty and abundance dance before my eyes. Tastes exploding upon my lips and tongue, I am bathed in the aphrodisiac of pleasures. My breath, this sensual smile emerging as I connect to the subtle realms of bliss I feel at the ecstasy of this manifest world, this miraculous journey. Sounds of birdsong and strings mimic the silent pulsing rhythms of existence, catching fire in my heart. The embers of the codes that live there in all of us are perpetual. You are a Magdalene by the very essence that animates your incarnate existence.

I am the daughter of the essence that birthed this world, that burns within every heart. How can I look upon nature and not fall in love when I am connected to its primal intimacy? The sacred act of creation, of mind interacting with matter, spirit manifest, cannot but embrace an immersion into sensual existence.

When I embrace the Magdalene within my womb to enact a reclamation of that law of sovereign sexual energy, of sovereign regenerative life force, and feminine creative power, I connect to the pure, blissful flow of my spirit. I am a mermaid dancing within the toroidal ethers, frolicking with the elemental primeval Kundalini dragons of creation.

This is the Magdalene dragon that dances life within the mind-spirit-body. Magdalene energy is the beating of dragon wings, amplifying the power of our toroidal vortices that channel spirit to descend into this dimension and give birth to life on earth, birthing the universe and mending the tear that splits consciousness to heal the birth trauma of the planet. I remove the cloak of burdens and radiate my light.

The awareness of the Magdalene alchemizing within my organic body becomes part of the quantum metaphysical alchemy of the collective. The transmissions that have come through for me as I write this for you are also a direct invitation from the Magdalene lineage for you.

Become a guardian and protector of life on this earth as a Midwife of Rebirth.

The Magdalene Codes are not written for us to read and understand with our mind. They are tools and portals for action and evolution, transformation and transmutation. Ingredients *and* formula, for a quantum shift of timelines to support the left-hand Christed path of being—embodied on earth. No education needed to align with life. Embodied awareness is all that is required to deschool the mind and reconnect with nature.

Feel and sense how the Lady of Magdala speaks to your heart and listen to your womb to heal and clear the path home to your heart's soul-fire. That brilliance stemming from within your heart is the catalyzing life-force Yeshua and Mary Magdalene spoke of that was later documented in the Nag Hammadi Codices. Religious historian, Elaine Pagels, has written extensively on this library's paradigm shifting revelations and the original message of Jesus. You carry that awakening light in your palms, within the chambers of your heart, seated upon the throne of your womb, in the temple of your body.

Do not perpetuate the rift of separation consciousness by focusing on, "What put out my fire?"

Ask instead, "What will feed the fire that burns deep within me?

What will light up my life, body, mind, and spirit?

What oxygen do I need to breathe my dragon fire?

What will lift my outspread dragon wings to soar the unseen currents my soul travels?

Awaken your Magdalene from every inertia. Exalt the Magdalene radiance whose keening moans and soft whispers of love are incantations that weave a medicine from loin to loin. Her codes await your attention like a fire-starter ready to ignite. Let your Burning Bush speak to you of love directly. That fire of transformation that alchemizes all that old programming, defense structures in their loops and repetitive phrases that dig their embedded trenches into labyrinths of unconscious psyche.

She Who Ignites the Christed Spirit Within resurrects herself from the betrayal of that corruption. She Who Parts the Seas continues to clear the way. Magdalena codes are the energy signature of a blueprint for the new construction of the world, a joyful vibe I welcome in my body.

I hold this generative vision and affirm:

I examine what is awakening within me and alchemize any

181

parts that remain unloved. Unwanted. Abandoned. Conditionally loved. Abused.

I transmute all of it within the crucible of my womb-body-tree-of-life.

I connect with my sovereign fire and visualize a gentle, loving disintegration of blocks in the river of unconditional love, and give my soul access to the flow of sensual bliss that arouses my love of life.

Continually clearing and creating pathways in the mind-body-spirit is a counterbalance against what we come into contact with in the world. I write of embracing the wild and letting go of imperfections even as I meet that desire to finesse the perfect chapter. Ha! That's why this work is often called a practice. It is a way of life to keep aligning with the nature of our sovereign soul. At EmRahMa Mystery College, the Embodying Divinity nine-moon womb consciousness apprenticeship supports this process of evolving, clearing, and catalyzing your DNA.

In the psychospiritual counseling work I do, my spirit dances beside you as I hold a sacred ceremonial circle for the whispers of your womb to be heard by you. I will not disempower you by dictating how to decolonize the rainbow light of your body.

You are invited to celebrate your wildest sovereignty! I offer metaphysical maps and keys. It's up to you to step through the Magdalene doorway and resurrect the gold beneath the roots.

The Magdalene who walks in her power among the men of the time after Christ is timeless, and she lives within us if we dare to embody her wisdom.

She comes speaking of ecstasy in her palpable transmissions inside the spaces between times.

She comes radiating a brilliant softness illuminating the way to shepherd the information aflame within.

She comes offering compassionate understanding with her reflection of the tales of weeping rivers.

The mycelial filaments are lighting up the sacred geometry on earth. All these mythic moments of flow and power-in-action dismantle the greedy commands that try to tame a unifying instinct, that ecstatic spirit of nature, which bridges our souls in an empowered collective experience: our evolutionary path of sensual liberation.

END

ABOUT THE AUTHOR

DHYĀNA KLUTH

Rainbow Mermaid Mystic Dhyāna Kluth, psychospiritual counselor and international best-selling author, bridges worlds to decolonize the mind-body-spirit and heal the rift of separation-consciousness.

She guides women to listen to their soul, establishing a safe space for deep psyche embodied rebirth through intuitive processes of radical self-love alchemy with the Isis Womb mentorship and Embodying Divinity womb consciousness apprenticeship, in addition to signature masterclasses like Sovereign Soul Foundations.

Rooted in love, Dhyāna's clinical methods draw upon foundational therapeutic approaches to wellness. Buddhist psychology and somatic body-oriented therapy empower clients to liberate themselves.

A blend of dreambody, Taoism, Jungian psychology, physics, and deep democracy concepts of Dr. Arthur Mindell's WorldWork facilitates flow, unlocks your pure potential, and heals relationships.

The Reverend Priestess lives in Bloomfield, NJ with her husband and two daughters. In addition to psychospiritual client work and writing, Dhyāna can be found ushering kids to homeschool activities and hikes, or tasting dandelions in her wild medicinal garden.

Opportunities to thrive in ecstatic pleasure!

Embodying Divinity ~ Gestational Womb Consciousness Program of Remembering
www.emrahma.com/embodyingdivinity

Isis Womb Mentorship
www.dhyanahealing.com/motherwomb

TikTok
@holistichealingsupport www.tiktok.com/@holistichealing
support

Instagram @DhyanaHealing
www.instagram.com/Dhyanahealing/

YouTube https://bit.ly/dhyanakluth

MARY MAGDALENE STANDING IN POWER

EHRIN PARKER

WHAT IS THE LIFE EXPERIENCE? WHY DO OUR SOULS choose to come to earth in the first place? Did we do something wrong, so we were sent to Earth as a punishment? Or is it because our soul had a lot to learn, and we were the equivalent of a preschooler or was it a college student? Why are we in this experience called life? What is the point? It is very easy to feel the pointlessness of our experience on Earth, when you look around. Everywhere you look, no matter what the year, decade or century it is, there's sadness, pain, hunger, fear and anger and evil with just a smattering of love and joy sprinkled within. Why would a soul choose to be a part of this madness? There must be some reason that so many souls are here on earth. There must be a purpose. The purpose is the experience.

But what is it we are supposed to be experiencing? We are experiencing it all. The sadness and grief, happiness and joy, separation and togetherness, powerlessness and power, and

186

all there is in-between. Earth is a place of polarity unlike anywhere else. These experiences increase our knowledge and understanding at the deepest level. As we experience, not only does our soul grow and expand, but so does Source. It is said that we are all one with Source. We are connected to Source even if we are unable to remember. As a result, what we experience, Source experiences. In coming to Earth, we experience the illusion of separation and powerlessness. Part of the journey is finding our way home. Back to power and togetherness. But that still doesn't explain why our souls choose to come here to Earth. What makes Earth so special?

It has been said that Earth is the great experiment. What does that mean? What kind of experiment? To come to earth, we must jump through the veil of forgetfulness. We all do so willingly so we can have this experience of life on earth, forgetting. What is it that we are supposed to forget? We are to forget the great power we all carry within our souls. We forget that we are all one and even the reason why we chose to be here in the first place. Plus, to make it more interesting, we also have free will. We are guided but not told what to do. But for what purpose? As mentioned earlier, Source wants to experience it all for the greater good of all. But also, the question has been asked, can a soul find its power, source power when it feels so disconnected? Can the soul feel connected again? Can it find its true power?

Life on Earth is full of challenges. It doesn't matter what century or decade you are experiencing your life. Many believe that your experience is your destiny. You have no control over your life and there is nothing you can do about it. Once you start on the path you have no control over what happens to you. You are like a beach ball on the sand being blown to and fro. Others are of the belief that hell or high water I will make life happen as I want. I oversee my own path! But does it have to be either of those two ways? Is there

187

another way? Can you have the flexibility of a beach ball on the sand and control over your life? I believe you can. An example of this is in the story of Mary Magdalene. She is a shining beacon of light.

The story of Mary Magdalene has withstood the test of time. Her story has been told and retold, the story has been changed to fit the purpose of the storyteller. But no matter what the purpose of the speaker or the politics of the time, her story is still there. Her message has withstood all the renditions. She has been depicted as a whore, a wife, a mother or a sacred friend to Jesus. She has been reflected in both the best and the worst light. Much of her story seems lost. There is no accounting of her performing any great feats or miracles, no majestic greatness. Yet her story is still there, no matter what you hear in her story. She is still standing, standing in her power.

Mary Magdalene is symbolic of a woman who stands in the background, almost an afterthought. She stands in the power of the Feminine. The Feminine Spirt doesn't need grand gestures or credit for its greatness. She stands in her quiet fierce power, influencing all around her. Mary Magdalene is standing in her own power despite all the drama that is swirling around her. She stands in her quiet fierce power, influencing all around her. She stands in the truth and love of who she is, the truth in her heart

Mary Magdalene represents the power within all of us. But what does standing in your power mean? When I first thought about it, I imagined a girl in the schoolyard punching a boy in the nose. But that isn't it. Power is the belief of knowing and being who you are. Can anyone do it? YES. If so, how does one do it? How do we have power in the swirling mess of life and its events around us?

As with learning anything, begin with the small things. We must crawl before we can run. In mastering the minutiae, we can master our lives. There is much power in mastering the small around us. Consider that the big and grand surrounding us is just an extension of the small. Controlling the rain is no more difficult than controlling one drop of water. The rain is many drops of water. Even a rainbow is still just drops of water. It is all in standing in the power of the "small."

My journey began when I was born. I had no understanding of my power back then. I became aware of the beginnings of my own power when I was a freshman in college. It was the beginning of finals week. I had been up for days pouring over books, looking at notes and just plain studying. I never felt very confident in my brain and its mental capacity. It took all I had to fill it full of figures and facts. Suddenly, I started to feel the beginnings of a cold or worse the flu. My muscles were a bit sore and the back of the throat a little scratchy. When I was in college, there were no retakes on final exams, if you missed a final you failed the course. I had perfect attendance as I was motivated by how much each hour of classes cost me. By golly, I wasn't giving the college a free dime of my time. As I felt the first stirring of sickness, I remembered back to my last finals week in high school. I went armed with a down coat and pencil as I took my biology final with a fever of 102. My brain was sluggish and foggy that day. I barely passed the final.

Braced with the fear of failure in my first year of college, I made a deal. Not with the devil, but with my body. I acknowledged my body's message, I understood that it was telling me I needed sleep and less stress. I promised to give it that in just three days. "Just give me three more days fever free, long enough to have a clear mind to take the final exams ahead of me." I went to bed and I thought nothing more of it as I took all my finals fever free over the next three days. Later, as I was traveling home for the holidays, the fever hit hard and fast. Once I recovered and could think clearly again, I realized that my body had agreed to my deal. It gave me three fever-free days to take my finals. It was the beginning of what I called, "let's make a deal." I understand what you want, and I will give it to you if you give me what I want.

Are you clear about what your body wants? Do you understand the language of your body? I started by paying attention to my body. Is it thirsty or hungry, too stressed or tired? How could I help it? For me, the body was a safe place to start. No one would know if I got it right or wrong. The body is always communicating with you. Can you "hear" what it is saying and understand it? Take a moment and clear your mind and breath into the body. Clear away the swirl and chaos of life around you, to "hear" your body.

Then I wondered, could I have power over any other areas of my body or just over sickness? I started playing with my menstrual cycles. I knew when I was supposed to start my cycle, but could I start it two days earlier or three days later? It was another version of "let's make a deal". I knew that I needed to cycle and clear out the blood in my uterus, but if I had a trip, or a special event or date coming up, could I menstruate on a different day? I struck other deals and I found that they worked. I acknowledge what the body needed and what I needed so all needs were met.

I then took the controlling of my cycles a step further. After I was married, I only saw my husband on weekends and I really wanted children. Could I ovulate only on the weekends so I could increase my opportunities for getting pregnant? I struck another deal. I felt the power within my body. I was not the beach ball on the sand and in the wind. I felt more like seaweed. I had flexibility and control. I was like Mary

Magdalene, despite all that was around me, I had subtle but fierce power.

If you are thinking, that's nice that she could do that, but I could never get my body to do what I want. Start noticing your thoughts. How do you think about your body? Have you ever thought about your body? Your body is your partner in this life. Have you ever considered that your body can be your partner or friend? Or is it just something you were stuck with? A body is an amazing compilation of cells. I recently came to understand that our gut biome is its own consciousness. They are live cells, and they too have a consciousness. This places our body in a whole different perspective. Sit with yourself and check in with your body. It is not something that you have to do for hours. Just be present with yourself. Once you can sit with yourself you can begin to understand the language your body is speaking. Notice what you are saying to your body and how the body responds.

The power you have over your body can be used for problem-solving as well. I had a patient once that did not have a great home life. To get a break, she had migraine headaches that were so bad that she had to sit in her quiet dark room all weekend. I don't know exactly how she started this, but I imagine that it began with the thought that "I want to get away." I will keep you safe if you can get me away. Hence the migraine in the quiet dark room. She spoke to her body and the body responded. After noticing this we discussed ways of changing her "deal." Could she have safe space without a migraine? After some work on her part, she found she could.

Once I felt that I mastered the power I had in my body, I then started looking around noticing where else I could have power in my life. We live in a world with so many people and chaos, how can we have power there? You can have power over what types of people you interact with. I work with the public as an Osteopathic Physician. Many people see me when they are not feeling their best. I came to understand early on in my residency that I feel very uncomfortable and unsure when I am dealing with direct loud confrontation. Like when people attack me. In my residency, I didn't realize that I had any control over who I saw. It wasn't my space. But once I was in private practice, I gave a lot of thought to what type of experience I wanted to have as a physician. So, I had a talk with the space at my office, after a mind-numbing confrontation that left me shaken and unsure of myself. I really looked at what I did not want to deal with in my life, people yelling and attacking me. I feel comfortable around people who are hurting, angry or upset with life, but not at me. I was very clear and specific stating my intention, it is not Ok with me for people to attack me verbally or physically. I stated that I was surrounded by people who supported me. Lo and behold the feel of my practice changed overnight. I realized that I was standing in my power of what I want to interact with in my professional life.

This idea can extend into all interactions. I held it when I went into the grocery store or Walmart. It was very easy to see during the COVID mask insanity. I did not wear a mask unless I was specifically asked to. No one confronted me. I could go about doing my business. This was great confirmation that I had power over the experiences around me.

It felt more complicated when I started working with my home life and children. For me the complication came with the feeling of guilt. I felt guilty that I could not give my undivided attention to my children because I worked, But I absolutely loved working. But I discovered that I could stand in my power there also. I have two boys and two girls. Getting them off to school felt like controlled chaos. They wouldn't get dressed quickly, fought about breakfast, picked on each other until all were mad or crying. One day I was thinking about how nice and calm my office was, and I wondered how I could have it here at home. I began thinking of how I wanted my morning to progress. I called it "setting the day." In the morning after I woke up but before I got out of bed, I would take a moment and envision how I wanted the morning to go. I envisioned my children getting up happy, dressing quickly and eating, making their lunches and treating each other with kindness. Lo and behold it worked with them too! They would get all the way to school with smiles and laughter. Sure enough, every day that I imagined this, it happened. I am not controlling my children. I am asking for the environment I want to participate in. Happiness and harmony felt so much better than anger and frustration. I had the power to interact with all types of people on my terms. I was no longer at the whims of others.

I had the power to influence my bodily experiences and interactions with others, but could I also have the power to command the space I occupied? I had an office next to a restaurant that piped out horrible smells. It smelled fake and chemically. I didn't notice it when I looked at the space, but it hit while I was moving in. To make it worse, the back door of my office was the cigarette and marijuana smoking spot. Smells permeated into my workspace to distraction. I thought of canceling my lease before I even moved in. Unfortunately, it was January and there was very little office space available to rent. I could not afford to not work while I continued looking. So, I decided right that my office smelled nice, and I only breathed clean sweet air. I never smelled the awful smells again by my office or within it and neither did my patients.

I had power over my space. Once I declared it, I never thought about it again until a couple of years later, a forest fire nearby was sending smoke all over the town. One day, I had my office door open to bring fresh air inside, a patient came in and couldn't believe that I had the doors and window open letting in fresh air when the town was so smoky. I looked up and responded, there is only clean sweet air in here. The patient agreed and wanted to know what kind of filter I had. None, I responded, I hold the power over my space and there is only clean sweet air inside. Sometime later, I was walking along the main street with a friend. After a while she turned and asked me how I could walk on the street with all the smelly exhaust from the cars. I truly had not noticed it. I had gone so long with the idea that I only breathed clean sweet air that I thought that cars' exhaust had changed, and it no longer smelled. Mary Magdalene had power over her space, she stood in her truth and allowed life to swirl around her.

Another way to command your space is by ordering the weather. I live in a mountain town and to get to most big cities, I must drive over mountain passes with drop-offs. They can be scary in bad weather. One day in May, I had to drive over a mountain pass to get my girls to a gymnastic meet. The clouds in the sky did not look good. Before I left, I declared that I would drive on dry roads. I was willing to have them wet, but I did not want much water on the road because I didn't want to worry about hydroplaning. When I hit the pass about noon, I saw a little snow, maybe ½-1 inches of snow on the sides of the road and cars off to the side like they might have slid. I even saw the snowplows. I thought that was odd for how little snow was on the ground. My girls and I arrived safely at the gym. I sat next to two mothers who also drove the past that day. One went over at 11:30 am and the other at 12:30 pm. Both moms discussed the blizzard conditions they had driven through.

194

Power is all around us. Are you using the power or reacting to the power? Notice the power we all have within. You can be a warrior fighting to hold your ground against the foes of life. You can beat people with your power or just stand there with it. When I think of Mary Magdalene, that is the power that I think of. Standing in the power of who you are and what you desire in life. Can you stand in this power despite what is swirling around you, what people are saying or doing? Standing in your power begins in your mind and thoughts. Power is the belief of knowing and being who you are. It doesn't have to be showy or grand. We are here to experience the triumph of discovering our power and being one with Source. One drop of water is just as powerful as a whole rainstorm. For rain is just many drops of water.

ABOUT THE AUTHOR

EHRIN PARKER

Ehrin Parker has been a family practice osteopathic physician for 23 years. In this capacity, she works with her patients to find their balance and health. She empowers all to embrace their healing powers within.

As a mother of four children, she was very concerned about the power of medicine in labeling and dictating her children. She began a quest of discovery both as an inner journey and outer, discovering how her very energy influenced the behavior of her children. Plus, the influences of nature and real food and a clean home. Through this discovery, she discovered her own inner power for health and healing. She has been sharing it with all who connect with her ever since.

Ehrin Parker is a medical intuitive. She uses this gift to guide her "healing practice" of her patience. She uses it to help her patients discover their own hidden blocks to health.

https://ehrinparker.com

FROM SURVIVING TO THRIVING

ILONA POKA

MY CHILDHOOD TRAUMA BEGAN WHEN I WAS IN
MY mother's womb. We were both mentally and physically
abused by my father. My mom finally left my father when I
was two years old. Just because she left doesn't mean the
abuse didn't show up in many other people and experiences
throughout my life.

When I was seven weeks old, I almost lost my life due to
having meningitis. I couldn't eat so the doctors had to feed
me through a tube in my ankle, I still have the scar. Luckily,
they caught it early, so early they could not detect if it was
viral or spinal meningitis. Doctors said I may be delayed in
walking, talking and/or any development kids my age would
do. Turned out, I did everything earlier than everyone else! I
was walking by nine months and talking by my first year.
Imagine, I was fighting for my life at the age of seven weeks
old and how that has affected who I am and how I behave.

I have no doubt that the Women's Movement in the 1960s

gave my mom the courage and strength to leave an abusive marriage in 1975. Divorce was not the common way of thinking in 1975, my mom was taking a stand for herself. There was a ton of shame around getting divorced during this time especially being raised in an Italian Catholic family. During those times you didn't let the world know your problems. You took beatings and kept your mouth shut knowing in the back of your mind that you deserved so much more and there could be one time it could lead to your death.

Every couple of years my father would fight for his parental rights, and it always ended in a heated argument, sometimes physical. I clearly remember when I was seven years old and my sister was sixteen years old, my father told my sister that since she was sixteen, she didn't have to go to his house every weekend. So, one weekend she decided not to go. I remember taking the elevator downstairs with my mom, telling her I was scared and didn't want to go. I didn't want to go without my sister, and I knew my father was going to be angry. She comforted me and told me I probably wasn't going to spend the weekend with him. Well, she was right! He was SO angry that my sister wasn't joining us. He and his wife were screaming at my sister who was standing on our outside balcony of the fourth floor of our apartment building. My father then threw me in the backseat of the car. My mom went to get me, and he grabbed her and left a horrible huge bruise on her arm. They left right before the police arrived. Forty years later, it's amazing how I can remember all the details of that day.

I became the fixer. The fixer who wanted everyone to be happy, and that included allowing myself to become a pretzel. I would bend and twist and stay stuck to make everyone else happy, that included family, friends, coworkers, bosses and boyfriends. I've had numerous failed relationships. I've never been married. Most of my 20s and

30s I was promiscuous, having had my first sexual experience with my stepsister when I was younger. She took the innocence of that little girl. My father had actually given me a photo album of different pictures. I saw one of the pictures and my heart sank, I felt sick to my stomach. There was a picture of me when I was 10 years old and in a negligee. It was a picture my stepsister took of me. I don't understand why my father didn't question the picture. It wasn't until my 30s when I was in therapy that I realized what had really happened and that it was inappropriate. When I told my mom, she comforted me. When I told my father and his wife, they said I was lying. They said I was being vengeful. Vengeful is not a word anyone who knows me would use to label me. I didn't spend more than three months before finding a new boyfriend, yet I never felt so alone in my life. I didn't know how to communicate, let alone express how I felt or ask for what I really wanted. My experience was if you spoke what was on your mind, you'd get whacked.

I attended Marymount College in Tarrytown, NY, an all-women's Catholic college. My major was psychology with a minor in women's studies. There was a woman who came to speak at our Women's Studies Workshop, and she told us how on the day of her wedding, she was putting her mascara on, looking at herself in the mirror, and she knew she should not marry her soon-to-be husband. She was educated, came from a great family, and had a great job. She said, "I was terrified, how could someone who looked like they had it all together, be living this way. That's the thing, abused people look just like everyone else." She did marry him and went through years of physical and mental abuse, which inevitably ended in them divorcing. On the outside it appeared they were one of the happiest couples–meanwhile this woman lived in fear more than not.

I had some random notion in my head that I would be

married by the time I was 25 years old. That came and went, and I cried at that time; however, a few years later I was grateful. Five out of six of my best friends were married and divorced by the time I was 30. We do the best we can with what we're given. I get it. No one is perfect and we learn and grow along the way.

Have you ever had this feeling? It started when I was a little girl. I felt this knowing inside of me, a knowing that there was more in life than what I experienced. There was more to life than what my parents had chosen, more to life than some of the marriages I experienced growing up, even what my own life was like! I was tired of the inconsistency in my life. I wanted a relationship and kept choosing the wrong men for me. I do know that all of these experiences in my life (and others not specifically mentioned) led me exactly where I needed to be to make a DIFFERENT CHOICE. Just like many of you reading this, you know there's something more out there than what you currently have. You feel it, you know it in your heart. Listen to it, I'm sure grateful I did.

It was 2001 and the universe was very clear it was going to shake up my life a little. My boyfriend and I broke up. I got laid off from my full-time job, the bar that I bartended at closed, and September 11 happened–all in four months. I was sending 40-50 resumes out a week and getting no reply because all of the jobs are going to victims of September 11th who lost their job, understandably so.

One day I was sitting on the couch staring out the window and I got this feeling inside of me, calling me, telling me to do something different. I decided right then and there, I would rather say that I tried and failed than I wish I would have taken the risk. So when I was 28 years old, I moved across the country from New York to Arizona. I knew one person who lived here and had $2,000 in my pocket. I can honestly say it was one of the best decisions of my life.

Being away from my family gave me an opportunity to create my life, on my terms. I knew I wanted a peaceful, loving, nurturing and supportive life so that is what I was on the journey to create. I started to feel more like an outsider looking in on my family dysfunction. I attended a personal development workshop and began unraveling what wasn't mine. Just because that was my parents' story, it didn't have to be mine. I had no idea how my family and society's impact and conditioning had on me. I had gone through YEARS of talk therapy, resolving concerns and issues that I was experiencing at that time. I thought I had talked about it and thought I was free from it. I was clueless that I was holding myself back. So, I began to peel back the layers of the onion on my family dysfunction and began my process of self-discovery.

I started realizing my negative automatic-pilot thinking and began to change my thoughts to be more positive. I put reminders on my phone throughout the day to remind me to be more positive! Sometimes I would add a song and dance to the positive message and really FEEL IT. I learned that saying and writing empowering "I am" statements to counter the negative thoughts helped too! I learned how my breath could help with the anxiety I was feeling. I realized how powerful my brain is and how to rewire it to create the life that I really wanted! I learned how to communicate and how to express my feelings. I could say how I was feeling and it didn't have to be a fight. I use these tools in my seven-month Thriving Academy where I show my clients how they can create their thriving lives.

Within my first year of living in Arizona I got my real estate license. I was in corporate America for many years. I have a great work ethic, I always gave 125% but I never did well kissing ass so corporate Americans were not for me. Becoming self-employed was a huge accomplishment for me. It has allowed me so many levels of freedom. I can create my own hours, I can be on vacation and still be able to work. I have created a peaceful, loving home for myself. I currently live on a property that has two tiny homes. As close as my mother and I are, we both know we wouldn't do well living in the same house. You know you can all relate. However, having her 60 feet away from me allows her to be close enough as she is getting nearer to retirement. I have loving, supportive people in my life. I have learned to clearly communicate with them and ask for what I want. I can express how I feel and it doesn't have to be a fight. It feels amazing to be able to speak my mind and say how I feel without the fear of getting whacked. It truly is liberating, along with being able to do the work that I do. I've staffed the life success course many times, as well as the women's leadership seminar. I get to work with clients that I can totally relate to, and helping empower them to overcome their trauma is such a beautiful experience for me. It's what's led this chapter to all of you today. My passion for coaching and supporting others to move past their trauma.

On this journey of unraveling and self-discovery, there was still more to uncover. Applying these tools and strategies to my everyday life was the most important part. Anyone can be aware and learn, it's about using and applying it to my life.

Unknowingly, I dated a man who really wanted to live a gay lifestyle. I knew him five years before we started dating, we had mutual friends. He had a girlfriend most of that time I knew him. He was previously married and had a daughter. A few months later after they broke up, he and I started dating. There were SO MANY red flags that I just ignored. I woke up one morning and he was gone, said he couldn't sleep and went to his friend's house. He got kicked out of a casino for being an obnoxious drunk. I wound up ending the relationship because he was an alcoholic. The last straw was when he threw up in the shower and didn't clean it. He had owed me money so I was checking his email. Yes, I was snooping! I have no problem admitting that. I saw an email from adult friend finder website, and I opened it. His username was cossucker. His profile had a pull-down menu – man seeking – woman, man, both. He had chosen he was a man seeking a man. I almost dropped to the floor. I thought to myself that there is no way a straight man is going to make that mistake!! The first thing I did was get an AIDS test, it was one of the scariest experiences in my life. I was negative and a few days later I received a paycheck for him in the mail. I went to his house and told him he needed to cash the check so he could give me the money he owed me. He told me to take a long walk on a dark road. I said OK, if you don't give me my money, I am going to tell everyone your secret. I walked towards the front door and said it again. I got in my car and left. Five minutes later he called me and asked me how much I wanted. I just didn't understand, we were such good friends beforehand, I wish he would have told me he was gay, I would have totally supported him. He came from an Irish Catholic family where that wasn't allowed. I spoke to him nine years later and he was still living a lie, dating a woman.

It was the week between Christmas and New Years, I met a friend at a hotel casino to have some drinks and catch up. We sat by the hotel pool, laughed and had a great time. I was leaving the hotel and was very confused by the signs and blew a stop sign. The police officer pulled me over and gave me a breathalyzer. It didn't work, three times. They made me get in a paddy wagon and took me to a Walmart parking lot where they drew my blood. Since this happened on casino property, it is owned by the Indian Reservation. They have very different laws and can pretty much do whatever they want. I could not get a copy of my ticket. They would only allow an attorney to obtain the info, which I would then have to pay for. I spoke with friends who had experienced this, and one of them told me just get over yourself and agree to the DUI. My business includes me driving clients around, that was not an option for me. If I was going to pay an attorney $10,000, they were going to get the charges dropped!

About 30 days later I attended a personal development seminar where I learned about the power of setting my intentions. I had spoken to a friend and said the only way I was going to get out of the DUI was if my blood results came back invalid and unreliable. I wrote on about 10 Post-it Notes 'Invalid Unreliable Results." They were all over my house – front door, bathroom, bedroom, in my office. As I passed them, I would think about the results coming back invalid and unreliable AND I felt what it would be like when the results came back that way. Three months later, on April Fool's Day, I received a call from the Department of Motor Vehicles that my results were under the limit. So invalid and unreliable?!?! Whatever the connection, I was going with it!

There is so much more to life that we all get to experience. If you would like to release trauma and build a toolbox to support you on this beautiful journey of healing, I am here for you. If you have experienced trauma and you're ready to release its hold on you, I can lead you to have the life that you want. I have been wherever you have been. I understand your pain. If you are ready to move forward and build a thriving life, I would be honored to support you.

ABOUT THE AUTHOR

ILONA POKA

Ilona Poka is the Queen of Inner Peace. She is the Creator & Owner of Truth Be Told, a public speaking and coaching company. She is also the Creator and President of Mental Illness Refined, her 501c3 non-profit. Her mission is that the world becomes aware of the importance of mental wellness. She has been a multipreneur since 2006.

Women who attend Ilona's Thriving Academy have experienced childhood trauma and are ready to release the past. She gives women tools and techniques to claim their power so that they go from trauma to trusting themselves and others. They feel psychologically, physically and emotionally safe.

Ilona is originally from New York and has lived in Arizona since 2002. She owns a property with two tiny homes. Her mother will be retiring soon and will join Ilona and move into one of the tiny homes. Ilona has a cockapoo named Marley who's smart, fun and spunky. They enjoy walks around the neighborhood and playing ball.

If you are a woman who is experiencing childhood trauma and is ready to go from surviving to THRIVING, connect with me.

Linktree: https://linktr.ee/TruthBeToldOneWorld

Join Our Facebook Community Group – The Thriving Sisterhood
https://www.facebook.com/groups/TheThrivingSisterhood

Facebook https://www.facebook.com/TruthBeToldOneWorld

Instagram
https://www.instagram.com/TruthBeToldOneWorld/

SHE SPEAKS

ISABEL MORALES

AS I SAT HERE TO WRITE THIS CHAPTER, I WAS flooded with a steady stream of creativity and ideas. I wrote a beautiful, compelling (or so I thought!) story of how I grew up in Colombia in the 80s, in the midst of the greatest civil war the country has ever seen and absorbed the lack mentality around me which I carried through my younger years, and how I uncovered my personal magic to create an extraordinary life experience that more than pleases me.

What I got to write was filled with humour - something I adore about the way I write. I love writing deep stuff layered with my own energetic signature of fun and sarcasm. However, something felt off. What I wrote wasn't...bad. It just wasn't meant for this book. It was such a weird yet familiar feeling to know that the greater plan wasn't for me to distill a chapter of this book, but instead to *receive it*.

So, I connected with her. I called her into my heart. And I let her guide my fingers on the keyboard as the words poured.

"How do I know this is coming from you and not from my imagination?"

"Just trust," she said.

"Trust?"

"There's no accident that you were called to do this work. There's no accident that you are the interpreter of this portion of the codes. Trust that what's needed to be imprinted will be imprinted. Take this as a joint venture and let the stream of thoughts run from me to you. You know what to do. You've done it before."

I have. That's pretty much how I write. I get in the space where the words just come, but they feel *mine*. What you're about to read is a compilation of thoughts that came from a different place, yet they're somehow, also mine. They feel more grounded. There's a part of me that wants to say that they're missing the element of fun–the giddy stuff my personality always brings to the table. But that wouldn't be quite accurate, as every message delivers a key to getting back to our divinity, which is rooted in joy, freedom and play. So, even though the tone is different from anything that comes directly from me and my writing "team" this chapter was written from the heart of Magdalene, through Isabel's vessel.

Scan the following pages as you are intuitively called to. Set your eyes where your soul guides you because what's next will not read as a story in itself, or in a specific order. It was brought forward for you to receive the message that resonates with you, specifically for where you are in your spiritual growth. And every time you read a message you will receive it in a different way, but always in perfect orchestration with

209

the calling of your soul.

You may choose to read every page as it's laid out or read one or a few messages at a time. Listen to your intuition, run your fingers through the pages and check within to know what resonates the most. Trust that what comes up is exactly what you need to hear.

Enjoy!
Isabel

The amount of love that is poured onto you exceeds any stretch of your human imagination. You're never alone. I want you to know that you have a group–a team–that is available to you from the unseen at any moment in time. When you feel our love, when you feel our admiration and adoration for your willingness and excitement to be here, now, then you can *feel* the whisper of the guidance that is our gift to you. Because everything that you do has a deeper resonance on the greater *all*. Because this is your time to create heaven on earth.
-She speaks

1. The power of your magic exceeds any form of expectation you place on it. In other words, you're magical beyond your own imagination. However, from the personality perspective, you only have access to that which you can imagine. When you unlock this code, you'll understand how ridiculously powerful your own imagination is, even considering you only have access to what you can imagine. Imagine intentionally. Imagine wisely. It is your sacred connection to your own divinity.

2. What you see outside of the self (your world) is only a

perception of the inner self. If you desire to see a radical difference in what you experience outside, change your perception of self. This is the work of a lifetime, and it is the challenge of a lifetime. And even though there's no shortcut, start with compassionately and lovingly evolving your perspective of your outside world.

3. Your ego is only an identification with the world of duality. When you practice neutrality in the observation of all things, events and circumstances in life, you'll experience unlimited peace and happiness. There's no good or bad, only what you make it be.

4. Changing your perception of self requires radical responsibility for two things: the environment *you have created* and *your magical power to change it*. You owe it to yourself to own both.

5. Your body holds infinite wisdom for health, wealth, love and self-expression. Your body has been designed to experience bliss and pleasure in all its forms, and to aid you in the ascension process. However, the ego mind has been falsely deemed Queen which, in many ways, limits your physical experience of bliss. In all cases, consciousness overrides the ego mind and the body. You are THE consciousness. As you learn to break free from the restrictions of the ego, your body will be set free to do what it's meant to do.

6. You unleash consciousness by holding neutrality in the midst of apparent duality. By observing events, rather than experiencing them. By feeling the emotions in the body without identifying with them. It's ultimately the relentless steadiness of the 'observer' in you that will set the Goddess free.

7. Life is always working in your favour. That is a guarantee. It only might feel like it's not when the ego insists on giving meaning to the emotions felt in the body. I'd love for you to understand that an emotion is the result of a connection the ego has made to a past memory, and you can create new connections by contemplating new memories. That's when the magic of your imagination comes in.

8. You command matter. Infinite particles are constantly rearranging themselves to materialize the infinite algorithm that culminates in your life experience. They run back and forth, orderly, as you think, decide, change your heart and decide again. They organize the chaos and the beauty you direct. Every 'moment of now' is the culmination of creation, the birth of matter, the expansion of thought. Every 'moment of now' you experience is a mini-orgasm of life. Let that sink deep into your soul. You have more power of influence over everything you experience than you've been led to believe, including the realm of the unseen.

9. There's no need for prayer when assertion creates in the tangible reality. I understand this might confuse you, as you might have heard time and time again about the power of prayer. Prayer only works if it builds faith. Faith only works if it reinforces assertion.

10. You cannot forcefully change the reflection in the mirror but you can change your perception of the reflection in the mirror, which will change the reflection in the mirror. The perception of self is the key to fulfillment.

11. You have access to a spirit team that is constantly communicating with you. Come to the space of neutrality where you can hear their wisdom. You may call it intuition, a nudge, a sign. They call it a conversation with Goddess herself.

212

12. There's nothing outside of you. Nothing. There's no one up in the sky testing you, judging you, keeping score. There's only you making all this up. The shitty, the glorious, the infamous, the extraordinary–all you, all made up. Make good shit up.

13. A belief is only a rule you've accepted as your own. A distortion through which you experience life. The best way to defy your own beliefs is to apply the "universal rule" as only a rule if it applies to everyone. No exceptions. If you can find ONE exception, there's no rule. Do you have to work hard for money? Find someone who doesn't. You can't be happy and wealthy at the same time? Find someone who is. Be a rule breaker. Remember, you're making it all up anyway.

14. An emotion is painful only because it wants your attention, hence the physical discomfort the body feels. What most people do is avoid the pain of an emotion by numbing themselves to it. But you won't find the growth potential a painful emotion brings in anything else, nowhere else. Each growth opportunity a painful emotion brings is very personal and unique to every individual. It is the signature your soul has planted in you to continue the expansion that was planned for you. What do you do, then? Sit in silence with the emotion for as long as it's needed. Pay attention to it. Listen to it. The wisdom it brings is invaluable.

15. I understand the challenge of sitting in silence with a painful emotion, when all you want to do is NOT FEEL IT, and move on. However, it is in the act of *holding space* for it, lovingly, that you grow in wisdom and character. If you're new to the practice of holding space for the little one inside of you crying in pain, here's how you start loving her more: 1. Ask the emotion how old it is. 2. Ask what it needs from you, how it wants you to help. 3. Be open to what comes up

for you. You might get a flood of images, words that might seem random, a song, a movie scene. Whatever comes up, honour it. *She speaks your language*, only you haven't listened for too long. The progression from asking questions to sitting in silence and in observation will blend seamlessly. Remember, you are consciousness itself. You are the observer.

16. You can observe in pain, or you can absorb in suffering. Those are two very different things that are easily confused. The first one implies you can re-parent yourself by holding space and observing, with no identification with the event which caused the pain, but deeply *feeling* the pain. The latter implies the mind is highly involved, justifying, blaming, victimizing (often the self) and trying to find logical meaning to the event that brought the emotional response. The first one will translate to consciousness, being, liberation from the mind. The second one creates a stronger tie to circumstances and reinforces the attachment to the ego-mind. None is better than the other. They're both part of the human experience. It is up to you and only you to decide which one you'll contemplate.

17. Contrary to what you may be inclined to do, consciously lean into the pain. I promise you, the only thing it wants from you is your attention. And as you lean, you'll open portals to deeper connection with your own divinity. There's tremendous, untapped wisdom in human pain. That's human pain, not human suffering.

18. Every day, take some time to decide who you want to be. What does it look like to be this version of you? How does she talk? What does she think? What does she do? Who's with her? What does her day look like? How does she feel? Play with the idea of being her in all her glory. This is who you're becoming, and this is how you start becoming.

19. Focus and consistency–not effort–will bring you to realize the next version of you you're creating. Make a point to embody, fully, your new self for 90 days and see what happens. [Hint: magic, magic, magic will unfold].

20. Open your heart several times a day. Opening your heart prepares your body to receive the consciousness that you are more fully. Do you remember Jesus's words: "Let the children come to me. Don't stop them! For the Kingdom of God belongs to those who are like these children?" There it is! Open your heart to more play, hysterical laughter, walks in nature, presence, daydreaming, magic spells, dancing. When you go back to your heart, like a child, life finds a way to show you your magnificence.

21. The voice within has more creative power than a million voices without. Can you hear it? Is it loud and clear for you? A very simple practice to unveil the voice within is to quietly whisper in meditation "Who am I?" life will bend over backwards to bring to you the full experience of that, and the breadth of who you really are–the goddess, the queen. Including the voice within.

22. Daydreaming will transform your life. More people are positively changed by the art of daydreaming than by physical work alone.

23. Repetitive conscious daydreaming. That's all there is to it. When you unlock this code, the universal mind births life *through you*, not to you.

24. You are a part of me. You are a part of the *all*. One crucial key to life is to learn to love the depths of you, even the parts that seem unlovable. That's why it is so magnificently important to give disidentified attention to your emotional wounds for as long as it is necessary.

Attention *is* love.

25. Do the inner work as if your life depended on it. Because it does.

26. Awareness is the practice of observing different parts of you. It's the witnessing of the different aspects that make up your personality, your ego, your individuality. Witnessing without an opinion or judgment is the beginning of potentially the most beautiful love affair ever created, for when you get to observe with no judgment, you cannot help but fall in love with your entire life experience. Honour your humanness and love everything out of it!

27. There's nothing that will move the needle further in your spiritual growth, and in your humanness than the awareness of self. Become so intimately acquainted with your current thoughts, behaviours, reactions, preferences and quirks that none of your own self-created drama gets past you. I promise you, you will blow your own mind by practicing awareness regularly, because then and only then the next step to get you to your ideal self will become crystal clear.

28. Practicing self-awareness: Start by noticing how you feel, how you think, how you react. Make a note to notice your opinions, biases and perspectives about yourself, the people in your life, the people around you and the circumstances you've created. Notice which ones you love and which ones you don't. Notice what seems like a thought *you choose* to think vs. an automatic thought that happens without much consideration. Notice what seems common sense to you. Notice how you can notice.

29. Practicing self-awareness: Stop several times a day, for two minutes, and notice how you feel. Notice what your state of being is. Scan your body, from head to toe, and notice

what's going on physically and emotionally. Just observe without opinion.

30. Practicing self-awareness: Several times a day, ask yourself three questions: Who am I? Where am I? What am I doing? This simple trinity is more potent than you think. It will get you back into your body and into the present moment.

31. Let's have a full circle moment: Only YOU can be the catalyst for change in your life. Only you can make the moves to get from A to B. As you strengthen your awareness muscle, you widen the space in consciousness where long-lasting change CAN happen. In other words, as you become more aware, you create space between the old and the new potential. Then it is up to you to decide which way to move. It is as simple as that. Awareness increases your range of view of who you're being at any point in time and gives you the freedom to choose who you BE in the next moment. It is incredibly powerful!

32. There's no human desire that doesn't have the potential to become manifested in three-dimensional reality. Life wouldn't plant a seed for a desire in you, if it didn't have full-force potential to deliver it to you. In other words, if you can imagine it and desire it, then it can manifest. You can't imagine something that doesn't already exist, even if it exists in a timeline that you haven't yet accessed. The path to your desire will be revealed to you as you practice assertion of the desire, often as imperceptible minimal adjustments of your assertion into it.

33. Micro-shifts: The art of compassionately and continually looking within to adjust your internal state of being. It's not a matter of "believing" something else in one try or forcefully deciding to like this instead of that, but a *soft*

217

look within to decide "is this worth my attention?" And if it is, consciously choose how your attention is laid out. The way things run behind the scenes of self-awareness is to repeatedly contemplate perceptions that have been formed on past, unconscious decisions. So, in the name of having an opinion or a thought about something, lots of these perceptions slip unchecked because they feel true to your nature. This is far from your truth. The feeling of resonance may be an indication of how you have looked at things in the past. A micro-shift is a mini act of courage to make a decision to hold a new perception even in the midst of the old resonance.

34. A micro-shift in perception is often all that's needed to set the pace and build momentum in the direction of what's desired. Big leaps aren't necessary, although they happen. However, more often than not, a leap is the result of multiple conscious micro-shifts.

35. There's no right or wrong way to go about life. Only you decide if your life choices and perceptions are right or wrong. Only you can decide for yourself what's good, bad, proper and improper. And only you decide to hold your current perceptions, or micro-shift into more pleasing ones.

36. Your laughter opens portals to the unseen. Laugh daily.

37. Your admiration of the world you are creating opens portals to the unseen. If you're pleased with what you see, express gratitude for it. If you're not, laugh about it. Either way, you're opening portals and strengthening your connection to the unseen.

38. Take care of your body. Feed it well, breathe it well, dress it well, sleep it well! Every sensation felt in your body enriches and expands the entire universe. Your body is not

only your instrument of consciousness, but your instrument to consciousness.

39. Feel the love life has for you, always and in all ways.

40. Play more, laugh more, daydream more. There are passages in your body that open up when you do this. And as you do this, your life experience expands.

And so I am trusting that the magic of these words has hit your heart as it's hit mine. We are truly infinite beings that tend to wander, lost in the infinitesimal yarn of the mind. The irony and the ridiculousness of it all is that it is in the *infinitesimal pause* that we start to rebuild our connection with the higher consciousness that we are.

This transmission feels to me like a bridge between aspects of the ascension process, and each person gets to hear it differently as they move through their own path.

On the one hand, the duality that comes with desire–the having and not having. The experiencing and not experiencing is such a common denominator for all of us. The quest for upgrading the programming so that we can be and have more, while continually rotating through the same life cycles–like a video game where winning through the levels is needed to move through it.

And on the other hand, there's the proposition of an exciting way to truly BE and experience the bliss we're designed to BE by accepting the mind as it is although disassociating from the fuckery of it - my words!

ABOUT THE AUTHOR

ISABEL MORALES

Isabel is a wealth consciousness coach, with an incredible passion to guide women in living a free and abundant life. In her 1:1 mentorship and group programs she provides a space for women to OWN their wealth leadership, and embody their *tits up, rich bitch, badass* selves - for good.

Her brilliance in guiding women to deeper self-awareness, to identify how they relate to wealth, and to finally LEAD with their energy from a place of consciousness, is the catalyst for extraordinary transformations. Just as easily as it is to code our cells with scarcity, we can intentionally re-code them with wealth, health, and the *foundation for an extraordinary life*. She believes that life wouldn't give us a *desire*, if it didn't have a way to *make it a reality*.

Growing up in Colombia in an environment where a "lack" mentality was ingrained in *every cell of her being* was the initiation to the evolution of her *greatest desire* to break the patterns of scarcity she learned and coded in her childhood, and mentor others to do the same.

Isabel suffers from endless wanderlust, however, she calls Ottawa home where she happily lives with her husband.

Feeling the call to do the work? connect with her at www.thedaydreamco.com or isabel@thedaydreamco.com

MONEY ISN'T WHAT YOU THINK IT IS

JENNA BROWN

MONEY ISN'T WHAT YOU THINK IT IS.

It's taken me years to understand, to play with, to try on different approaches to money and wealth almost like a child playing dress-up, but I have seen what I have seen, and I cannot unsee it.

I hope and intend that this chapter will bring you into the wealth frequency that the spirit of Mary Magdalene has always been journeying you towards.

HER STORY

To be honest with you, I do not actually know that much about Mary Magdalene's story. I have never read any books about her, her writings, nothing. I know of one story from the Bible, the story of when she comes to wash Yeshua's (Jesus's) feet. Perhaps you may have heard it.

She was coming to him on a day when he was feasting surrounded by his friends, his students. She had prepared for this moment by bringing an entire bottle of fragrant oil that she would then pour on his feet. She used it all, the equivalent of thousands of dollars was poured over this man's feet. She washed his feet with her tears and wiped them with her hair.

When I heard this story as an awakening young woman from religion, I didn't quite see the connection to wealth, but now, it's obvious.

Mary Magdalene sat in a room full of men who, inside of their own conscious understanding, considered her to be a fool with money. Not only was she completely inappropriate for being there, but she was also wasteful, she was depleting something of value, and for what? Love? They turned their heads, turned up their noses and even tried to tell her to leave, but Yeshua insisted that she stay. As the story goes, he told her how beautiful her offering was to him, how this was a statement of true love. In my interpretation, of true wealth consciousness.

WHAT IS WEALTH ANYWAY?

The very first thing that most people think of when I say "What is wealth?" is MONEY. But I want you to think for a second, why do you want money? Why do any of us want money?

We want it so that we can get (fill in the blank), and do (fill in the blank)... so that we can do what?

So we can FEEL SOMETHING.

We want money because we believe and live inside of, a paradigm that says once I have this money, I will be able to feel this feeling that I so deeply need and desire.

For the majority of us, that feeling always comes back to safety, security, and freedom.

You have been trained and raised your entire life to live in the paradigm of scarcity, and the most interesting thing about scarcity is, it's an illusion that you create in order to stay safe.

Now, you might be asking, how do I stay safe in the feeling of not having enough? Surely, that cannot be true. But it is safe, it's safe to the mind, to the matrix of "how things go," and I'd love for you to journey with me into the layers beneath the conscious mind, and the ever-evolving connections I desire to help you make through your wealth consciousness in this chapter.

THE SUBCONSCIOUS MIND

To understand how your mind could be keeping you stuck in a pattern and consciousness of scarcity, you first have to understand the beauty of the subconscious mind. You have both the subconscious (also known as the unconscious) and the conscious mind. The conscious mind is the part of your thinking that you are aware of. For instance, "I want ice cream for dessert" is a conscious thought. "Money is not safe" is an unconscious thought, it is *under* the awareness of your mind. You are not aware that you are thinking it, yet it's controlling your life. The subconscious is responsible for all of your dreams and creativity, all of your emotions, and most of your bodily functions.

The subconscious mind houses millions of belief systems that run like programs on a computer. One of the easiest ways for you to start to feel empowered with your mind and your life is to understand that your brain is a computer, and once I describe to you how the hardware (in a sense) works, it will help you understand how to change the inputs on that computer, to shift and change everything about your life.

Most people think that they are walking through life completely conscious and making all of their life decisions through the power of their thoughts. They are not. You are not. We are all little kids with grown-up skin on, as I like to say, because our subconscious mind is fully developed at age eight. Before the age of eight, we are an open sponge, taking in all of life completely as matter of fact. Everything we see and everything that is said becomes a program in our brains, and in our bodies, that dictates the rest of how our adult lives work.

In order to change this, we must be able to access the subconscious mind. Then through the accessing of the subconscious mind, we are then able to see what programs are there and begin to change them.

The subconscious mind is responsible for your whole life. Over 95% of your reality is created by the subconscious mind, and it's completely impartial. It's just doing its number one job, which is to keep you SAFE, and wouldn't you know it… "safe" to the subconscious mind is the SAME as childhood.

Our brain's job is to keep us safe, so if we lived in a sea of chaos growing up or understand the money matrix as scarcity the way most of us consider it to be, we will keep recreating that in adulthood simply because our brain is doing its job.

PROOF OF A NEW PARADIGM

I can imagine that if you are the type of person who is reading this book, you are already on this journey with me, with all of us breaking through old beliefs and stepping into new paradigms. I invite you even a few steps deeper, beyond the matrix that you very well may still be creating.

The way that I love to talk about money and teach about money is through wealth energetic foundations, so let's go there, back to the beginning, back to the foundations of why we grow up to struggle with creating wealth the way so many of us do.

Money is not what you think it is.

Let that sink in.

Money is not what you think it is.
One more time,

Money is not what you think it is.

As children, we are hardwired to survive, and the funny thing about being a kid is that you are not even consciously aware money exists (shhh because it doesn't, and kids actually know everything), and you are learning to observe your caregivers to understand and manipulate and contort to get the only currency that mattered to you at the time–LOVE.

If our entire subconscious mind is completely formed by the age of eight and is controlling our entire energetic reality, how we push and pull for money, how it's here and then it's gone, how there is simply never enough, what if it's not money that we are pining for?

What if it's love?

What if it's a program that has been under the surface underlying every move that we make, deeply embedded into the collective consciousness and into the web of our nervous system, we are little kids, acting out what we did for love, with money.

The funny thing is, money is inherently neutral. It has no energy; however, it allows us to project our energy onto it. Money is cool like that. Would it not be safe to argue–with the evidence I have provided to your conscious mind–that you might be acting out with money the way that you learned to perform for love?

What if this entire paradigm that you have built as you push and pull for money, or perhaps ignore it altogether, wasn't about money at all? What if money was so safe and pure in love that it allowed you to project all of your love trauma onto it, simply responding to who you need it to be to fulfill the computer program of the subconscious mind of, this is how it works, this is how the paradigm is calculated, this is always how it goes?

MY STORY

Four years ago, from the time of the release of this book, I was lying in a hospital bed, fighting for my life. I was pregnant with our third child, seven weeks in utero, and had gone septic from an unnoticed kidney infection. Before this moment I was operating in the most bizarrely contrasting consciousness, that it's hard for many people that know "this version" of me to wrap their minds around.

I was running a non-profit organization that I had started five years prior, a leader in my church and a well-regarded community figure. I had spent years living from the paradigms of lack, terrified of money and genuinely thinking I was better than everyone else because I didn't have any of it.

I kept money far from me, it felt safer that way, yet at the same time deep down I always wanted more of it.

At the time of being hospitalized, my husband and I were both working for the non-profit, had given our entire lives up to try to serve other people, were living in a spare bedroom in a generous friend's house, driving a $1,000 beater van, and making $600 a month that we raised from asking people that knew us to support our life and our mission.

At this time in my life, it was regular that I would have seasons where money would flow to us unexpectedly in huge amounts, and because money felt so unsafe to me, somehow I would manifest situations where it all needed to fly out of our account just as quickly as it had come.

It wasn't until after this spiritual awakening, my Saturn return, that I began to understand these deeper truths.

Money didn't matter, but it mattered so much to me, why?

How did I always find myself in these cycles of wanting money so badly while also hating it, with money coming but only sporadically, and when it did I felt like I was suffocating? How did I get it to feel safe to me? I genuinely had no clue.

Even inside of religion, before we left that way of expressing our spirituality, I was obsessed with understanding money. I would read books and do studies, and prove to myself logically why money was safe, but no matter what I did, it always was the same cycle. I knew something had to change, and subconscious reprogramming is what changed my entire reality in such a short time, genuinely, I do not recognize this person anymore that I write about, even though I love this former version of myself dearly.

I will never forget–after I signed up for my first course to subconsciously reprogram my money trauma–what I learned. I went into a hypnosis that was designed for me to meet money. She led me into a park, where I was walking and feeling so safe in my body, and invited money to join me.

I never could have expected that money would show up as my dad

.

He came into the picture and I was so confused. Why was he money? Why did it have to be him?

I cried. I released. I remember feeling after that hypnosis that I had been changed forever. I had seen something I could never unsee, and it would be the foundation to wealth energetics that I would teach and carry for the rest of my life.

To bring that stark contrast to understanding, at the time of writing this chapter I am running a multiple six-figure business in my second year running it, traveling the globe with my husband and three healthy children, am the healthiest I have ever been and have the skills to not only manifest whatever reality I desire, but also teach them to other people. IN FOUR YEARS from the moment listed above.

MONEY IS LOVE

As children, we did not worry about money. We worried, and didn't know we were worrying, about love. When would we get it, would we get it? I have to perform for it. *Oh, this* is what I have to say for mom to hold me like that, or smile at me like that. Children are inherently wired to survive, and the number one survival need for children–beyond food, clothing and shelter–is attachment. Attachment is the way we learned to love. It is the way we learned or did not learn that our caregivers were safe, and if we would be held and nurtured.

These love patterns are stored deep within our nervous system, which dictates and creates the patterns we see developing in our world.

As an example, what happens when you see a police officer pull up behind you? Your hands get sweaty maybe? You look at the dash wondering how fast you were going, and your nervous system is activated. I have never gotten pulled over and not cried for an hour afterward (talk about stored trauma haha).

This is the same exact patterning that happens with you and money.

If you can peel back the layers, if you allow it to be safe to peel back the layers, I could try and speak to your trauma. I could reinforce what every other finance teacher is teaching you about why you suck at money because you aren't budgeting and you aren't doing X, Y, and Z to get more money, but those that are "really good" with their finances in the world typically are stuck in a fight-or-flight nervous system pattern with money. I am going to guess that you tend to lean more on the flight side, or maybe you are a little like how I was, where it comes in and it's scary so it goes out.

Even though it feels like it's about money, it's actually about love–and money is simply the easiest thing to project your love, also known as your attachment trauma, onto.

Your subconscious was created before the age of eight, and it is creating 95% of your reality right now.

You were not a manager of money at seven, you were a

manager of love.

If this is resonating, I want to take you one step further. If we can conclude that our relationship with money is simply a projection of our unhealed trauma and attachment relationships with love, we can also conclude that our desire to have more money is simply a feeling that we are longing for, that we never actually received to the measure that we needed.

I want to ask you something, and when I ask this, I am asking your inner child right now.

What did you need that you didn't get?

What are you longing so deep inside of you to feel?

What do you wish your parents or caregivers could give you that they just couldn't, or perhaps they didn't know how to?

This–these answers–are wealth to you.

Safety, Security, Attachment, Freedom…these are not extra toppings on our sundaes of life, they are the ice cream. They are the currency that our entire world has always operated on, and the currency that their entire world desires to operate on.

This is why you can meet the richest man in the world who is also filled with misery. Because he never wanted money. Money was the illusion that kept him performing and chasing and striving to get the thing he was hoping he would get from love. The hole continues to be created because money is serving him, even when it feels like it may be destroying him, as his mirror to see that it was never money he was searching for, it was love, it was security, it was freedom, it was safety.

231

I'd like to be the woman who comes in with the flashy budget system and helps people hustle their way to a million dollars sometimes, but I am not that woman.

I am the woman who knows the energetic foundations of why you do not have what you so deeply desire, and I am also the woman to tell you what it is that you think it will be that gives it to you is an illusion.

It's an illusion that you created, at a young age, in order to do what the entire world is trying to do right now: survive.

MAGDALENE

Her wealth goes beyond what the disciples–the men couldn't understand, but Christ consciousness understands. He, and we when we step into our Christ consciousness, understand that absolutely everything is in constant flow.

They were offended at her impolite attempts to interrupt and frustrated by her lack of respect for how much something cost.

But she got it.

She understood that in order to receive love, her true love, partnership with Christ–or for us, Christ consciousness–she would need to let go of the paradigm of lack. The paradigm of "running out," is the paradigm that we are all living in.

Afraid that if we give, if we serve, if we let go of the money in our accounts that we will never see it again.

She got it though, didn't she? Are you starting to see?

Her story is a story of love. A washing of the feet of love. A service and gratitude to love, to wealth, in the way that her heart desired.

Wealth consciousness is not making friends with money and seeing it as some object that you are contorting. You may have been beating yourself up for an entire lifetime wondering why you can't figure it out–it's time to hack the code, to be like the person you admire with money.

But what if you aren't wrong?

What if money is showing up as the only thing it knows how to be, LOVE, to mirror to you the deeper wounding of childhood that you just haven't quite yet been ready to see?

What do you do? How do you move forward?

Play with reality.

Money isn't what you think it is.

Money is love.

See what happens.

ABOUT THE AUTHOR

JENNA BROWN

Jenna Brown is a business coach, spiritual mentor, and known as a wealth energetics queen. She specializes in subconscious reprogramming which allows her clients to manifest their dream lives, heal their generational trauma and step into their destiny. She is the creator of Wealth Embodied and Feminine Alchemized Business which allows the modern feminine entrepreneur to heal their subconscious drama and trauma with wealth-building and business.

She supports her clients to completely revolutionize their foundations within their bodies, their programming, and shift to be able to hold the wealth, the clients, and the impactful leadership that their heart desires and knows is waiting for them.

Jenna is currently traveling the world with her husband and three children who are nine and under.

If you are a feminine entrepreneur and want to feel safe in your body as you experience a business and wealth beyond your dreams join the waitlist for Jenna's core program, Wealth Embodied at

https://www.iamjennabrown.com/opt-in-for-wealth-embodied-waitlist

Follow Jenna on Instagram at:
https://www.instagram.com/iam_jennabrown

Enjoy Jenna's podcast, Expand with Jenna Brown at:
https://podcasts.apple.com/us/podcast/the-manifestation-process-the-energetics/id1610393323?i=1000568707938

PATH OF THE PRIESTESS

JESSICA SAGE

"YOU ARE HERE TO SAVE THE WORLD."

That was one of the first things I was *told* at the start of my awakening.

In June of 2020, I had a spontaneous spiritual awakening. My preprogrammed "alarm clock" had gone off at the predetermined age of 38, to awaken and activate me into remembering who I was and my specific soul mission.

One night, I turned to my husband, and I said, "I am not from this Earth. I am from a different planet, and I am here on a mission. A mission to save the world! I'm like a superhero! With superpowers!"

I honestly had no fucking idea what the words meant that had just come out of my mouth, but I DID know how it felt.

It felt like TRUTH.

And you definitely couldn't tell me otherwise....

My spiritual awakening happened in 2020, but I believe that I first started on the awakening path in 2012.

I grew up in a very dysfunctional family and suffered a lot of trauma from a very young age. There are many memories from my childhood and young adult life that have been blocked from my memory, and I have no recollection of them. My mind doesn't remember, but my body certainly did. My physical vessel held a lot of suppressed anger, rage, sadness, hurt, betrayal, pain and trauma, deep within every single one of its cells. I may have looked OK to those on the outside looking in, but really, I was nothing short of numb.

It is my belief that we spend many, many lifetimes with our families, our soul families, and each time we swap roles depending on what each of us wants to learn. I might be the daughter in this life, but the mother or father in another. While some of us may have had a tough childhood in this lifetime, it is very humbling when you awaken and realise that even if you never had a good relationship with your mother or father growing up, they are most likely your biggest supporters on the other side. They love you SO much that they volunteered themselves to become the narcissist, the manipulator, the abuser, the abandoner...all for YOU! They did it for your spiritual growth and ascension. You needed to learn these lessons on Earth to evolve and they did that for you! They each put their hand up, even though they knew it would also cause them a lot of pain. This is very hard for the human mind to comprehend, but that is an act of unconditional love.

It does break my heart that my own parents cannot comprehend this (yet). They suffer very much because of it. I see this suffering in them. Their hearts are heavy. They are riddled with trauma, pain and sadness. They probably think that deep down I hate them, but that couldn't be further from the truth. I admire them, for the brave souls they are and the huge mission that they came here to do for me. I am thankful for them and I love them. It was all part of my destiny. My traumas had to happen. We wrote the script together. If only they could see what I see, they would be healed in an instant.

In Sept 2012, I said goodbye to my mother, my father, and my siblings and left my hometown for good. I moved to Darwin with my husband and two young boys for a new adventure.

This was actually the furthest place in Australia that we could move to, although we didn't plan that. Ironically, Darwin is also one of the rare locations in which Lemurian energies still exist today. This was the perfect place and energy for me to begin on my healing journey. Lemuria, or Mu, was a highly evolved, highly spiritual, fifth-dimensional, ancient civilization. Lemuria was the ultimate expression of the Divine Feminine. A place of the Goddess and the Mother. Of nurturing, love and compassion. A place where nature was revered, and everyone and everything lived in peace and harmony. Where they were all ONE.

The day I moved away from my family was such a significant one for me, even if I didn't realise it at the time. This was the day I took back control and ownership of my own life. I was finally standing in my power and breaking free of the shackles! It was the day I realised the importance of boundaries and saying NO. My healing journey had begun, and my soul wished for me to address the mother wound and my inner child first. There would be no more people pleasing. No more codependency. No more trauma-bond attachments. No more toxic relationships. No more sacrificing my soul. I was now on a trajectory to transmute my dark past into love and light.

THE PATH TO WHOLENESS

The Priestess path is one that starts with inner healing and raising your vibration. It is a path back to wholeness.

"Holy shit! Is that really me? Is that what I look like?" I asked my husband on a family holiday in Singapore.

As I looked at the photo of me, tears streamed down my face. How could I let myself go like that? How had I not noticed before? I was so unhealthy, and I didn't do any type of exercise. I hated my body, and I had disrespected it for way too long. I was shocked and angry at myself. As soon as we arrived back in Australia, the first thing I did was sign up to a boot camp.

One time in my hometown, my husband had tried to make me go for a run with him. I ran about 100m and then started crying. It was too hard! Imagine how I felt when I arrived at my very first bootcamp workout and the trainer, who incidentally is a very good friend of mine now, made us run in a line for a whole 5 kilometres! The person at the back of the line would have to sprint to the front and it continued on like this for an hour! It was like a lucid nightmare!

When it was finished, a funny thing happened though. I felt amazing! They say the only bad workout is the one you didn't do. It's true! The endorphins you get from exercising are so worth it!

From here, I went on to learn about fueling my body with good nutrition and clean eating. It felt so good to fill myself up on vibrant and high vibrational foods, rather than processed, packaged and junk foods that were filled with sugar, salt, chemicals and preservatives. I taught myself how to and got really good at reading labels on foods and then on everything else from skin care to cleaning products to sunscreens and clothing.

The excess weight continued to drop off me until I had lost a total of 30kgs (66 pounds). I felt so good. I felt confident. I loved my body again. And of course, I wanted EVERYONE to feel like this!

I am entrepreneurial by nature. When I had my babies in 2008 and 2010, I studied to become a childcare educator in my free time, so that I could open my own family day care at home and not have to be away from them. I could look after my own children and have an income coming in too. I named the business "Little Cherubs" and it succeeded and did really well. I put my heart and soul into it and met some beautiful children and their parents along the way, but most of all, I was able to be there for my own children and not miss out on their important early years.

In 2016, I started up my current business, Core Body Health and Fitness. This was my ultimate passion. My aim was to create a fun environment where people could workout to get fit and healthy. I ran my workouts in parks and schools, so that my clients would have access to the added mental health benefits of being outdoors, in the sun and in nature. Unlike other gyms in my area, I promoted the group as family friendly, because this was especially important to me. I wished for parents to be role models for their children and for children to also be able to enjoy the benefits of play, fresh air and the grass under their feet instead of being inside and on technology all day.

The very first day, I had 20 members sign up! The following year it had grown to 100. The next year it was over 200! With very minimal advertising, my baby was growing just by word of mouth and my own magnetism alone.

We both evolved alongside each other. With a whole-body, holistic, health-centred approach. A mind, body, soul connection. I went on to introduce nutritional education and physical body transformation programs, which helped hundreds of women lose their excess weight, learn how to read food labels, ditch societal conditioning and start to love themselves again.

Over the years, each time I would do something that I loved and that had helped me, I would add it to my business, so that all of my soulmate clients could benefit also. Yoga, Pilates, meditation, women's circles, sound bowl healing, women's empowerment retreats, plus self-love and awakening programs. We had started our journey at the base chakra (physical fitness) and worked our way all the way up through them all, to the crown (meditation).

I went on to become a certified crystal energy healer and reiki master and started taking clients for healing sessions too. I am so passionate about helping people, especially women, heal from the inside out. When you heal your inner self, your inner child first, the rest will just all fall into place.

My own path to wholeness had led me to create a system for others to take the journey, too, if they chose. A way for them to start on their own path to wholeness. To evolve. To awaken and ascend.

WHEN THE GODDESS CALLS YOU BACK HOME, YOU ANSWER

The Priestess path is full of initiations, purifications and pilgrimages to your soul. It is a sacred path that leads you back to your Divine Feminine energy, your ancient wisdom, your magic and your own power.

"You must remember who you are. It's time to remember."
– Isis

When you heal your womb, it feels like you are coming home.
Coming home to yourself.
Home to your TRUE, authentic self.

*

I rolled over and turned off my lamp.

"Good night my Goddess." My husband, Ben, has called me this since the day that we met. He leaned over, gave me a kiss and then placed his hand on my stomach. On my womb.

"She is very powerful," he said.

"What do you mean?" I asked him.

"I can feel her power. It is so strong." And then, "Your womb births powerful beings into this world."

I kind of knew what he was talking about. I had also felt her power. I had been doing a lot of womb clearing and healing, and since then I could feel her energy too. This was a new level of awakening for me. I had no idea about the power of our wombs before then. Mine had been sabotaged and hijacked since childhood. By men. By doctors. By social conditioning and by the patriarchy. She was also very numb.

With his hand still on my womb, suddenly, he was catapulted into a past life vision. Ben is very clairvoyant. He also has the gift of clear hearing, or clairaudience.

"Oh, my God," he said. "Wow! I see you. You are so beautiful. You are a Queen. I am your bodyguard, or some type of protector. I am also your lover..."

He went on to describe his vision in extremely vivid detail. This was an Ancient Egyptian lifetime. He was in my chambers. It was a very stormy night. There was thunder and lightning. We were practicing sex magick. I was to birth a very powerful king into the physical world and although I had many lovers at that time, I had chosen him (Ben) to provide the seed. We made love. When it came to the point of climax, a loud thunderclap sounded and at the exact same moment I took out a dagger and stabbed him in the heart. I killed him. But it was for the greater good. He knew this would happen. He agreed to it. He had done a great service to the people of Egypt, for they would now receive a very powerful king.

This was such a profound and intense spiritual experience! To share it with my husband was next level and a form of very deep healing for both of us. I had not told him, but about a month prior, I had had a similar vision in a quantum hypnosis session. In my vision, I had also seen myself in Ancient Egypt with him as my lover/bodyguard. I saw my quarters where I was training at a mystery school. Here, I was learning the art of sex magick. This was extremely confusing to me, because my human mind could not comprehend what sex magick was. I would come to know shortly after that, yes indeed, sex magick and sexual healing had been practiced and taught in this time period. Mary Magdalene herself had been a high initiate of the temple of Isis and her teachings.

As Ben continued to describe his vision, the room around us transformed and I started to have a weird, intense feeling in my yoni. It was not something I had ever felt before. It was almost quite painful, yet also not. Like something was building and needed to be released. I believe it was trauma, that had been trapped for a very long time and it was finally about to be set free. After the vision had finished, Ben and I made love and it was a beautiful, magical experience. The pressure in my yoni dissipated. My womb felt lighter! Something had shifted. In that moment and the days to come, we both intuitively felt and knew that we had just healed our Ancient Egypt timeline.

BIRTHING A NEW WORLD

To express your truest self is a beautiful expression of the Divine Feminine and the Goddess herself.

Divine Feminine is rising, and the awakened women are birthing a new world into consciousness. We are remembering our long-forgotten wisdom and magic. We are healing ourselves and speaking our truth. We are feeling the power of our wombs returning, and we are creating new ideas and nurturing new ways of being onto this dying planet.

"You are my sister. You have travelled with me through many lifetimes. We have learnt from each other. For I am you and you are me. Now is the time that you will remember and you will light the way for others as a divine, powerful priestess. One who holds the Mother of All template. You are a very strong nurturer. Now is the time for you to answer the call." - Isis

Lying in bed one night, shortly after my spiritual awakening, I turned to Ben and said, "I think I am going to fall pregnant." He laughed. This statement was absurd! For one, our sons were almost in their teens by now and secondly, Ben had already had a vasectomy. "I know it sounds insane, but I know deep within me that I am going to have another baby."

The next day, I was instructing a fitness class. Ben and I were jogging together at one stage and one of my clients ran past us and casually said, "Oh, Jess! I had a dream about you last night. You were pregnant!"

Ben's jaw dropped. The look on his face was priceless. For me though, it was just another sign from my spirit baby. She was communicating to me in this way. By synchronicity. She would continue to send me more signs, such as cherubs in the sky, messages in songs, conversations with people, oracle cards, tarot readers, in dreams and through my youngest son, who would not stop talking about her.

One day whilst I was doing my food shopping, I was walking down the aisles and a name literally *dropped* into my head. It was Ruby. It didn't come from within me, it came in through my crown chakra. I hadn't been thinking about her at all, yet she had found a way to intimately communicate with me. I didn't know it at the time, but I believe this was either a download or a form of telepathy.

Although my memories are few and far between, I have never forgotten the time I went to see a very well-renowned tea leaf reader at the age of 18. She told me "You will have two, actually, maybe three children." I know it may not seem odd to the reader, but to me it was. This woman had a pretty good track record of being right. So why wouldn't she just tell me straight? Why make a wishy-washy comment like that? It has always stuck with me and now 20 years later, it finally makes a little more sense.

A spirit baby can be a child that has passed from illness, stillborn or from a miscarriage, but it can also be a baby that has not been through the conception process yet. They are *future* babies. Communication from spirit babies with their parents happens more often than you think, however the parent may not be conscious, aware or open to what is happening.

Since healing my womb this year, in 2022, I have had yet another ego death and awakening. It doesn't stop at one, you can have many. For me, it was another step up towards Zero Point resonance. To achieve equilibrium within. My spiritual path started becoming clearer. I started to innerstand where I had been, where I had come from, and where I was going.

I've been the leader, I've been the teacher, I've been successful in business, but the Goddess was now calling, and I couldn't say no. Now it is time for me to nourish and nurture myself. To nourish and nurture my inner child AND my own children. To love myself unconditionally so that I can radiate that frequency out into the world and help others to do the same. To connect with my Divine Feminine essence, follow my intuition and flow. To ground peace, harmony and healing into this world. To work with Spirit and bring back sacredness and ancient wisdom to this planet. To just be in the world, and not always doing. To let go, live and love.

"Remember the times that we walked together?" – Mary Magdalene

How do you become a priestess?

I believe you are born one, not made.

It is your destiny. It is your past, your present and your future. It is a culmination of all of your soul gifts, magic, abilities, ancient wisdom and knowledge. Nothing is ever lost. A Priestess is a woman that remembers who she is and what she is here for. She acts as a vessel for the Divine Feminine energy, the Goddess, the Mother of all, and the supreme nurturer, to be channelled through her and onto the Earth plane. She is connected to the Spirit realm and is guided by her intuition. She is a woman that remembers and re-integrates her abilities and powers of knowing, clairvoyance, magic, healing, manifestation and unconditional love. She is here to be of service. To help humanity and the Earth evolve. The Priestess woman is here for the evolution of the human. Body, consciousness and soul.

The pure hearts are awakening at this time and we WILL save the world!

With our pure hearts and unconditional LOVE.

Divine Feminine is rising.

And so it is.

ABOUT THE AUTHOR

JESSICA SAGE

Jessica Sage is personal trainer, health and wellness coach, crystal energy healer, Usui Reiki Master, ascension coach and galactic guide, as well as the owner and founder of Core Body Health and Fitness.

She is the creator of The Health & Happiness Journey and The Self-Love Sanctuary, both holistic programs that teach women sustainable techniques on how to deeply nourish their bodies, fuel their mind, and light their spirit.

She holds space for women to rise in their power and learn how to feel good in their bodies, release emotional baggage, grow spiritually and start feeling unconditional love and self-compassion for themselves again.

She currently lives in the hot and humid tropics of Darwin, Australia with her husband and 2 boys.

Are you ready to activate your true, authentic and happiest self? To discover the most empowered YOU that exists? YES Goddess, you are! And when the Goddess calls, you must answer.

Links:

https://linktr.ee/jessicasage144

www.facebook.com/jessica.sage.44

www.corebodyhealthandfitness.com

DREAMS, FLAMES AND ANCESTRAL LOVE

JULIANA LAVELL

HIDDEN IN MY DNA ARE UNIQUE CODES. A CODE IS a key to unlock a door revealing a new pathway. Love can unlock these codes, opening my senses to a new world, a new resonant frequency.

Magdalene energy has shown up in my life like sparks of divine feminine flames that ignite my intuition. Her energy is compassionate yet fierce. I believe she is woven through each of us as an archetype rooted in love.

These stories reveal challenging moments in my life where I have discovered codes that have helped me alchemize dark into light. I hope they inspire you to see your own unique codes and how they light you up.

DREAMS

I woke up one morning with beads of sweat running down my face. My heart thundered in my chest. I reached over to wake up my partner. "I had the craziest dream, I just woke up to my death. Red and orange flames surrounding me, hot

250

crackling embers beneath me, voices yelling in a crowd–I was burning at the stake."

Immediately I knew there was something strange about this dream. I had never experienced anything like that before. Rarely do I remember dreams so vividly; this one stood out to me in an intense way. As if it were a message from my ancestors or the universe. It felt like a wake-up call. I was twenty-six years old and approaching my Saturn Return astrologically, where often one redefines and reassesses who they are, which often triggers big life changes.

I asked my aunt quietly at a family gathering about our ancestry. She was a safe person to share my dream with at the time, as I knew she had an encounter with a little boy's ghost who lived in her home (which had been a children's daycare for a little while prior to her owning it). She told me she had done a lot of DNA research around our family lineage. She said it was no surprise that I had these dreams, as we were in direct lineage to an ancestor who was executed in the Salem Witch trials in Massachusetts in the 1700s. Her death caused an uproar because she was an elder, a midwife, and well-loved by her community.

SINGLE MOTHERHOOD

The following year after my dream I went through a divorce and began a chapter of single motherhood. It was a very painful period but full of growth and freedom to get to know myself. I had been seventeen when I partnered with my daughter's father. Our love was so playful, deep and pure. We were so young and naive to the lessons life had in store for us. We lasted for nine years before parting ways. I was terrified to be on my own. To be a financial provider and attentive mother at the same time felt impossible. I often felt I had to choose between growing my career and being a good parent. In an ideal world, we would have strong support networks so families with young children would be able to survive and thrive. I was blessed to have extended family to help, but I often felt stretched thin.

My priority was being the best mom I could be. To me that meant having the flexibility to be physically present for my daughter and have quality time with her in the precious years of her childhood. The cost of being a good mother is often undervalued. When she was sick or stressed, I canceled work. She was my top priority. Forgiveness had to become a routine practice, for myself and her father for our imperfections that created this stressful situation to raise a child. Holding on to anger and resentment, I learned, is like drinking poison and hoping the other person will be sick. My daughter's father and I ended up reuniting romantically 10 years later, we discovered deep healing and growth as we learned to love each other more unconditionally.

I was raised by a trailblazer solo mother and I knew my inner fire could get me through anything. The fire I'd dreamt about was coursing fiercely and passionately through my family line. My mom practiced the fire walk many times when I was a kid: a bonfire spread into a bed of hot coals, a group gathered and intended with deep knowing we can walk over fire without being burned, a transmutation of that energy can happen. A form of alchemy through the human body that can allow us to channel the energy of fire through our thoughts rather than be burned by it.

I decided to do a fire walk when I was in my mid-thirties, and it changed my life. It made me realize my powerful ability to walk through any challenges when I trust myself with unwavering focus and breath. Finding the calm eye of the storm. The storm being my fears, chaotic life drama in the outside world, and the eye of the storm being my focus and resolve to get through it courageously.

PRAYER

As the years passed, I was forced to depend more on myself. In moments when life became challenging, I leaned into my spirituality to get me through—I learned to pray. One day I found myself praying out loud in my car, tears streaming down my face, uncertain where to go, or how I could get by. I decided to drive to the cemetery to visit my grandpa's gravesite. I was asking for help from unseen forces. Any spirits on the other side that might be listening.

I felt stuck, struggling to prosper and unsure of my next move in life. These moments knocked me to my knees. I surrendered and trusted that the universe would take care of me, that miracles happen. Little synchronicities would surprise me, filling me with joy—this was how I knew angels were near. Whether it was a familiar song lyric on the radio at the perfect moment, a feather, or a black and yellow monarch butterfly that would stay near me for an hour. Some of my grandfather's last words were, "I feel like I'm floating like a butterfly." I always feel a twinkle of happiness from him when I see those butterflies. Synchronicities feel like a code of good luck, a blessing and a gesture from the universe that I am on the right path.

I trialed through another fire when I was diagnosed with an autoimmune disease that almost killed me. At the age of thirty-six, I had to have my entire large intestine removed. I wore an ostomy bag for six months and underwent three surgeries to put my plumbing back inside. My life-saving surgeon happened to be named Magdalena, another sign from the universe I was taken care of. This was by far the most challenging time in my life. I knew I had to make the choice to be a survivor and let go of being a victim, to surrender my "why?" and pray. It was a deep letting go and another

253

opportunity to do a metaphorical fire walk. Not only did I pray, but I experienced others praying for me from many church denominations, as well as group intention from spiritual science-based people. I was deeply moved by the love I felt in group prayer. It truly helped me to regain the belief in myself to heal.

PSYCHIC SPACES

Throughout my life, I've often heard messages from people who have passed on, as well as a strong inner voice. It takes a lot of courage for me to admit this now. As a child, the wind spoke to me. Rainbow prisms made my heart glow and opened my daydreams. I channeled my great-grandfather at the age of five, sharing things with my mother that I heard him say, which left her in shock and happy to feel reconnected. I learned to stifle that side of myself because of religious fear imposed by my father and the church we attended at the time. I was taught that hearing voices or connecting with my imagination was the devil, and I must stay away from anything "new age" or esoteric as it was dangerous territory.

My mother and father divorced when I was two, and they went down very polarizing paths. While my father was in his fundamentalist Christian views, my mother was a free-spirited, firewalking, eagle-spotting, tarot-reading woman. She was a nurse turned master's-in-counseling psychologist. My dad and stepmother loathed her magic; they painted a picture of fear around her, and even told me I had demons attached to me because of her. That became very confusing to me as a young child, as I loved my mom and could never see her in that light. I have learned to forgive them, as they were stuck in an ancient cycle of fear. I don't think they had bad intentions, but they needed more love and compassion to heal the fearful wounds painting their realities.

By my late teens I finally started to question everything, rebel against the fear-based reality, and start to reclaim my own sense of magic. It is a healing process to this day to not fear my own innate metaphysical gifts. I believe that my dreams have helped me to heed the call of my ancestors, the women labeled as witches or prostitutes who were persecuted, cast away, and murdered. I believe many were goddesses, psychics, and healers. They carry the energy of Magdalene; if you are reading this book, you likely carry these codes too. I believe our intuition is the key to unlocking these codes.

In my adult life, I turned to yoga and meditation, practices that have offered a way to cultivate inner peace, detachment, and a safe space for me to connect with myself. I often receive intuitive insights on my mat, especially during Savasana, when my brain is shifted into a subconscious state. Journaling is another way I tap into my intuition. I let myself write freely, clearing away the cobwebs of repetitive thought, and then a flow state kicks in. I believe this is my greater intelligence channeling through. Art and creativity are pathways as well. I often keep a notebook beside me while I paint, as I receive messages that come and go quickly. Any creative focus can open up my portal for intuitive sense: dancing, cooking, and being in nature.

I started to do tarot readings for people at an early age. I trusted the call to use them as a tool for reflection but not to give away my power to them as all-knowing. They are meant to be used as a tool. I feel it is important to trust oneself as to when to take breaks from seeking answers from divination tools. I am often guided to be still and cultivate my sense of trust and faith in the universe.

It is fun to explore our five senses and be curious about what shows up when we meditate on people or objects with our eyes closed. I have often tuned into pregnancies in women and the gender of their babies. I had a few occasions where I meditated with a deceased person's items, like eyeglasses or jewelry, and messages have come through. You can do this with the personal objects of living people as well, such as a necklace or ring a person wears all the time—hold it in your hands, close your eyes and be open to receive. I feel that these moments have brought healing and wisdom to others when channeled with good intentions. This is how I know they are codes…they are guided by love and initiate healing.

PLANT MEDICINE

My spirituality led me to explore plant teachers. I explored psilocybin, iboga, and ayahuasca over the course of several years, with plenty of space and time for integration in between. I don't crave to use these anymore, which is why I don't like to classify them as a drug. They are medicine and often don't need recurring doses. Iboga in particular works wonders with addiction. I went to Costa Rica to sit in an iboga ceremony. It was like someone hit a reset button on my energy field. It showed me clearly what needed to change in my body: harsh toxins like hair dye on my scalp, and my IUD, needed to be removed. It showed me crystal clear/ movie-like memories from childhood, igniting love and connection for my parents. It is easy for us to stay stuck in a blame/victim cycle with our parents, but I realized that also keeps us stuck in karmic cycles that hold us back from experiencing our purpose. I saw my grandmother in prayer, in purple light; the message was clear that this was how she could persevere through challenging times.

One night during an ayahuasca ceremony, a woman came to me burning alive in the same vivid imagery as my dream many years earlier. She was an ancestor on fire. She said to me, "Look at what they did to us. Tell the truth. You are free

256

and you're safe to tell the truth in your time. Don't be scared, be brave." She was fiery in more ways than one. Her spirit was strong. She was full of feistiness. She was an energy of transformation and she inspired me to go forth and create my own yoga teacher training program called Into the Mystic Yoga.

INTO THE MYSTIC

I noticed wisdom teachings from many lineages carried common threads. Yoga was my main medicine. I learned to move with intention and breath, to focus my mind and ground my own energy. I noticed that yogis prayed with mantras, repeating statements, similar to the way Catholics count prayers on a rosary, the way personal growth teachers use affirmations.

I wanted to create a new program that was non-dogmatic. No hierarchy or gurus on pedestals. Just experiences, the sharing of ancient teachings and open group conversation. I wanted to gather experts from a variety of healing traditions. A buffet of tools and experiences to offer people from reiki to transformational breathwork, First Nations teachings with elders, therapeutic yoga, Ayurveda, and traditional yogic philosophy. We could explore the many diverse rivers that lead to the same great ocean of yoga. It was time to share an innovative recipe for healing, through the practices of physical movement, journaling, meditation, mantra, art therapy, and indigenous wisdom (to name just a few).

These were all practices rich and dear to my heart that I felt were important medicine to bring forward in these times. The connection to my ancestors gave me the courage to create this program. That woman on fire ignited something within me. She was me, I am her. My ancestors and I and the women who will live after me. My daughter's children and their

257

children. On a genetic level, we are all tethered and intertwined in this greater fabric of life. It felt important for me to create that training. I know that the projects we create carry resonance and can have a ripple effect in the same way my ancestors have managed to ripple through space and time to visit me in dreams and ceremonies—supporting, advising, and igniting my soul path.

PAST LIVES

Signs of Magdalene energy showed up while I was traveling in London, England. I visited an ancient church where an inscription in the gray stone wall captured my attention:

"Veritas Vos Liberabit"

A Latin Bible quote from John 8:32. The translation is:

"The truth, written in your hearts by the Spirit of God, shall make you free."

This quote resonated with me deeply. I wrote it down and I had to know the story behind it. I spontaneously walked into a tattoo shop in London and a Scottish man tattooed the words down my spine. It was the story about a prostitute who was brought to the village square to be executed, stoned to death. I learned this through research after I discovered the quote. She may have been a sinner or a powerful, beautiful unwed woman—in those times an unwed female was a danger to society. If you looked at a man the wrong way or moved your hips in such a way, it was a crime. Jesus came to stand beside her in the village circle where everyone was prepared to stone her. He said, "Those of you who have never sinned throw the first stone," and everybody dropped their stones, teaching us that there is no one without sin in our human experience.

We can feel remorse for actions that hurt others and choose to atone for our actions. We all will inevitably have to face our imperfect actions as lessons if we want to break karmic cycles. Staying in shame and judgment towards ourselves or others will keep us from moving forward on a path to healing and evolution.

The message from the Bible quote is revealing that our freedom lives in the truth blueprinted in our hearts. When we see through the eyes of unity and love, we transcend this war of duality and balance it with love and compassionate understanding.

I recently learned about the Magdalene Laundries. Historians estimate that by the late 1800s there were more than three hundred Magdalene institutions in England and at least forty-one in Ireland. It was discovered in the '90s when one parcel of church land in Ireland was sold to a developer. As the land was excavated, the remains of hundreds of women were found. They may have been raped or pregnant and unwed, and therefore sent to the Magdalene Laundries.

Women were sent to the Magdalene Laundries to work without pay and live in confinement. I don't know the full stories of what happened, but the oppression of women titled as "Magdalenes" speaks volumes to me. The paradox of the story from the Bible to the actions that were taken by the Church are so contrasting and hypocritical. It seems as though control over women was desired by the traditional Church, overpowering, overbearing, shame-placing and freedom-stealing. Women's magic and creative powers were seen as a sin, as also seen in the mass execution of "witches," often burned, hanged or stoned. I believe these stories have come forward as an awakening to our divine feminine consciousness.

Over the years, I dated men and also spent a lot of time single. I found myself protective of my womb space. Mirrors of lifetimes past where I may have been executed for such things, even just being a single beautiful female was intimidating in society. I feel that it's important to reclaim our power, our sovereignty, to wake up to life. To courageously share our powerful medicine as intuitive beings. We create life and we have been shamed for this power in generations past.

It is time now to release the shame to step back into our fire, that fire that burns beneath our feet and transforms us. The millions of women that were executed as witches throughout time are now free, reincarnated, and we're finding each other. This book is a collection of these women. And I hope that these stories work to ignite your inner fire, to disrupt, transform, and awaken you to the powerful loving consciousness inherent in you.

May we now be free to shine in our bright light, to share in our love and our sexuality in a safe and sacred way. May we have each other's backs as women and men—we don't have to turn against each other anymore. There is no competition. We are sisters and brothers on this planet, and we need each other to grow.

If we are meant to continue on this Earth, love must prevail to balance out these outdated structures of patriarchy. The awakened feminine inspires the sacred masculine. We can inspire each other through love rather than fear.

May we find the balance of masculine and feminine within ourselves. Then we can arrive in a relationship with another more deeply anchored. An intertwining dance of polarizing energies that create harmony. This power comes from being held in spaces that feel safe, where we feel adored, treasured, and appreciated with tenderness, compassion, and unconditional love.

I believe that when we meet ourselves with these qualities it builds a foundation of courage to follow the cobblestone path that leads us toward our deepest and greatest destiny. Our soul's path. These Magdalene codes that came to me through dreams, memories, personal trials, and reading stories have helped me to pass my own Earth school lessons. I make myself a priority and listen to my body and intuition. I continue to create unabashedly and speak my truth. I navigate painful experiences with grace, as I know my ancestors are rallying behind me.

I return home to the sanctuary of prayer and the power of my intention. I gather with my soul tribe to intend together; we amplify the coherence of our hearts and miracles happen. May we embrace the chaotic mess of change, trusting in these earthquakes to unlock codes required to shift and act as catalysts toward our greatest experience of love and growth. Healing each of our lineages and anchoring in the present moment where we are held in love. We are safe now to speak our truth and our timeless freedom depends on it.

With Love,
Juliana

ABOUT THE AUTHOR

JULIANA LAVELL

Juliana Lavell is a yoga educator, intuitive mentor and artist.

She offers intuitive readings channeled with tarot and astrological insights. Her yoga classes, sound healing sessions and workshops are online and in person. You can find her with a paintbrush in hand, creating original and custom artwork sold internationally. Find her on your podcast platform where she shares free guided meditations with sound bowls plus interviews and recordings to light you up.

Her new projects include ergonomic furniture design, publishing her writing and art in books, training manuals, oracle cards and home products.

Her purpose is to inspire you towards a deep, soul-level return to your highest Self. Using the ancient tools of mysticism to mirror and awaken your inherent wisdom.

So you can align with your purpose and return to love - that is who you truly are. Together we cultivate physical, spiritual and emotional well being through embodiment, practical tools, fully felt wisdom and artistic inspiration.

Find her at www.julianalavell.com

Tune into her podcast called "Into the Mystic" available on iTunes and Spotify.

Instagram: @mystic.jewel

GROWING MY GARDEN OF HOPE

KATHY ELLER

YOUR LIFE IS YOUR MEDICINE. HOW YOU SHOW UP in your personal atmosphere—how you show who you are in this great big world—this is your life. Yes, it takes time to get here. It takes work. It takes turning off the outside world at times. It takes going inward with your sensitive and messy thoughts. Let your journal be your confidant, your buddy that lets you write freely—uncensored. Your personal space to be brave to confront your intimate life.

For me it's when submitting my chapters, they become an extension of my journaling and using words on paper as my voice. My voice of expression—my voice for having those sensitive conversations. My chapters are just as much for me as they are for you...the reader. I hope that by sharing my story it will bring light to your experience.

When you are having internal conversations with yourself, this is it you talking to that little three-year-old you. I find for me it is. I'm talking to that shy, frightened girl who was in her grandmother's kitchen so many years ago.

Can I take you back in time to share a story about myself? A peek at why I have made the decision to make a change.

It was the day my twin sister and I arrived at our new home, my grandmother's home. This day was more significant than I thought it was. I always seem to skim over it in my thoughts. Now I know why—it was really where my struggles began. Even my gut has a tug inside it when I relive this moment. I look back, and it's as if the older me is looking at the three-year-old little girl. I look at her with love and compassion. Like a big sister. I tell my young self that you will get through this. Hang on a little bit longer. You see, it was a time when my family fell apart. My mom was sick. My dad was out the door to find whatever he needed. It was a time when us kids were shipped around to be looked after by family and close family friends until my mom was well enough to have us back.

That night of coming home to my grandmother's was the beginning of my unconscious beliefs that I was in the way, a burden to my mom and family, including my grandmother. I was scared. Everyone was looking at the twins. The story that I must have told myself way back then was, *now what do we do with them?* I now realize that when I feel like I'm being judged or left behind, it triggers me back to this moment. A moment where I felt like I didn't belong—I felt out of place, out of love. This moment is when I became a daydream believer. I went inside to a safe place.

THE FALLEN YEARS

Over the past few years, I have taken a deep dive to fix that younger me. It did take a mental crash after my mom passed away, as well as some other major events and relationships.

It has been a struggle at times. Today, though, I feel like I have finally come out of it.

Writing my three chapters are as much for me as they are for you, the reader. A potential tool to help you make the choice to make a change, to help you move forward.

A short time ago, I re-entered the mainstream workforce with a temporary position. Although it helped pay some bills, it also reinforced my need to follow my dreams. When your tummy starts to churn, you know you are on the move to follow your dreams. Don't fight off these feelings. Don't bury them. Let them go through you. Feel them - hear them - be with them. When you sit still and let the shit flow through you, you can come out of it with new hopes and desires. Shift happens when shit happens.

The story of my past will tell you that I always felt like a stranger among family and friends. Looking into my world from sitting out in left field. Always the observer. I have come from being that outcast weirdo kid who lost her mom, then dove into a relationship that ended with the snap of a finger. This ended up in a burst of grief. Boom—it all came out. Being rejected, the sorrow and grief gushed out in waves of sorrow. Yep, she burst wide open. Living was getting out of control, spiraling down. Crash. Boom. Collapse. Now where to turn?

This fall was the turning point to the start of my healing journey. I can say that I am still a work in progress, but I have arrived at a peaceful time in my life. What a journey it has been. Now I have the tools to help guide me through the ups and downs. Life can have a way of keeping you in a state of constant mindset combat. This combat somehow keeps me in the present, reminds me to keep moving forward. I'm alive, sometimes messy but also in a state of gratitude for where I have arrived. Living life my way. Following my dreams.

Since taking my deep dive, I have found comfort in knowing what energies to attract myself to. And knowing when to move along my merry way when I'm headed into a dangerous energy zone. Hand goes up, and a voice inside me says, *not today*. And I swiftly move away to safer ground.

YOUR LIFE IS YOUR MEDICINE

Make it a practice to consciously look outside yourself from the inside out. Go beneath your root system. Dig deep. Most of your living comes from the surface of life. To do the work you need to, go deep below the surface. It is easy and convenient to live in a superficial state. That's where we stay, and that's where people often want to find you.

For me, journaling keeps me from being on the surface of life. It helps me dig deep into my thoughts. In life there are so many out there that are coming from a place of being on the surface—aka surface feeders. I choose to be below the surface with the roots. A tree needs its roots to survive. The roots allow us to see the tree's leaves and branches growing above the surface. A tree with no roots will have no life to grow its leaves. We can learn so much from our native roots. The next time you are in the woods, imagine the circuits of life that are below the soil. Give your imagination room to roam free. Be a DayDream Believer.

Take the time and be still with those thoughts. Take notes. Take note of how you are feeling at that very moment. Let your imagination flow. Once you begin your journey of taking notes and writing your thoughts down on paper, the way you look at your peace of heaven here on earth will change.

267

My thought is that if you stop and observe how things are going, you might just start putting the intention to move forward in your daily life. For me, journaling is the tool that can help you to move forward. In your journal you could jot down daily intentions. Who do I want to show up as today? An intention could be - today I intend to look at the way the clouds are forming. Or my intention today is to give one of my smiles away to a stranger on the street. I guess you could say an intention is similar to having a daily affirmation. For me, an intention is an action. To achieve an outcome that you have made a promise to do for yourself I believe stress is the leading way to sickness. If you stay in a state of superficiality or a state of overachieving to satisfy someone else's vision of who you should be for them, this will keep your mindset stuck. Your body already tells you when enough is enough. A tightness in your belly area, always fidgeting, your body is in a constant fight-or-flight mode. You can't even relax at the beach, let alone get a good night's sleep.

When facing a difficult situation, this is where you can start making the continuous effort to make the intention to stop. Take some focused deep breaths and state an intention to slow down. Look inside out - ask yourself how this occurrence makes you feel? Are you super anxious right now? What can you do to reverse this anxiety? Excuse yourself and step away from the situation. Avoid a reaction until you have given yourself time to question if you should pursue this any further.

Another intention is to make better meal choices. I've made the intention to eat healthier and to make better snack options. To have foods in the house that need to be slightly prepared instead of popping open a bag of chips or sliding a frozen dinner into the microwave. I have made these options a practice that is now a normal thing.

Speaking of normal, one other intention that I set is to make seeing the good in life to be a normal feeling. Make it normal to see the good in everyday life. By doing some of these actions that I have been mentioning, your mindset will shift. You will start to enjoy life, relax, and in turn your body will feel your shift. Your mind plays such a big part in your well-being. It can even be very affordable to make these simple intentions. Bottom line, be mindful of your thoughts. You have thousands of them in a day. Make the good ones outnumber the not so good ones.

Not everyone is ready to jump ahead, I do realize. I have been noticing, when having caring conversations with certain people, that there are more of you out there than I realize, that are searching for something new. You may not have moved yet because it isn't time.

Finding my peace comes from letting go. And rediscovering myself. Time to finally calm down. Stop playing everyone else's game. Start living your truest life - start living. If those around you don't like your change, then I guess they don't get to come along to see your transformation. Let that be as it may.

How often do we stay in a job or relationship out of fear that the other side will be upset with us if we leave or move on? I felt this one day when I went out for lunch with my friend Mary. She asked me if I stayed in a certain situation out of loyalty. I said it was the fear that they would be angry at me and think less of me. I love how my friend was able to bring out my truest self. By realizing what made me stay somewhere that I didn't want to be anymore, this took the guilt away.

How often have you been in a job or relationship where your value, your worth, is silenced because it is expected of you to just do as you are told? This has happened many times to me. I remember a dream where these three words came in loud and clear: *enough is enough*. After hearing them, I can tell you it was a new day to shift my mindset. Do you listen to such dreams? I have taken them as an extension of my intuition. Know when to move on, even if you start with small changes. You weren't meant to be silenced.

MOVE ALONG YOUR MERRY LITTLE WAY

Recently I made the choice to move away from some relationships. I was going through the grief of knowing I wasn't fitting in well before letting go. Have you ever just kept holding on to something, always making the moves to get together, always the one to hold on tight? Holding on for fear of losing the part of who you were in that relationship. For fear of being left behind...rejected? It takes great strength to move along from a relationship that has hit a dead end. Sad—it's just that...sad. After the release, let the guilt fall away. You don't have to carry it around like a ball and chain. You will move forward and grow new relationships with a new crew of people that have similar interests as you. You will also grow a new loving relationship with yourself.

A meditation I once participated in was going into the future. Having a conversation with me, 20 years into the future. This was a couple of years ago, and can I tell you it has stayed with me. Each day, I make an intention to keep moving forward and being excited to meet me 20 years from now, because I took the effort to make a change.

If you want to see a change, it starts by making the choice to pursue some mindset work. It is worth it, and I am here to say that it has made a world of difference for me. Does this work stop? Do you ever get to "the end?" Not really. It does, however, become second nature. Your choice to make a change has already started by you finding and reading this book. At some point in time, you must have made an intention to move along for yourself.

BECOME A DAYDREAM BELIEVER

Journaling those sensitive conversations is what has helped me to progress along my changed mindset journey. Writing your thoughts down on paper brings them to life and makes them real. You are committed to you, to bring your life...to life!

My journaling has led me to submit three published chapters. A few years back I would have never thought I would be involved in one let alone three multi-author bestselling books.

I love writing nowadays. For me it has brought freedom to my being. When I sit and am still with myself, the words just flow through me. My voice has come alive, and I have grown so much over the past few years. Writing has helped me to come out of my shy, timid shell.

Before you start your daily journaling, take five minutes with this little exercise I created.

Five minutes of deep breathing. Inhale for a count of five through your nose and exhale through your nose for a count of five.

Become connected to your body with each breath and exhale.

Start from your toes, and feel the sensation travel up your legs to your belly, to your chest, arms, fingertips, to your neck, up to the top of your head. Feel the light move through your body. If you have thoughts enter your mind let them move through you. Just let those messy thoughts flow through you.

Always keep breathing, keep focused on your body. Feel your breath move to each part of your body from your toes to the top of your head.

Do this for a minimum of five minutes a day—before you start your day, on your lunch break, or before you go to sleep each night.

My journal writing has helped me realize that we must get busy living our lives. STOP wasting your days wondering why people are not always around. Like when envisioning a big day such as your 60th birthday, stop hoping and wishing someone takes the initiative to ask you first for dinner or to plan a special outing. Yes, that sounded princess-like, but I think you will have gotten the idea of what I was thinking. Realize that not everyone is thinking about you. Be more the queen in your life, not the princess. Be assertive, head held high. Be your true, authentic queen self.

Go do something for yourself. If there are certain people in your life that aren't even thinking of you—let alone, you and your big day...why would you go to great lengths to tell stories to yourself about them not thinking of you? Stop it...just go live your life. Long after that big day. And you know darn well you will have had a better time anyway just living for you.

Stop waiting around for someone or some people to make room for you in their lives. Your life is yours with people that you invite into your circle or you as a singular being. Go be you!

Have you ever stopped to think that over the last little while you have been going about your business and you are the one that has moved along, unconnected yourself. You are the one that has kept moving forward and not everyone from your past will be moving forward with you. That's okay. You are already making your life happen, and you didn't even recognize it.

To keep yourself on this forward moving path, keep telling yourself new storylines. This is a new story about you, so describe how you see yourself in your daily life. What is the picture you see in your mind of what you look like going to that nice restaurant, for instance? Or how about that cruise you have been dreaming of? Maybe the picture is you meeting new people on that cruise. Just look, you are laughing and having great conversations. It's also okay to be selfish with how you want to see your life play out. Once you start on this changed mindset, you will start to notice how the universe sees you and has been guiding you along the way. This is part of you manifesting your own destiny.

GROW YOUR GARDEN OF HOPE

We all have knowledge and talents that represent a seed. Grow your garden of hope by exploring your thoughts. When you spend time musing about your day, you will be inclined to reflect and journal. Take the time to venture into your own mind when you are out in nature or out for an urban walk around town. Writing down your thoughts stimulates you to grow and to learn about yourself. You will begin to grow and open your thoughts to new ways of thinking. You may just make the choice to make some changes in your life. Stepping out of your ordinary way of thinking. Creating a new way of life with new thoughts. Changing the stories of past events can guide you to make these changes.

Once you get going on exploring your thoughts, who knows…you may want to share some of your story. A reader of Musing About Stories to Live By might just be looking for your story, as it could be similar to theirs, or it will make them realize that they are not alone in their thinking.

One of my passions has been creating my own publication. It is called Musing About Stories to Live By. A publication with uplifting content to guide you to nurture yourself and to become empowered to make the choice to create a better today. To grow your garden of hope. Creating my publication has been a dream come true.

Do you relate to having felt like you are about to burst at the seams if you don't move forward?

Your body is telling you that it is time to move. You are about to climb another mountain.

You have a will about you. Listen to your internal guides. They are guiding you to move forward.

I get so excited about what is to come. At times, I just amaze myself as I keep moving forward. Moving along my merry little way. Yes, little Kathy (my three-year-old self), dreams do come true. You are living your authentic self, way to go girl.

I leave you with these thoughts...

Start your journey of moving forward. Be present with your here and now. Allow the messy bits to be present. This allows you to come up for a breath of fresh air. Come up to the surface—face the mess, allow your mindset to tidy up, clear the messy energy.

Journal your thoughts. Take a notebook on your nature walk

or use the notes app on your phone or now you can even record your thoughts. Just keep moving forward. Be alive, be real, it is good for you.

At this time in my life, I say to that little girl, be brave little one and a big one for me still today is do not shrink yourself in order to make others feel comfortable.

Whenever you find yourself doubting if you can go on, just remember how far you have come. Remember all that you have faced, all the battles you have won and all the fears you have overcome. Then raise your head high and move along knowing that YOU'VE GOT THIS!

A quote I recently read, though I'm not sure of who the author is, but it goes like this, "I heard you were focusing a little more on yourself, and worrying a little less about everyone else. That's beautiful."

ABOUT THE AUTHOR

KATHY ELLER

Kathy Eller is the owner/creator of MusingAbout.ca

When Kathy created Musing About Stories to Live by, she was thinking of all you creative beings.

To create a space to be brave with expression, creativity showcased. A space to make the choice to create a better today.

Kathy's thought is "wouldn't it be great to lead by example on how to live a good life with uplifting content and resourceful and informative stories?" Make it normal to see the 'good'.

Kathy's daily practice of journaling has brought her to new paths in her life. She has become a best-selling author: Magdalene Rising: Feminine Leaders Guided by Her Fierce and Unconditional Wisdom was created to bring together the magic of empowering feminine voices. Isis- Her second submitted chapter was in the best-selling book Mother of Magic. Now her third submitted chapter in the Magdalene Codes. Published by KIVA Publishing.

Become a Day Dream Believer. Kathy is currently creating a journaling community at Musing About - Journal Your Way to a Better Today. You never know where your journaling and writing will take you.

www.kathy@musingabout.ca

https://musingabout.ca

https://www.facebook.com/musingabout.ca

https://www.facebook.com/Sociable60s

SACRED EMBODIMENT IS TO KNOW YOURSELF

LISA CURTIS

THE BLACK SHEEP

I HAVE ALWAYS BEEN AN EMPATH. AS A CHILD, I was perceived as shy because I tended to shrink back from the world. It all felt so overwhelming at times. People were too loud, things moved too fast, and I was picking up on things I didn't yet understand. Adults called me "Little Lisa" because not only was I physically smaller than most kids my age, my voice was soft and I preferred not to speak. I remember seeing adults tower over me with their large presence and big smiles, announcing to the room how shy and quiet I was, looking down on me as if I was a curious object. It made me want to make myself even smaller so I could disappear. I remember believing that being small and shy was an unwanted trait and that I was supposed to be loud and take up more space, but I didn't know how.

The only time I would take up space and raise my voice was during my tantrums. Something would trigger me and I would erupt; running to my room to throw everything to the floor, seeing red, and not knowing how to manage all of the intense emotion that was running through my body like fire. No matter how loving and supportive my parents were to me growing up, I did not feel understood or accepted in the society I was living in. I couldn't help but compare myself to my older sister, my friends, classmates and neighbours who all seemed to be better in school, more social and active. Stuck in a perpetual state of not feeling good enough, my body became a container holding these bad feelings that had nowhere to go. I was too young to be able to describe what I was feeling or why I was feeling it. The only way out was through these tantrums.

By the time I began school, a pattern emerged when it came to friends. I would identify a problem in the group and decide they weren't good for me, so I would move on and find new friends. Whether it was because I found one person was being a bully to the rest, or I knew they didn't care for me as deeply as I needed my friends to care for me. The decision to change my path always came clearly, and I wouldn't waste any time in taking action. It left some bad blood with schoolmates, I'm sure, and it confused the adults in my life. They moved on from calling me "shy little Lisa" to questioning, "Lisa is different, isn't she?"

From childhood, I always knew I was not like most people. Although, I could never define it because I was never shown *how* to define it. It seemed like society's definition of an acceptable personality was one who was confident, energetic, smart and happy. Those were the words in my vocabulary. Those were the labels that received positive feedback. I was (and still am) an emotional and intense person. I am sensitive to my surroundings and what other people are feeling. I love deeply. I am stubborn and committed to finding my own path to feeling happy and accepted, no matter what that looks like.

I was born with this internal flame in my belly and was put to the task of navigating life with this body, mind and spirit, as we all are.

I believe we are put on this earth to experience a series of lessons. Depending on the choices we make, these lessons will appear as obstacles and challenges, inviting us to step into and explore what they are here to teach us. With each challenge we overcome, we have answered the call to heal a part of ourselves that was holding us back, whether it was generational or in this life. By facing our demons, we release what is no longer serving us and take one step closer to living a purposeful and fulfilled life.

Having a family, a successful career, discovering the world...it is rare to know your purpose at a young age. Growing up in an environment that was consistently placing me in boxes that didn't fit only made me feel further away from feeling a sense of belonging. Every day after school my mother would ask me how my day went and I would reply: "It was the worst day of my life." From school to extracurricular activities, none of these boxes fit. From childhood to the age of 20, I spent these years of my life numbly going through the motions of what was expected of me, endlessly in search of the places and people I felt at home with. When I was old enough to make my own decisions, I was still disconnected from the divine lessons that were hidden in plain sight.

REBIRTH

When I was 21, I lost my apartment and all of my

280

belongings in a fire. I was home that night with my roommate. We heard the distant alarm and took our time putting our shoes on, thinking it was another false alarm. I opened the front door to find a wall of black smoke. We raced to the fire escape only to find it was engulfed in bright orange flames. We grabbed our cell phones and ran to the balcony to call 911. By the time we got there, the black wall of smoke took over the entire apartment.

I don't know how long we were waiting on that fourth-floor balcony for help to arrive, but time seemed to slow down. My eyes were seeing the world in slow motion, everything went quiet despite the roaring heat of the burning building around us. I wasn't aware my body was hyperventilating until I called my dad and wasn't able to speak. The words were coming out as desperate sobs. I looked down to see everyone else who made it out of the building and was overcome with helplessness. Not knowing when help would arrive, or when the building pressure inside our apartment would break, shattered any feeling of control I ever had. I couldn't accept what was happening. I couldn't accept that this was how it was going to end.

As the smoke grew thicker and the soles of my sandals started melting from the heat rising from the apartment below, I spoke to something outside of myself for the first time. I was never a religious person and I considered myself an atheist at that time, but in that moment of utter helplessness, I didn't know what else to do while I awaited my fate. I told this Higher Power that I am not ready to go. I am meant to do something great and I need more time to achieve it. I need more time. Give me more time.

Moments later, the fire department arrived and brought us down from the balcony to safety. Once on the ground, my roommate and I sat down on a curb and looked up at where we just were. The pressure inside then shattered the windows and engulfed the balcony in flames.

That night changed my life forever. I no longer felt invincible. I adopted a new sense of urgency to live my life in the fullest way because it can end at any moment. Now, anything can happen. The fire had incinerated everything I had ever owned. Photo albums and family heirlooms burnt to ash. My bed had fallen through the floor to the apartment below. All I had left was my body–and suddenly that was all that mattered.

Having experienced living with nothing to my name but the clothes on my back, I began appreciating the little things. My emotions came in with such intensity and fullness, I felt like I was meeting myself for the first time. That experience broke down the barriers I had put up around me and reminded me that life is short, so live it the way you want.

It took me some time to recover from the shock and work through the initial PTSD, which made it nearly impossible for me to leave a lit candle unattended, or not have a panic attack when I heard any sort of alarm, which was difficult to avoid living in the city. I knew I didn't want to be a victim of this trauma, so I did what I could to heal with the tools I had at that time. I walked past the site of the burned building every day on my way to work purposefully in order to heal my body from the memory of that night. The first few days triggered panic attacks; my body would return to that night and all of the fear and panic that came with it. Until one day, I walked by without falling into an attack, and I started to feel a little bit more grounded.

I didn't know at the time why a part of me knew I had to expose myself to the traumatic experience in order to heal, but this was before I understood intuition and its magic.

282

What I didn't know then was that this traumatic experience was the greatest gift the Universe could give me. I needed a wake-up call, and it had to be dramatic to catch my attention. My time here IS meant for something great, and I needed to find it. My old self and everything connected to it had to burn to ash in order to make space for my rebirth.

AWAKENING

The deeper healing began two years after the fire. I had met a man and fallen deeply in love with him, knowing he was leaving to travel the world with no return date. He left nine months after we met. Not knowing if he would ever return left me heartbroken because I knew in every part of my being that he was my person. I spent the first two months wallowing in my own heartbreak in my studio apartment.

One of the first times I left my apartment to socialize was to visit a new friend. She read my Tarot cards and, for the first time, I felt hope. With this newfound hope, I bought my own deck and started to explore their mysteries.

The Tarot Cards gave me new perspectives on what I was going through and helped me out of the funk I was in. They guided me to heal in the highest and best way for myself. I was blown away and inspired by the magic behind these cards. I wanted to learn more because I knew there was so much more to discover about myself.

Seven months into his travels, my love came home and we wasted no time in continuing where we left off. My heart was full and I was ready for whatever was next. I was working in the fashion industry at this time, pursuing my field of study. But I hadn't expected the feeling of complete unhappiness I felt going to work every day. One day, in particular, I came home and told my partner I was quitting with no plan. The next day, I gave my notice. I had moved through this decision with such certainty in my gut while my logical mind was in complete turmoil.

I kept thinking about that moment on the burning balcony when I was speaking to an invisible force telling it that I was meant for something greater. I knew following my gut would lead me to the right place.

I spent three months unemployed, reading self-help books, taking online classes about topics from project management to palm reading, and speaking with a career coach. I loved my experience with the career coach so much that I decided to get my Life Coaching Certification and explore the idea of entrepreneurship. Part of the Life Coaching program included a weekend intensive introduction to Theta Healing, a meditative technique that channels Source's energy. We spent the weekend tapping into each other's energy and connecting to our higher selves. I had no idea what I was doing or if it was legitimate until one moment changed everything.

We were asked to face the person next to us and connect to their energy. We were prompted to invite their personal angels and guides in. I went through the motions with a mix of openness and self-doubt. Focusing on my third eye, everything was black and expansive. I immediately saw a russet-brown, long-haired dog. I tried pushing it away, thinking it was just my mind playing tricks on me. The dog stayed in my vision. Moments later, the activity ended and we were asked to share what we saw. I told the person next to me that all I saw was a dog. I described the dog to him and without saying a word he took out his phone and showed me a picture of his childhood pet. There it was, the russet-brown dog, exactly as I had seen him in my meditation. I nearly fell out of my chair.

After that experience, I knew there was more to life than meets the eye. That weekend had cracked me open in ways I never thought possible. I walked out of the class feeling tuned into every person on the street. I was amazed and inspired.

HOLDING THE FLAME

Like an explorer, I dove into understanding crystals and their properties. I started Life Coaching my friends, giving Tarot readings, meditating daily and attending Intuitive Development classes. Along the way I was healing parts of myself I didn't even know existed. I was discovering the beautiful depths of myself that were dormant. I was learning how to connect to others and help them with their personal journey, just by intuitively reading their energy and telling them what I felt and saw. I have never felt so fulfilled as I did when I walked out of those experiences. So I kept exploring and landed on an opportunity to learn Reiki, an energy healing modality.

I soaked up Reiki Level I like a sponge. I didn't fully understand what chakras were or what to do with them, but by the end of the training, I had experienced firsthand the energy of Source flowing through my hands like a warm electric charge. I could physically feel the concentration of energy in the palms of my hands, like tiny flames.

Flames once lived in my belly as a child, uncontrollably bursting with nowhere to go. Flames once threatened me with death and taught me how to overcome trauma. Fire, which can both destroy and purify, has appeared in my life in many forms. Initiating me into the next rebirth, the next initiation into self-growth and self-empowerment.

The energy healing arts taught me what an empath was and that I wasn't alone. I could finally put a name to my ability to pick up on what people are feeling. I started identifying energies in the environment and learned how to ground and protect myself when it felt too chaotic. In that process, I started to honour my boundaries and overall energetic health. I could finally tell my younger self why she was feeling so overwhelmed and angry. I could hold her and comfort her in the ways she had needed back then. I use this gift of hypersensitivity to improve my life but also help others improve theirs. It is my superpower.

Within two years I had attained my Reiki Master Certification and was calling it my life's work. I started my own Reiki practice in 2020. Global pandemic or not, I had found my roots in energy healing and the world needed it more than ever. With every session, I grow more fascinated with the world of energy. This thing we cannot quite see, hear, smell or touch, but has a great effect on how we engage with the world around us and within us. It is equally fragile as it is powerful. This system is dynamic and interconnected and it makes us who we are. It is our spark of life. It's how we carry ourselves in the world, how we communicate, love, and live. To understand it is to know yourself.

WELCOMING THE DARKNESS

I can't logically explain half the decisions I make because they are moved by my intuition and how they affect my energy. These decisions have disrupted the environment around me. It has invited skepticism, doubt and even fear from loved ones. It has challenged me in ways I never expected.

My journey so far has not been linear and has not always been easy. I believe it is meant to be challenging, because without challenges you don't have the opportunity to learn, and without learning, there is no growth. Now, I invite challenges in–I welcome the darkness with an open mind and heart. I have been through the discomfort enough times to know that the other side is always brighter. I deliberately stir the pot in order to initiate change in my life. Through every obstacle, I choose to not only face the darkness but to walk through it.

I choose this path because it challenges me. I choose this path because it leads to a greater understanding of myself, where I come from and where I'm headed. Disrupting the status quo has brought me closer to self-liberation. I will lead by intuition no matter what other people think because I know it will feed every layer of my being. It will bring me closer to myself. That is what I wish for the people who choose to work with me.

Through my Reiki practice, I provide a safe space for people to land exactly as they are, to dive into their internal depths and explore the layers of their being, face their demons, heal their energetic bodies from traumatic experiences or the daily interactions that can make us feel off. Wherever they are in their story is exactly where they need to be. Whether it's for deep relaxation or deep work, I guide people on how to read their own energy and collaborate with it.

By doing this work, I am nurturing my younger self, who had always felt empty, angry and misunderstood. I am showing her that this emptiness is actually expansiveness; this anger is actually a passion and inner fire that should never be extinguished, and this feeling of being misunderstood will be filled with unconditional love. I am now the person who can tell her she is expansion, fire and love.

Now I look back with immense pride on her abrasive decisions to cut ties with friends who didn't make her feel loved or cherished. She was honouring her boundaries. I think about how many jobs I resigned from because they simply didn't feel right with a grounded heart. I was unapologetically forging my path to fulfillment. The pattern was always there to show me I was meant to disrupt, and join the tribe of those who choose the same path.

ABOUT THE AUTHOR

LISA CURTIS

Lisa Curtis is a Certified Reiki Master, Published Author and Spiritual Entrepreneur. Through 1:1 Reiki sessions, she helps people around the world engage with their energy so they can move through life in a meaningful way.

Offering both in-person and distant sessions, Lisa guides her clients into deep relaxation, while scanning their energetic body for imbalances. She provides intuitive support on how to nurture their personal energy for everyday life. Her unique approach incorporates crystal therapy, aromatherapy, tarot reading and life coaching to help her clients achieve heightened personal awareness and spiritual connection.

Lisa created the Reiki Bundle program, which is designed to facilitate a deeper dive into energy work. It includes three consecutive sessions and oracle readings with detailed recaps and unlimited post-session support to help you track your growth and stay accountable throughout your journey.

Lisa lives in Montréal, Canada with her life partner in their beautiful home by the canal. She is honoured to facilitate self-healing, self-discovery and self-love with her clients.

Are you ready to deepen your connection to your energetic body?

Sign up for the Reiki Bundle: tinyurl.com/reikibundle

Follow Lisa: instagram.com/lisacurtisreiki

Let's work together: lisa-curtis.com

POWERFUL LOVE & LOVING POWER

MĀRCIA DĀROMCK MERMA

WE ARE WITNESSING A MASS WAVE OF A MAGDALENE awakening on a global scale today. The woman who spent almost 2,000 years excluded, rejected, judged as a sinner and as a repentant penitent, "saved" by the masculine from her sinful and lost ways (read: feminine), is now sitting on the throne next to him as the Feminine Christ. The codes of Mary Magdalene are being delivered to women willing to awaken their wombs, heal their broken hearts, and open to love again…women who are ready to remember and trust their intuition. Do you feel the call?

I have been working with Magdalene energy my whole life…first very much unconsciously as she softly whispered to me for 13 years, and then very much consciously and purposefully over the past 8 years, like a waterfall. The Magdalene Frequency translates to feminine energy embodied meeting in sacred union with the inner and outer beloved, daring to Love.

In 2018 I surrendered in devotion to HER after diving deep into a Magdalene Vision Quest. It was part of my training as a Womb Priestess in the former Fountain of Life Mystery School, founded by my dear teachers Seren and Azra Bertrand. My Magdalene Womb awakened, my heart opened to love again, and I embodied her frequency of Powerful Love and Loving Power. A Magdalene is someone who can open the heart, awaken the womb space and live in a state of sacred union. This is my story of how I became one.

GRIEVING WOMB AND THE SEED OF SACRED UNION

I start my journey in a grieving womb.

That was my first sense of home. Quite challenging and quite paradoxical. The place supposed to hold me in safety and love was sad and torn with emotion from my brother's death, just over a year before I was conceived.

I was a rainbow baby, conceived on Valentine's Day after my grieving parents visited a newborn. They were so thrilled to hold a new life again, the baby's light gave them hope and courage. Their concern about how their surviving daughter would cope, adjust and heal from suddenly losing her brother also guided them to have another baby. It was the best they could do for her. I was a wish, a dream agreed upon by both of my parents to heal a broken, grieving family, devastated by the loss of their firstling. The power of life and the power of love work in such mysterious ways that all it took was for my parents to get hit with a spark of life from a newborn baby, and their first reaction was to make love and create life.

They were conscious, willing, and open. They loved each other very much and had just passed the death portal with one child…and managed to choose life again. I am a child of a sacred union. And pleasure! In the deepest crevices of my memory, I can hear the gasp of my parents climaxing as my father released his seed into Mom's sacred womb to create new life. Eyes meeting in love. Hearts beating together. Sacred Conscious Sex unifying two lives into one.

DEATH DOULA

That spark of divine light carried me through my childhood and adolescent years. Then Lady Death came to visit again, this time taking my most precious treasure away from me way too soon: my beloved mother. As life had it, my intrauterine experience inside a grieving womb was only preparing me to face one of the most difficult events of my life. After nine months fighting cancer, she passed, and I became a soul and a death doula. I had just turned 25 and had no formal teaching or acquired skills on how to facilitate the passing of a loved one, but my intrauterine training taught me.

For hours before she stopped breathing, I stayed by her side in the hospital, guiding her gently back home, whispering into her ear soft words of love and release, allowing her to transition safely and in peace. Holding her hand with my heart broken from seeing her drifting as I watched her spirit go. At the same time, I was comforted with the opportunity to be with her at her crossing. I realize now I was chanting her back to the spirit world and she left her body guided by the sound of my voice. How wonderful it must be to hear a familiar voice when crossing the bridge between worlds. She was cremated and her ashes buried in a cemetery, as our family did not know what to do with them.

Thirteen years later I knew what to do...and Magdalene and Yeshua sure were my guides. Meditating one day I remembered my mother saying, "I don't feel like traveling much, but if I could I would walk the Holy Land and follow

293

the footsteps of Jesus in Jerusalem." It was important for me to make that dream come true taking her to a place where she would enjoy being in honor of her memory. And just like that, I was scheduled for a huge initiatory trip. A pilgrimage where I made my way from Brazil to Israel to scatter my mother's ashes in the Holy Sepulcher. Holding a red pouch with her remains in it, I walked the stone streets from the Gethsemane Garden to the Golgota, the place of the Skull, and this experience made me cross a mystical threshold and feel as if I was Mary herself, walking those stone paths, foot by foot, making the record for human history.

Surprisingly, I arrived at the same time the Pope visited Jerusalem, a very unusual fact. A most sacred site for Christians, Jerusalem had not been visited by a Pope in 50 years. We both landed very close to each other, on a Magdalene portal day (I arrived on the 22nd and he on the 23rd). I did my funeral ceremony overcome with emotion spreading my mother's ashes over the Via Dolorosa, starting at The Church of the Assumption and then from Mount of Olives all the way until the holy of holies inside the Holy Sepulcher: a tomb carved into the stone wall...some believe this was the place Yeshua's body was put and where Mary Magdalene found him or assisted his resurrection. As I cast my mother's ashes to this empty tomb on the left, inside a cave located in a small chapel in the building, a group of carolers entered the room to sing...I felt in my heart it was for her, my mother. Later I understood that just like her human transition was sung by me, her ashes were being sung by the carolers to welcome her to her new home. My mom was from a priestess lineage. I feel it. And now I understand what it meant to have the womb that birthed me buried inside the earth...wow...it is profound as we become one with our ancestors.

THE MAGDALEN DRAGON AWAKENS

I was first introduced to the idea of Mary Magdalene being a companion to Jesus when reading the Da Vinci Code. At that time, I was a 26-year-old dentist working on my Ph.D. thesis. Regardless of its accuracy, this book unearthed one of the biggest mysteries of humanity for a multitude to read. I was one of those 80 million people who bought this book carrying the message that there was something else to that Christ story being told. Something was missing in this whole story around Jesus, the Bible, and the system, hierarchy, structure, institution and organization...that missing link is exactly the Feminine power, particularly expressed by Mary Magdalene. It was through reading the enchanted words "Divine Feminine" in the book that something shifted immediately within me.

I was touched...from that moment on all I cared about was that I felt the scent of the Rose.

Divine Feminine! I had never heard of that expression before. I had never heard that the feminine could be divine. I grew up hearing that women betrayed God when eating that apple and offering it to Adam. We are cursed to birth in pain and we are less, guilty, and dirty. We are not as equal as men. Sadly, that was my programming. When I heard the words "Divine Feminine", it was so profound! I contemplated the idea that I am divine just for being a woman, and not separated, or guilty or the one to blame. I felt the Feminine essence percolating that book unto me, something that was kept inside for many years. I welcomed it, like a seed put into the soil. It takes time to sprout and develop.

Years later, as I prepared to give birth to my son, my dragon wild feminine awakened. Birthing is a dragon experience: we can't control it, or rather, a wild feminine force is controlling us–the same wild force required for a volcano to erupt or a rose to bloom. This force can't be tamed. And yet...I was robbed of that experience by being under an artificial and interventionist medical system. When the "sentence" of an emergency C-section was declared during my labor, I had to surrender in great frustration and disappointment. Went for the surgery feeling I was about to die although I was about to give birth. My arms were restrained wide open as if I was Jesus on the cross. The birth was effortless and painless, but I was literally feeling ripped from the inside…and I knew. I had just lost one of the most powerful experiences a woman can have, my chance of experiencing the force of the dragon birthing through me.

But my dragon sure did awaken. And she was furious. And sad.

After my son was born, I felt the elation and ecstatic joy of being a mother, having a baby and a family. I also felt my frustration and hurt for not being able to birth naturally and not feeling supported in my motherly role. I had no parent to teach me, my mom was gone for eight solid years. But I experienced, again, this wild and fiery dragon force in a mother where she just "knows"- she can sense her child, she can know whether her baby is comfortable or not, she can perceive if the baby needs a hug, a drink, a safe place to rest or just to be in the presence of the mother.

With this silent grieving many more wounds surfaced: from people not trusting my instincts, to me not trusting myself, nor feeling respected, heard or honored, and having to fight for my voice and space in my marriage. A sense of guilt, for allowing my precious baby to cry to sleep, and not having enough strength to protect him. It was all so paradoxical again: I was in touch with my wild feminine and was completely crushed by it. I knew I had to heal. Solemnly I took a vow to work on myself. Less than two months later I started to awaken spiritually.

Two years into couple's therapy I sorrowfully realized I couldn't be myself in my marriage. I was either submissive or controlling, and either shrunk or rebelled. In short, I did not feel accepted for who I was. A divorce was the route taken. Not an easy one, for sure, but I promised my mother and my ancestors I would live in my truth.

MOVING FROM FEAR-BASED TO LOVE-BASED

In 2010, my teacher suggested I read a book called Magdalen Manuscripts, about alchemical sexual practices performed by Yeshua and his beloved. I did, and it was another mystical portal for me, felt as if I was stepping into a past life so vividly, visceral and real. More keys to the energetic nature of meeting in union and love with the beloved were awakened. A few years later I began my path of healing my womb, studying at The Fountain of Life.

My training in the mystery school was profound and intense. It put me in contact with the wild feminine as I had never seen before, not with tantra and not with any other practice or spiritual healing I've done. I visited the three realms of the tree of life (underworld, middleworld, and upperworld). In the underworld I learned about the trickster archetype and understood many distorted relationships I had attracted into my life in order to heal. I could gauge the amount of trauma I was holding inside. I had to grieve the betrayal I felt for being put in a grieving womb, for being left out, for having never known my parents without the grief cape, for not being taught proper sexual and menstrual education and being programmed to be an obedient "good girl" in a patriarchal society. Also for losing my birthright of having a natural childbirth and my family collapsing twice: when my mom died and with divorce and other abusive relationships. I made a pilgrimage to Avalon, Mexico, Hawaii, Israel, Italy, Peru and Easter Island. With Magdalene guidance, I dissolved my guilt with Camomile tea, remembering we are all innocent in Ma'at's scales as she holds us to open our hearts and our return to Innocence.

We have an amazing power ready to be discovered, released and integrated into our lives: our sexuality and the pilgrimage through our inner labyrinth and grail gates, leading us to pleasure, bliss, and the black-hole womb portal within. The integration I had on the polarities of dark and light was immense! Eventually, the mystery school was menstruated and closed, but their teachings remain. My teachers published two books on womb shamanism: Womb Awakening and Magdalene Mysteries. I translated both books to Portuguese and held study groups and book clubs with them. I was healing and in time attracted a relationship totally guided by her, my beloved Mary Magdalene, from start to end.

SACRED UNION AT LAST

Mary Magdalene and Yeshua were the spiritual pillars of our school. Although I was experiencing a powerful womb awakening, it was only when I took time off to rest, do her Vision Quest, and commune with the sandy beaches of Serra Grande, in Bahia, Brazil, that I truly felt Magdalene and her Mary lineage of ancient mermaid dragon mothers awakening within me. I could hear her whispers in the wind and her song, her mermaid songs on the waves. The ebbs and flows of the tides and the sound of the waves in the ocean became her voice and her breath. Only when I devoted time, she came to meet me in dreams and visions; giving me feelings, reawakening memories, and most of all, teaching me how to love powerfully and how to be powerful in a loving way. After this initiation two major shifts happened: I met a soulmate and we were together for 3 years in a sacred relationship; and my work with MM officially began with my channeling the Magdalene Mandala, a journey through the Magdalene womb and the elements.

Over the past years, her guidance led me and my students through paths and portals never visited before. Magdalene is a magical weaver and she midwives our pilgrimage within, to our wombs and haras as well as to our hearts. Since working with her frequency, I had real-life initiations in my close relationships, each opening a medicine and a sacred portal in my human life. With her anointing alabaster jar and the work of my dear teacher Aletheia Pistis Sophia, who lives in the Cathar region in the south of France, she awakened the myrrhophore within, teaching me oil and scent medicine of the death doula, her ancestral line that goes back to Inanna, Ísis and Sofia, the sisterhood of the Rose, the Cathars and gnostics and more. She taught me how to be a womb vessel of love and let love embrace all wounds to be rebirthed.

She showed me the path of embodying a love relationship rooted on Earth. I experienced sacred loving sexuality, surrendering and trusting in love as I offered my womb as a vessel of love to rebirth both my partner and me: the Pod Consciousness. Experiencing this sacred union was a pearl that Mary Magdalene gifted me. It brought me to hope for a more balanced and loving world, where we can embody and birth our children with respect, time and space, educating them in a more loving and gentler world as they learn and grow with us.

THE PRIESTESS PATH

The very first spiritual work I did with MM energy was on her Feast Day in 2014, as a womb apprentice. A work called Healing the Grail wound and healing abuse in wounded relationships.

299

Eight years later I was serving as the host for a magnificent celebration of Love, Sacred Union and Sisterhood for her on July 22, 2022, Magdalene Feast Day, a date which has been celebrated worldwide for over a thousand years.

We were over 150 people vibrating the holy name of Mary Magdalene, concentrated in the same place, embodying her. Our hearts pulsing together, praying together, dancing to Venus notes, drinking Cacao medicine, singing together, being blessed, smudged, and receiving a bath of plant leaves and crystal singing bowls from amazing Magdalene priestesses. As the number 22 holds her frequency, 2022 is the year of Mary Magdalene, a code in itself.

Joy was expressed in each sister's smile! We danced in abandon with our long skirts under the sound of the Fire Rose and Sarah la Kali. After some Magdalene songs, a sister priestess echoed a tune calling the Spin-Doves (Pomba-Gira in Portuguese), ancient and popular female power spirit symbols in Brazilian dance rituals. She was Enthroned.

In these eight years, since my first Magdalene ritual, I was taken on a spiral feminine journey, which can often look like a dance of two steps backward, one forward. Those were years of intense, visible and invisible initiations and remembering the art of relating, the art of walking my talk, and the path of love. The remembrances and experiences of sacred union frequency are forever sealed in my heart-womb. Magdalene initiated me into the art of writing, speaking, moving, crying, singing, and working. She shows me that a life of bliss is just one choice away, one feeling away.

As I step into my Crone years with pre-menopause on the horizon, I am in awe of all that Mary Magdalene is offering to us at this time. Having mentored and taught hundreds of students especially in Brazil, I see people looking for the

Magdalene essence within them like I did, curious and wanting to learn more about this untold feminine story in the Bible, and ready to embody her frequency.

MAY SACRED UNION RETURN AND REBIRTH LOVE ON EARTH AGAIN

Mary Magdalene is listening to us and giving us rose seedlings. Gaia is inviting each and every woman on Earth to plant their own rosebush and tend to it. This is a global invitation I am proposing to you, reading these lines to be shared worldwide. Care for roses on every 22nd day of the month to awaken your Magdalene power individually and as a collective. Even if you don't have a rosebush, you can buy roses on that day or find a garden with it, and talk to your rose, ask her how she is, stop and listen to her, and tell your rose how you are doing. Every time we connect with the Earth, we gain access to her, as Magdalene is contained within the Earth; she walked here before and her remains are scattered across our planet.

Every time we connect with water, we are connecting with the codes that ancient priestesses, witches, healers, peasant girls, and herbalists left for us. They prayed for the waters and the land just like we pray for our future generations.

I invite you to connect with the prayers Magdalene left for us.

This is an invitation to all of you, Magdalenes.

She is on Earth, in Fire, in Air, and in the Waters.

We are all roses planted in this garden of Magdalene Sophia, the Body of Gaia.

I am walking this priestess path as anyone else. Together with my sisters, we are walking and dancing, awakening, feeling, living, experiencing and, in Union, we are carrying together a wave of love. We are bearing these waters and holding a wave of love. Each Magdalene awakening receives her medicine from the waters and becomes part of this wave.

All of us who resonate the word MAGDALENE in our mouths vibrate her frequency. Every moment we speak the name Magdalene the planet is vibrating her powerful love and her loving power.

Let us love anyway.
And always respect ourselves!

Breathe deeply in self-respect, sister.

Experiment Love in All Forms.

Open and Trust

In Magdalene's Great Love

Absolutely.

We are weaving her golden threads.

Fire roses have this power,

The power to Love.

Love covers all that exists!

We all are all Magdalenes!

Inanna Rakhma!

ABOUT THE AUTHOR

MĀRCIA DĀROMCK MERMA

Márcia Dáromck MerMa is a Sacred Weaver on the Way of Love, a Rose Magdalene Womb Mystic, Grail Mermaid Priestess, and a Spirit keeper of the Feminine Mysteries. She has been dedicating her life to awakening, healing, embodying and restoring the ancient feminine frequency and pre-patriarchal ancestral wisdom and anchoring the return of Sacred Sexual Union. She has worked with hundreds of people facilitating healing and transformation with Mary Magdalene & Yeshua, sound healing, yoga, plant medicine and shamanic practices. She loves to sing and write Magdalene and Mermaid songs and poems.

Teacher, translator, and artist, she created the "Temple of the Feminine Arts" in 2017, a space dedicated to the return of feminine wisdom with love, art, pleasure and respect, serving as a uterine space for healing, creation and awakening of men and women.

She leads study groups, ceremonies, retreats, group and individual journeys with Mary Magdalene and Yeshua, Ma'at, and Sophia. She created the Menstrual Education project and is a faculty of the University of Biomancy, a school of magic founded by Dr. Azra Bertrand uniting science and spirituality.

She lives in New York and Brazil with her son Daniel, and her pets Cat, Crystal and Dudu.

Links:

Facebook: https://www.facebook.com/marcia.daronch

Instagram: @marcia.merma

Website: https://www.marciadaromck.com

RETRIEVAL OF FORGOTTEN WISDOM

MELISSA ANN

OVERVIEW OF MAGDALENE RISING CHAPTER: RECLAMATION OF LOVE

IN THE CHAPTER I WROTE IN THE BOOK MAGDALENE RISING, I shared how the passing of my grandfather in 2017 initiated a change in the direction I thought I was heading in life. It led me to the decision to leave all I had achieved in business, love and relationships behind at the end of 2018. At the time, I was feeling called to work on helping to heal not only my ancestral bloodline but also to work on behalf of the collective, to assist with the shift and creation of New Earth. The intuitive guidance along with the synchronicities I received at the time made it hard for me to ignore what was being shown to me. So my journey back to love and oneness began…and, along with it, forgotten gifts of bloodline and past incarnations.

DARKNESS OF THE INNER JOURNEY

In 2019, after leaving my long-term relationship, it was quite an intense year spiritually as the physical changes my body went through were challenging. I found myself triggered on a nearly daily basis by the world around me. It brought up situations that reflected back to me trauma I had been through. I was experiencing what many would call the Dark Night of the Soul. It had me questioning everything. It pulled me into the darkness in order to no longer fear it but also help me understand my own inner light.

During this time, I was unable to ignore it I had the emotions surrounding the trauma that came to me so strongly that I was forced to sit with it until I was able to transmute and dissolve it so that I was then in a place of peace with the events which had happened in my past.

The past events I'd experienced came not only from this life but also brought up a deep recall of past life events which had impacted me, as well as those that showed up as either dream states or in visions. My sleep dramatically changed. I never felt like I had slept soundly. I was always deep dreaming or in an astral state in my sleep, which was exhausting to the point that I often had to take short naps during the day just to get through it. I also found myself slowly releasing myself from the toxicity of my previous relationship, realizing how the continual negativity of the long-term relationship I was in had impacted my beliefs around my self-worth. This lack of self-worth had become a reflection of my reality, particularly evident in my workplace where there seemed to be constant division and conflict with the staff. As I let go of the desire to take control of the work situation and change the dynamic and focus on myself, the workplace dynamic suddenly changed without me having to do anything really but work on myself. No longer did small stuff that others did frustrate me, and no longer did I keep wishing that those in higher positions did more because they were being paid more. I was able to accept them for just who they are. I also realised how my desire to work had become focused on money instead of actually loving what I did, simply appreciating the smaller things in each day such as practicing more gratitude.

The realisation of how much I had shifted from doing something because I loved doing it—instead focused on monetary gain—actually shocked me. I'm not sure when and where in my mental shift toward my professional life changed. It took place as I grew up, and when I was younger I always did jobs out of love before money. I also in this timeframe began to become more aware of how different people would make me feel. For instance, some were energetically draining, and I felt there was a hidden agenda, or I felt the opposite with a genuine sense of caring and compassion from them.

Because I was working in customer service, it became quite interesting to learn to read people better, and in doing so I was able to better meet their needs. I also didn't get as frustrated with the more challenging customer, as I had a better understanding that they were just presenting as who they were. With this new insight, I noticed that there were certain people I interacted with on a daily basis who were trying to tap into my own energy because when we interacted, I could feel my own energy being pulled from certain areas of my body while simply having conversations. I was amazed by how sensitive and aware of energy exchange I had become. I also mentioned in Magdalene Rising how at the end of 2018, I started to feel an influx of energy flowing through me and out of my hands. I experienced the following year the energy moving up my spine and hitting energetic blocks, which was at the time physically painful. I was also divinely pushed into a more physical job at the end of 2017, which helped me keep shifting the energy through me often with each shift would come some kind of emotion to work through as well.

As I reflect on this time, I realized that often I would find myself having to sit with my inner stillness to help move through whatever was coming up for me.

I had really turned within, during these 12 months while also focusing on physical activity, not just with work. I would ensure I was doing some form of physical exercise each day, but other than this I fully withdrew from the world around me and focused on understanding where I was being guided and my own internal environment and knowing. I learnt to listen to my intuitive gifts and the flow of energetic environments. I deeply questioned the good and bad around me, and I also found myself having to overcome the fear of darkness and mastering my own light in order to not fear that which seemed dark or my shadow self. I was also guided to start healing my womb space as I had just before leaving my last relationship when I experienced my monthly flow come to a complete stop. Little did I know this was the wisdom of my womb telling me this relationship was no longer for my highest good.

THE INQUIRY FOR KNOWLEDGE

It was the change in my monthly flow which intrigued me, leading me to want to learn more about the healing of my womb space. I had never actually experienced a regular period even from a young age. I always put this down to being very actively involved with ballet and dancing in my teens. I began searching for more information online on this topic and much to my surprise I didn't actually find much. I put the intention out there that I wanted to do training of some kind in feminine healing. Towards the end of 2019, I did Reiki training. This was great as it helped me regulate the energy flow coming from my hands while also giving me more insight into energetic healing. With this came a deeper understanding of working with energy.

It didn't take long for the intentions I had set at the end of 2019 to come into my reality. As it happened, 2020 became the year of learning more in the way of courses. Along with my soul family to now give me support on my journey, no longer was I fully withdrawn from the world around me and unable to openly talk about what I was experiencing. I was so grateful to have connected with like-minded people. This was also the year many people were in lockdowns due to COVID. Instead for me it enabled more connection.

I came across the feminine healing courses which I had put the intention out there months earlier to find. These courses normally probably wouldn't have been offered online however due to the COVID situation it meant many facilitators had no option but to use the internet for their delivery methods. These courses offered online enabled me to interact with beautiful women all over the world. One of the many courses I did was training in the shamanic medicine wheel course around the Sacred Feminine. This was a massive realisation for me about just how deeply I had rejected the feminine aspects of myself, having grown up on the farm longing for recognition or praise from my father, who was often absent due to the long hours worked on the family property. It resulted in my desire to do anything a man can do and to try and do it better. This meant as a result I had not nurtured my inner feminine, nor did I even know who she was. The course opened up a whole new aspect of self, which I worked on healing understanding and reintegrating, while also finding compassion for the relationship I had with my mother who was also not present or capable of giving love. Neither of my parents really was capable of giving the love my childhood self yearned for—and now I had to learn how to give myself the love I had missed out on.

During the previous year, I had a past recollection of a past life based in Egypt where the sacred feminine arts combined with sacred partnership was integrated with agriculture, along with the production of food and land fertility. This intrigued me. While I didn't cling to the Idea of what I was shown, I put intentions in place that if my path in this life was to incorporate some of such memories it would be shown to me. Later in the year I also did a nine-month womb wisdom training in a red tent again with women from all over the world. I was beginning to understand and feel into my feminine attributes for the first time. I grew to love and learn how to work with my monthly cycle not only just as a business tool but also as a form of healing and letting go of the past. I now understand some months, especially when they have been tough, are ones that can't wait for my monthly flow so I can release it and put the past month behind me.

I also began to have more understanding of the moon cycles while working with them to create intentions and let go of the old. I started to notice rain would often come with these cycles. This stood out to me a lot more as the drought in Australia came to an end. I viewed the rain as a cleansing of the pain not only held by the collective but also imprinted on the land itself. As a teenager and young adult, I always had a knowing of when rain was on its way. I remember when I was at university, I would often call home to let dad know it was going to rain. I would be in the ute driving around the farm with my father and have a knowing of what should be planted in particular paddocks and changes which need to be made in the running of enterprises. While he probably perceived these as an educated knowing from my formal studies, much of the basis of these conversations was from an inner knowing that I received from driving around on the land. Because this was something I had connected to my whole life I didn't actually realise it was a gift that not everyone has. I see much of this gift in one of my nieces who is growing up on the property. Her sensitivity, care, and love for the well-being of animals combine with her connection to the earth. It is beautiful to see and listen to her insight. Although she is only three years old. I also see the gifts of our family's lineage in all my four nieces. It's really quite rewarding to see it and understand the ripple effect it will have on the world around them one day.

EARTH ENERGY AND ANIMAL INTERACTION

At the beginning of 2021, I left my 9-5 sales job after I had learnt to love it and the daily interactions with not only the people I worked with but also the customers who walked through the door. Much about the business no longer aligned with who I was or the impact that the business had on the earth. There was also a lack of being challenged on a daily basis, taking up my time to listen to customers, and I knew the lessons this job was here to teach me had come to an end.

I actually on so many occasions tried to leave this job. What started as a casual two-week stint ended up with me working there for seven years. The job was divinely on my path for a reason. At the time I took the job, I was unemployed and knew the day that I was in town I had to go see a friend who was managing the business at the time, as she had a job for me. Little did I actually expect I'd be there for so long. I'd applied for many jobs while working here and always just missed out. It wasn't until the last couple of years working there, I realised it wasn't that simple. I had to learn the lessons to be able to move on to something better and more rewarding.

I handed in my notice, and within a week I had a new job with a friend I'd known for years. He and his wife owned an

311

agricultural contracting business they were expecting a baby in three months' time. They wanted someone to organise the staff and help with the admin side of the business while they tended to their new child. It was the first time in three years I'd had anything to do with agriculture even though my father and brother were still working on my family's property, and I hadn't helped them for close to five years.

It was really quite refreshing to view agriculture from a new perspective without the childhood wounding and installed beliefs and ego. After leaving the property my long-term ex-partner and I owned together there was a huge letting go of who I was and the ideal image of a country girl I had tried to live up to. When leaving I had an inner knowing agriculture couldn't continue in the same direction as it was going due to the continued taking from the land. The long-term drought to me was a key indicator of this. During the second year of the three-year drought, I was sitting with a cup of ceremonial cacao at my family's property when the similarity between a woman and the land was brought into my awareness. As a woman has more pressure put upon her she shuts down and dries up hence closing her heart and womb her fertile soil is no longer available. During the time away from the industry of learned knowledge and beliefs surrounding agriculture. I was now open to a whole new perspective, one that allowed me to take the canvas and create a new world for the next generation.

The new agricultural contracting job included shearing, dipping, etc., basically most things involving sheep husbandry. I did my wool classing certificate when I first left school, and I did a shearing course. Not that I ever took it up as a full-time thing. I really only did training in these for use on the family farm. I was now being asked to step into a leadership role in still a heavily male-dominated industry and those women within it ran more on their masculine energy in

312

order to compete in this space as I once did. It was challenging on a whole new level to now have to gain respect from predominantly male-dominated employees.

I was now on a journey to learn how to maintain the newly found divine feminine within while integrating it into a masculine world as a leader. It wasn't until I allowed myself to fully step into the shearing shed environment on a daily basis that I was shown the changes within the industry which need to occur. There were old outdated beliefs of having to work hard to receive money with the view of it being work of the lower class. Shearers were often looked down upon by wealthy property owners. Workers caught up in the struggles of fighting ancestral trauma hidden behind the masks of addiction. While sheep produce one of few natural fibers available therefore to me it is important for our future to maintain a quality natural fiber and the way it is harvested from the sheep.

I also began to discover an emerging energetic theme with sheep properties which had continual problems with lice. Therefore, the question of was more to the lice infestations than just management had begun to emerge. I also began to notice when coming onto properties significant impacts or energetic residue of trauma which had occurred to aboriginals and even during settlement. I also noticed changes in the energies within the differing landscape as I traveled between locations.

Later this year I spent five months working for a friend whom I had often helped on a yearly basis but with preparing cattle for shows and sales. I was also still doing the organising for the agricultural contractor from a distance. This was in a different state, during this time COVID once again flared up quite bad in my hometown once again it didn't have any effect on my daily duties. It was during this time I actually also did further training in another energy healing modality, it was while working with the cattle I was shown how energetic imprints on the property of where they were born and raised had negatively affected the behaviour of the cattle.

I also found the land in which I was staying became incredibly healing for me during these five months. I was able to heal childhood wounds as those from my previous relationships in regards to negative beliefs and self-worth around working on a farm or in agriculture. I was able to learn how to manage the balance between my internal masculine and feminine aspects of self through my daily work. I no longer held the negative thoughts and beliefs around working in the agricultural space as I had spent the past five months not being persecuted and yelled at like when I was growing up and in trying to run a property with my ex-partner. As the friends I was working with only ever built me up by increasing my self-worth.

SACRED PARTNERSHIP

When I returned home, I met one of the male co-workers who had been working in the agricultural contracting business the whole time, but I hadn't actually met him until October. Little did I know at the time he would bring me some of the hardest healing, while also gifting me with a glimpse of true inner peace, greater leadership capacity, and the most powerful creation tool yet.

As women, we often find ourselves holding space for men to open up and be vulnerable and reveal past traumas. We spend so much time building people up and the family aspect brought into the workplace...it ended up this interaction between us supported those around us to grow and become better versions of themselves. While I reflect back upon the last three to four years of my life, it seems as if patterns are repeating and the pain of healing continues. However, I have doubled my income each year, which has led to more love and peace.

It is truly hard to explain the pain each of us carries within our soul and physical body and just how deep it is ingrained within our cells and memory. That is…until you put in the work to fully heal and release it from being part of your reality. After doing so much work on myself, I now meet people and see them for who they are. We are all just trying to do our best. I see all the pain and trauma they carry. By fully investing in this work, we unlock the gifts and ancient wisdom at a soul level. We make the pain of retrieval may be somewhat similar to childbirth. The pain becomes forgotten, and all we remember is love.

ABOUT THE AUTHOR

MELISSA ANN

Melissa Ann is a leadership coach and energy healer working with earth, animals and humanity to create better health and work-life balance. Melissa's passion is working in the agricultural space to bring passion and new vision to the next generation. She believes what makes a true healer and leader is the extent you have moved through your own healing and embodiment. In this time of change, both for humanity and the Earth. It's time to speak up and reclaim the essence of who you are.

Links:

www.melissaannhw.com

https://linktr.ee/melissaannhw

https://www.facebook.com/melissaannhealingandwellbeing

FINDING ME

MONIQUE VETTE

THE INITIATION STEP

IT WAS OCTOBER 2017, AND I WAS AT A POINT WHERE everything in my life was nothing but darkness. The marriage was horrible, with constant abuse, mentally, emotionally, and sexually. Constant lies, control and manipulation–and with all this I had deep sadness, deep anger, and deep grief. I did not give myself the time to acknowledge it nor the time to allow it all to heal. I had lost my sense of self. I had lost my voice. I had lost myself.

I was tired of it all, I'd hit absolute exhaustion. I had miscarried my second baby seven months earlier. This was number two within two years. I had no emotional support. I had nothing.

I was working in a part-time job that just didn't give me any satisfaction at all. All my friends had disappeared, and I was all alone having to figure this out and understand why I had such a deep, dark sadness within.

I felt so lost, yet I knew there was more to life than how I was living it.

I had a husband that I never saw, and when I did, I was lucky he would acknowledge me, or even say hello. For the nine years we had been together, it became the one thing I hated the most. Living with him felt like a prison and not enjoyable. I was the slave, I was owned, and I was never seen as enough.

Yet deep inside me, I believed there was a deeper meaning to my life. A reason why I was here and what I needed to do. But before I knew where I wanted to go, I had to figure out who I was first.

So leading up to this time my marriage was getting worse day by day. He was always preoccupied on his phone, and I literally just vanished into the walls.

Until one day I was walking home from work to my car and it was like this huge bolt of insight came to me. When was the last time I laughed? When was the last time I went out with friends and had fun? When was the last time that I actually had joy in my life? The answer was...*I don't remember*, and that hit me hard.

All I could think was I WANT OUT of this marriage and I want out now!

I was officially done. I didn't care what it was going to look like afterward. I didn't care how I was going to feel. All I wanted was out.

318

I stomped my way to my car, with so much anger rising up in me that I had to contain myself from screaming.

All the years of abuse, all the years of broken promises. All the years I had put into this relationship, wishing and hoping that he would see me and everything I gave to him. Everything that I had sacrificed to make him happy. All of it, all of me!

I was absolutely broken…everything was broken. My heart, my soul, my dignity. Every single bit of me–gone, crumbled onto the floor like dust.

The reason why this hit me so hard was because I've been a clear channel most of my life. Since my early twenties, I have been channelling spirits, I did this as part-time work and helped hundreds of people with their problems. Yet for some reason when it came to mine, I couldn't see clearly. It was clouded by my judgement and my low self-worth I had at the time.

So that night I screamed at my spirit team to get me out of this marriage. All I remember saying was: *GET ME OUT of this marriage NOW! I need strong, clear guidance, and I need it now. I WANT OUT NOW!*

That night as I went to bed, I got woken up by the light of his phone. It was shining so bright that the whole room was lit up. This never happened, and I found it odd to wake up to this. So I started to flip his phone over to stop the light and all I heard very loudly in my mind was: You need to check his phone. I thought to myself, *No, I don't. I'm done with all this.* But again I heard the message, louder and louder and louder…until I took his phone.

This was unheard of as his phone was constantly locked and

319

always in his pocket. It never left his side. So I knew this was my only time to check. When he was asleep.

I walked down the hallway into the lounge so that I wouldn't be disturbed by him and began to look through his phone. I was shaking uncontrollably, I just about dropped the phone. My heart was pounding out of my chest, my mouth went dry, I couldn't breathe, and I was absolutely beside myself. I couldn't handle any more pain, then all of a sudden this huge wave of calm came over me and all the emotions stopped. I was sitting there wondering what had just happened. It was like someone had taken over me and said, *Here, just relax, I've got this. I'll take care of it.*

Then slowly I began to search through his phone. Checking all places I could think of to find information. There was nothing for a while until I remembered...the app he was on the most. So I went in there, and there they were, every single message in plain sight for me to read and see. Hundreds and hundreds of them–to one woman. I didn't have any anger toward her. It was all towards him and I then realised OMG it's HER!

The one woman I have been praying for, for the last three years. A prayer I said over and over and over. *Please, spirit, send another woman to take my husband away from me. Please help me. Send her to him and take him away.*

I had tried many times over and over to leave that marriage. Nothing worked. Everything I could think of, I tried and yet time and again I would get pulled in to stay. So for me this one prayer was all I had, and I prayed with all my heart. It was the only thing that I knew would save me.

I knew right then I had two choices. One to stay and keep being in this abusive marriage. Or finally leave. And I chose the latter.

From that point on, I kicked him out and had never felt so free before in my whole life.

Until I hit the ground on my knees feeling the darkness wrap itself around me and smother me until I couldn't breathe. There I was, finally a free woman. No more abuser around. Finally found my freedom and peace. Yet I was broken. Soul broken. I had nothing left in me.

I was done with this life. I was done.

Six months later when I went to my hairdresser I was still in a dark cloud, not knowing what was truly going on around me, and he advised me that I had too much hair falling out. So I went to the doctor to find out my problem and he diagnosed me with post-traumatic stress disorder (PTSD).

Even then I had no idea what he was talking about. He offered me some medication and therapy, which I immediately said no to. Because at that moment, all I could feel was my body telling me to RUN!

This was the beginning of my healing path of PTSD, later to be recognised as complex PTSD.

The initiation step had begun, my road to healing, my path of discovering what truly lay ahead.

While all this was going on, I was already on my road to meeting Mary Magdalene. Without me realising it. She had been interweaving in my life eight years prior to the ending of this marriage and the ending of the person I once knew.

THE HEALING STEP

321

Years on I was doing a lot better. My life had changed dramatically. I had a new job that I absolutely loved. I was looking after myself. I was doing all the internal work to help myself heal. I was doing all the workshops, tantra workshops, women's retreats, embodiment practice, yoga retreats, breathwork, shamanic journeys, healing courses, temple work, and non-alcoholic festivals. Mediation, exercise, nutrition...the list went on.

I was on a mission. A mission to connect to myself more deeply than I had ever before and to also wake up free from all the pain and symptoms of PTSD. I had no idea if any of this would work. All I knew was that it felt good and that I felt like a different person each time I left these workshops, retreats or festivals.

I felt something change in me.

So I kept going. No matter how hard it got, no matter how many times I had fallen to my knees screaming in pain. Feeling like my whole chest had cracked open. Feeling like I was about to disappear into the earth and be swallowed up whole. No matter how many panic attacks I had.

I kept going. Because I was determined to beat this illness. I was determined to get to my happy place. One that I had not known for more than 10 years...if not longer.

While I was on this path I read a few books about Mary Magdalene, and it was like I was literally there. There was something about her that made me feel loved. She made me feel at home. She made me feel at ease. These simple yet profound codes I got from reading books about her activated something with me, and it led me down the track to where I am today.

Four years later, I am totally healed from PTSD symptoms and have no resemblance to it at all.

I am now a new person. Whole, complete and totally in my joy, my freedom, and love for who I am and what I am about.

Each day is a blessing and I am so grateful I chose me and this path to walk. I wouldn't have it any other way.

What I learned the most was how to have the support I needed around me. Whether it was from a coach or from myself. The solid foundation that I had set up for myself was so important, and that is what has carried me through to today. I still make sure I am doing my daily rituals. As every time I use them, it helps me to ground back to me, why I am here, what my mission is about, and who I am as a person. It's an important routine for me, and always will be for the rest of my life.

Towards the end of my healing journey with PTSD, I decided I needed a change of scenery. I needed to go to someplace else and experience life in a different manner.

I didn't like where I was living. It reminded me of everything that I had experienced in that marriage. Everywhere I went, all I got were bad memories, and by then I was over it.

I was done looking over my shoulder constantly...just in case. Done seeing him around in my area, when I knew he lived 50 minutes away. Done being controlled by this unseen energy that was making me feel trapped. Done with it all.

So I packed up my three-bedroom house that I had lived in for 20 years and sold just about everything and moved to Australia with two suitcases in hand.

I had no idea what I was getting myself into. All I knew was that I had to leave Auckland, New Zealand.

Once I landed in Australia, I felt a sense of ease. I felt like I was home, my soul felt like it was home. Something that I hadn't felt in a very long time.

It was so exciting for me to now feel this newfound freedom, and I had no idea what was about to happen.

THE PATH OF THE PRIESTESS AND CONNECTING TO MARY MAGDALENE

After I landed in Australia, it took me some time to adjust to the different energy here. But for once I felt like I could breathe easily, and for me that was a huge comfort.

I landed here on January 31, 2020. In March we all went into lockdown.

I had two choices, either fly home back to New Zealand and not know when I could go back to Australia. Or stay in Australia. I decided to stay in Australia.
After that decision, I could feel my body settling into the land much more. The more I relaxed, the more I connected to the land here.

One thing I missed about New Zealand was the community that I had connected with, and I had to find my own way again. I also needed to keep me balanced, calm, and on top of my nervous system.

So while in lockdown I was using the tools I knew I could use at home daily. Some days all I was devoting myself to were these tools. It was the only way to stop me from going into daily panic attacks.

At times I would hear a beating of a drum around me and wondered who it was. It gradually got louder and louder and I started asking people around me if they could hear it.

To my surprise, no one could hear it but me. So I asked my spirit team to guide me and show me the way of the next steps I needed to take.

One thing led to another and I was buying myself a shamanic drum at 2:00 in the morning.

Once it arrived, I started to play with it, as I had no idea what it was for. Daily I would pick it up and just beat it. Slowly getting myself used to the feeling of having an instrument in my hands.

Then the idea came to me (thank you to my spirit team) to sit and channel while beating the drum.

And WOW the most powerful transmissions started coming through.

At that time, I was still having the odd panic attack. So I decided to do an experiment on myself and tune in weekly for six months. By the time five months came, I had noticed how much clearer I was. How much more in tune I was with Mother Earth and how grounded I felt within myself. Best of all, I had noticed that within this time, I had not experienced one panic attack–and from that day forward, I've never experienced any again.

I found with channelling the different sounds, voices, activations and energies, this had the most impact for me. The drum energy would instantly change my whole being. From being in a depressive state to then feeling open, alive and super clear.

It felt so divine and so natural, that I started to offer it out to the public to see how they would react to it, too, and they have received it with such gratitude.

I felt like I had been given such a huge gift, that it needed to be shared with others.

That's when I could feel the energy of Mary Magdalene come through so strongly. Every time I connected in with my guides, she was there.

Every time I felt this gentleness around me, such a loving energy and so strong, I could feel the ancient wisdom coming through from an Ancient Egyptian past life. And every time I connected to that energy she was there.

Our energy was so strongly connected, that now a few years down the track, I know with all my soul that we were priestess sisters in a past life. I just know it.

I can feel her divine essence around me all the time. Her soft loving nature, with a strong knowing and backbone, has had me in awe and in tears at the same time when connected to her.

Her presence is around us all. Her knowingness of what love truly meant, and how life was meant to be lived, has long been forgotten.

However, it's women like us who remember. Remember the priestess path, remember what our mission is. Remember what we are here to do. It is we who are here to show others what they too can achieve. How they can live their life now as a new age priestess. How they are the pure love and essence of Mary Magdalene herself.

Let her guide you. Let her shine her love through you. Let her be in your life. Because once you do. It'll change forever.

What I've learnt on this path is that the more I dive into myself and what I am capable of, the more I see. The ancients lived a certain way for a reason and it's time we learn it too.

The reason is because it takes us out of the pain and trauma that so many of us have been experiencing…and it brings us back to love.

Love for ourselves.

This is why I teach what I do now. This is why I am so devoted to helping others to transmute trauma into freedom.

Because the pain of it all is and can be too much to handle. Our bodies are not designed to hold onto trauma so deep. Our bodies are in resonance with love.

That's why life is so much easier and happier to live when we reside in love. Especially divine love.

This path is definitely not for the faint-hearted to walk down. But trust me on this. If you ever feel called—by the sisters of the rose, Mary Magdalene, Isis from Ancient Egypt, or even Ancient Egypt itself–follow it. Follow that guidance, follow that path.

As you never know where it may lead you.

For me, I am still walking this path of devotion and I will continue to the day I die.

MY FINAL WORDS TO YOU

The love and freedom I have within me now, compared to what it was like when I had PTSD, is indescribable. I'm also now in the most loving, caring and sensitive relationship I've ever been in. He sees me for who I am, accepts everything about me and respects me with the deepest honour.

Why? Because this is how I now feel about myself. Our relationships mirror how we feel inside. They tell us what is truly going on. Take note of where you are and what is happening with relationships around you. They tell you everything that you need to know. You just have to open your eyes.

You see, when we are going through such dark trauma, we think the whole world is going to swallow us up and make us disappear.

But what this is really calling you to do is to reach into those depths. It's asking you to get to know yourself better. Get to know who you are inside and out. To pull out everything that no longer serves you and to see the gold on the other side.

Alchemise that pain, like I did. Transform it to gold.

Because once you do, and once you get through it all, you will see the most magical, magnificent gift waiting on the other side for you.

It's always there. Underneath all that pain, all that trauma. There is always a gift there for you.

Don't give up. Keep going, keep asking your spirit team— god, the universe, whoever you want to use—to help you. Lean into the expansiveness of this unseen world around you.

Lean in and let them show you the possibilities of what else is out there.

Because like me, you could be given new things or gifts to try out that you would not have thought of doing yourself at all. And that could be the key to you living the life of your dreams.

Now I hold regular shamanic Journeys online and in person. Every time we do it together, each person tells me how powerful and transformative that was for them.

The fact that I listened to myself and what I no longer wanted in my life, helped me to get to where I am today. Every single step I've taken has led me here.

Ask yourself this. Are you listening and leaning into your inner guidance, to what could possibly happen? Or are you in total control of every single aspect around you?

Because of the fear of the unseen?

Check in with yourself and see. You never know, Mary Magdalene may just be waiting there for you, a sister with divine love.

ABOUT THE AUTHOR

MONIQUE VETTE

Monique Vette is a trauma embodiment coach and shamanic healer, helping people to shift trauma into freedom.

She works with men and women, one on one and in groups.

Her group Waking up Nefertiri is for women wanting to be free from the pain of trauma within and to rewrite their inner path to a life they have always dreamed of.

She guides people on how to connect to the dark shadows (trauma) within so that they can be transmuted into freedom. Showing them tools and natural modalities that they can use for the rest of their life and be the solid support for themselves.

With this new rewiring within, hidden gifts emerge, and she teaches them how to use these gifts in everyday life so they can step forward each day with love and confidence.

She lives in a small beach town, Tuncurry, in Australia with her partner, two dogs and two cats.

If you're a person who has hit rock bottom and you are wanting to change your life. To say goodbye to the trauma within and to live the life of your dreams. This is for you.
Join Here: http://www.moniquevette.com/traumawork

Links:

Facebook Groups:
Walking the path of darkness
https://www.facebook.com/groups/161508029160609/
and Alchemy Shamanic Ceremonies
https://www.facebook.com/groups/159100009532595/

Instagram: @moniquevettealchemist

Spotify: Guiding You Home
https://open.spotify.com/show/61W8XoCgZtBt9HBedzCG mj?si=7d0cec3c0627410b

Email: monique@moniquevette.com

RESURRECTING THE SACRED PLEASURE
OF EMBODIED MATER

NICOLE ISHTARA KATZ

THE RIPS, SPLITTING, AND OPENING ME APART HAVE been the doorways where my soul essence and her divine sparks could shine the way to my holy incarnation. The pain, the suffering, the traumas, crevices radiating flares of my eternal being, love, hope, and grace would walk along with me through the initiatory portals, the wounds, and wisdom of my lineages, of humanity.

Magna Mater—Great Mother Birther and Creatrix has been holding me and guiding me in the darkest moments. Her shimmering, dazzling radiance luring me back to wholeness. Her unconditional love bathing me as I courageously walk the forbidden road, her truth unveiling, revealing all that is ready to awaken within me, within you, within the world.

Do you feel her?

Close your eyes and feel her embrace.

I'm guided by my ancestors, their presence always with me. Together we retrieve the lost sparks, alchemizing the wounds, liberating and regenerating, birthing the Golden Age.

A call has been sent out across the multiverse for souls to descend to matter in service to the organic web of life. To restore harmony and the forgotten sacred wisdom of Magna Mater and Gaea Sophia.

I responded to the calling of the feminine soul of the world, devoting my incarnation to revivifying her harmonious and reciprocal ways. Healing the wasteland, the wounds of the world, my transgenerational inheritance, and rewriting HER-story.

Do you hear her calling?

We are here to awaken and spin new threads in our ancestral tapestry, to remember our feral feminine nature, to reclaim the magnetic ecstatic sensual essence of the body, to revive the wisdom of our lineages and incarnate our/her holy essence.

I invite you to descend to the body, to the Earth as you read the words scribed here. A sacred pilgrimage to discover and uncover all the places within and without that have forgotten love. Decolonizing the feminine landscapes to awaken the immaculate womb and the sacred flames of our erotic innocence.

A deep dive into the primordial waters of our womb consciousness to rebirth in the womb web that weaved our sacred flesh into being.

MISTRESS WEAVER OF BLISS

Consigned to oblivion, the feminine wisdom of Magna Mater would wake up from a slumber and return to the heart-womb and consciousness of people. My journey is part of this great weaving, I'm here to resurrect the sacred pleasure of embodied mater restoring Ma'at— Cosmic Harmony. You, sacred woman, are also part of this great weaving.

All the portals of loss, grief, despair, bliss, love, and harmony can merge in the cauldron of the womb. Life is a beautiful paradox, a spiral journey where we are active participants in this entangled dance of recollection.

To me, Mary Magdalene is a sacred woman, a womb priestess, a carrier of the feminine flames and the primordial wisdom of the Great Mother. Her archetype and the frequencies she beholds would rise within the collective unconscious to reveal the road maps back to wholeness and sacred union.

Her holy incarnation, along with her beloved Jesus, would trailblaze the way for the great awakening and the return of Womb Consciousness to this cosmic cycle on Earth. The way I commune with her is through the essence she beholds, and the lineages she is connected to.

MM is a spinner of red threads, the forbidden feminine that embodies the Holy Wild Immaculate Womb. I recall the way I first experienced those codes. I was five years old, a mystic child aware that within lies the mystery of creation. I was in my girlfriend's house, we were sitting in her mother's closet. A wall mirror in front of us, my legs open with curiosity my erotic innocence wondered about the mystery of my yoni.

The second time she initiated me I was thirteen, I longed for love, for the beloved to consume me, there was a pulse of life force surging within me. I was coming of age, my magical sexual hormones had awakened.

At this time rituals, prayers, and ceremonies were part of my life–so were magic, crystals, tarot, and the desire to become a woman. I was broken and eagerly searching for ways to mend those parts, to bring harmony to my life. I used to go to a Shamanic Shop to buy what I needed for my mystical practices. I wanted to find my beloved, to call prosperity and protection.

I was advised by the owner of the shop to commune with Pomba Gira Magdalena, an Afro-Brazilian spirit evoked by practitioners of Umbanda— a syncretic Brazilian religion blending traditions from Christianity and indigenous American beliefs. She, a lover of carnal pleasures, is often invoked by those who seek help in the matter of the heart and love. My offerings in exchange for her help: my orgasm, my sacred pleasure in the comfort of my bedroom, in ritual and ceremony.

Communing with her through self-pleasure, masturbation, and orgasm I consecrated my prayers for love. Reclaiming my sex as holy, my body the temple.

It was through the codes and frequencies of the liberated woman, feral in her nature, unbounded by the chains of patriarchy. The gypsy woman in red, sensual, sexual, and free. The archetypal wild woman, the wHORe— Hor in the ancient Semitic languages meant 'cave' and 'womb', in all her fullness, unbounded, weaver, and spinner of red threads and shimmering rays.

My first portal into grief happened when I was six years of age, the first rip that broke me apart. The separation of my

335

parents and the war between them. My life was abundantly prosperous, I was blessed to spend three months by the ocean, playing mermaid, enjoying the sun's rays with family and friends. There was light and joy in my life, this summer would be different and my life would never be the same.

My foundations were strong, I was blessed to study in a Montessori school, Our Lady of Sion where many of my gifts would blossom through arts, music, dance, ancient history, and hands-on learning. My best memories come from this period, my daily meeting with the blue and red Araras in the garden yard. All would change, this school year I would fail, and the ground below would collapse.

I was a psychic intuitive child, I wanted to be an astronaut mystically searching for a way out, perhaps. My home was free of religious dogmas, light but heavy with the weight of ancestral wounds. My father was a Hungarian Jew from Transylvania, atheist, in exile, nervous and shattered by war and communism. My mother is a Brazilian Miss, a priestess of the one with many names, broken yet spiritually aligned. I was in touch with the unseen world, aware of the wounds and the 'ugly' spirits that sometimes dwell here. I've begun to witness the dichotomies of life, painfully feeling the profound split in our consciousness.

During this period I learned in history classes about the ancient civilizations of Mesopotamia, Canaan, and Egypt. Something in me was activated, awakening the wisdom in my DNA a liminal space to dwell. I taught my invisible students about those cultures, igniting a lifelong passion, journey and research in ancient cosmologies.

In Catholic religion classes, I learned about the patriarchs, their God and his son, Jesus. The biblical myths and desert stories enticed my soul, I felt drawn to those lands and parables. So familiar, yet my intuition would wonder about the hidden stories, my curiosity suppressed with dogmatic answers.

How about our foremothers, who are they?

And the Divine Feminine, where is she?

Why do we say the father, son, and holy spirit?

Where is the mother?

Why do we refer to God as a father up above the sky?

Why does Eve come from Adam's rib?

Why is she the one that committed the first Sin?

"Because Jesus said!" the nun always responded.
I didn't believe it, I felt something was missing. Luckily there would be other roads to experience Great Mother and learn her-stories.

The Rose of my heart, my beloved mother Roseli Popper. I'm so grateful for her resilience and courage, her love, support, and her feral nature. Her constant soul radiance even in the darkest moments. I'm grateful for her knowing and I forgive her for the times she failed to remember.

I was a baby when she took me for the first of many times to the benzedeiras. Healers, curanderas, medicine women keepers of feminine wisdom. I feel deep gratitude for these experiences and the way they still reverberate in my consciousness. Their syncretic and multicultural medicine prayers weaved protective blessings, mantles around my being as they uttered sacred prayers gently 'hitting' me with

337

the Mother of Grace, the queen of the herbs my beloved Arruda, the name in Portuguese for Rue, is a powerful grandmother womb protectress, helper of witches commonly used in Brazil for protection.

When I smell womb grandmother Rue I relive this visceral memory, their codes still reverberating within my being. Another occasion of nature's magic was when I was sick with a disease, I was three years old, and my mother was so nervous and worried, her younger brother died at the same age from the same sickness. Besides taking me to the doctor, she also took me to the curanderas. The advised ritual was to make a cake and add my urine to the recipe, bake and give a piece every day to an anthill until it was over.

I smile thinking about the ants and how they are my ancestors, too. I thank them for weaving their medicine into my body. I am grateful for the spirit of the plants, the elemental beings, and all life in nature. I hear the voice of the ancient grandmothers and their primordial intelligence. Through the healing arts and technologies of Earth Mother, the power of ritual, ceremony, and feminine prayer we can regenerate. Here I was initiated into her Mysteries.

GREAT HOR

Night begins to fall in the land of Sin, the Goddess/God of the Moon in Mesopotamian Cosmologies. I feel a rush of energy, pulsing within my flesh, my heart-womb, I reckon the first time I've come to the land of the mistress of the Vulva, two days before my thirtieth birthday. HatHor–the Egyptian goddess of art, beauty, dance, and the feminine healing arts in all her facets would hold me, guide me and initiate me in her sacred ground.

Dahab, the gold city in South Sinai Peninsula - Egypt,

338

mystical ground that would support my ongoing journey of resurrecting my womb wisdom, and incarnating my creative soft-power and the birth of my Womb bli$$ness. For the last eight years I have been communing with this ground and the pulsing primordial wisdom it beholds. My first Womb Awakening Workshop was in Cairo, Egypt. In the land of Sekhmet, Lilith, Tiamat, Qadesh, the Great Hor, and her many facets, I reclaimed my throne, the tribal land of biblical stories where coexistence exists and the desert meets the Red Sea.

Ma'at called me home, The Goddess of Cosmic Harmony, Truth, and Justice in the Egyptian Pantheon. I declared my innocence in her hall during a womb shamanic journey while in Rome, and I was summoned to Egypt. A lifetime longing to return to Kemet, and journey through this ancient place. Synchronistically I arrived on the first day of my first Nine Moon Womb Awakening Apprenticeship with Seren and Dr. Azra Bertrand.

The triangular peninsula of Sinai is a land bridge, between Africa and Asia, a potent portal where the throat chakra of the Earth, together with the Great Pyramid of Giza and Mount Olives in Israel, pulse powerful codes in the dragon lines. I would travel this intricate ground while awakening, reclaiming the wisdom of my womb lineages, embodying the soft power of my heart-womb union, resurrecting the alkmey in my DNA and activating the many portals and wisdom of this land.

I scribe these words, feeling the embrace of all the women before me, the whispers of my ancestors, the Dragons of Creation, and the voice of Great Mother herself. A sense of wholeness and embrace. I witness the waves of the Red Sea, ebbing and flowing, cyclically birthing and crashing on the shore to only rebirth again in full expression. I reminisce how much I have been through, all the pain and blessings, the bliss and grief merged in the cauldron of my womb.

At the ripe age of thirteen years, I was already enduring the constraints of a patriarchal society. I was a whore even when I was a virgin, a maiden witch discovering her powers, opening her sensual nature, longing for love, and not conforming. I was a daughter of a divorcee, another rule breaker, a woman without a man. A Magdalene, trailblazing the way. Ironically on the patriarchal land of Sin, I would blossom and resurrect the feminine threads of very ancient alkemy, the wisdom of the Lioness Sekhmet.

Breaking free from a system that objectifies, persecutes, and exploits women can only happen from within by connecting to the flame of our creative feral nature. The old paradigm is collapsing, also within us. In our remembrance as women we must RESURRECT the innate wisdom of our bodies and our Sex. We are life givers, every person in this world was born from a Womban!

Yes, I am a HOR, I behold the gift of life. I'm a daughter of Mother Earth and Great Mother. I'm a weaver mistress of bliss, a Harlot.

Harlots, daughters of the Great Hor, do you feel your womb calling you home?

RED RIVER

Women are weavers and spinners of frequencies, we cycle with the moon, we ebb and flow. We hold the gift of birth, we are the embodiment of Creation. We are called to reclaim the sacred threads of feminine wisdom and journey to our primal instinctual sensual nature, to the womb, the body to resurrect the wisdom it beholds.

340

On my personal journey and working with hundreds of women, remembering our cyclical nature and reclaiming the blood that gives life, menstrual blood, as sacred is key to awakening the wisdom of the womb and resurrecting the sacred pleasure of embodied mater.

Conscious Menstruation has changed my life, the life of many of my clients and many women. A journey to remember the Art of being a cyclical woman, reviving the innate rhythms, currents, and flow of feminine waters. I began using the moon cup, twelve years ago, planting my moon, blessing the land with my blood, and asking for Mother Earth to guide me, heal me, and show me the way. Magnetically I began to attract the resources for my healing and transformation, my essence consecrating the land and Gaea supporting my rebirth.

We shed the lining of our womb with all the magical elixirs, every month until we reach our wise years in moonpause now holding the sacred blood. We are the embodiment of creation, vessels of the creative flow, the divine essence that animates all life. Our cyclical nature is a gift, our menstrual blood is a blessing from the Goddess. We are blessed with birth, the physical ability to create life, give life, and nurture life (babies, visions, and projects).

Allowing the Red River to flow down, and the energy to descend is crucial for our womb ecology and the world ecology. We hold our primal emotions in our pelvis; we can also shed the emotions, wounds, and generational traumas we inherited when we practice conscious menstruation.

Through devotional ritual, prayer and ceremony we can magnetize the support and resources for our inner alkemy. We can rebirth every new cycle, we journey through the seasons during our moonstruation and learning how to navigate our feminine waters is crucial for the embodiment of our potentiality.

The week before your bleed is autumn, and you may begin to inquire to your womb what is ready to be shed, listening to your needs and preparing for winter. The first day of your bleed, is time for retreat, nest, release, let die, rest and regenerate. Pre-ovulation is the arrival of spring, you begin to activate the fertility of your ovaries. Ovulation arrives, summertime, you are in full bloom, your ovum will descend to your womb, expansion and active creation, (baby or projects). Your womb is always calling you back home to the throne of your being.

Learning to honor your cycle will change your life, we hold the gift of creation, the cyclical sacred pleasure of embodied matter distorted as a sin. We descend to matter in the Womb, in the flesh of our mater—mother we are weaved into form forever held by the web of wombs all the way to the original mother. Our menstrual blood is the sacred blood that gives life, the holder of our magical stem cells, our ancestors, our genetic information, our quantum blueprint and mysteries of life-death-rebirth.

The truth is within our visceral intelligence, in the union of above and below, heart and womb, cosmos and earth. The primal voice of our instinctual sensual nature longs to guide us and share her radiance and magnificence. Through devotional presence and daily communion, we can begin to hear her voice and the voice of our ancient grandmothers.

HOLYWILD INCARNATION

I invite you to read the questions and affirmations below, pause in between being present in your body and breathing from your womb. Notice what visceral sensation arises.

How would the world look and feel if women remember they are sacred?

I reclaim my cyclical nature as a daughter of the Earth and Magna Mater. I'm sacred. I embody the truth and wisdom of my lineages, alkemizing the wounds.

How does your body feel when you whisper, "I'm sacred?"

I recollect the innate, sensual erotic innocence of my feminine waters. Through ancestral reverence, I descend to my body and heart-womb communion. I devote time to connecting with my sacred flesh, my heart-womb, to listen to her.

Do you feel safe in your body?

I witness and allow the flow of my emotions, honoring their voice and gifts. I return to my bliss instinct with presence and breath. I allow myself to feel the full spectrum of my feral feminine nature.

Are you free to express your sensuality?

I resurrect the sacred pleasure of my mater, my senses, I feel my body opening to the creative flammable flow of life. I explore the subtleness of my sensual elemental nature.

Daughter of the Great Cosmic Mother

Your Womb is a sacred Vessel, a hologram of the Great Womb that has birth all in Creation. You are Divine Bliss Blueprint. Your womb is beit-rechem— the abode of mercy in Hebrew, where you can immaculate, regenerate, rebirth, rewrite and awaken the wisdom within your DNA. You hold the sacred flames that blaze the path for your reclamation as

343

a sacred woman, full in your sensual nature, erotically innocent, and humbly devoted to the path of love and unity. Your waters are blessings to the ground, you are feral, sovereign, you are love and bliss.

We are summoned to decolonize the inner and outer feminine landscapes. To take a quantum leap in evolution, rebirth and embody our divinity. Divine Mother calls her daughters back to the throne of their being, the soft power of their heart-womb union. The Queendom of love and the inner alkemy of divine feminine and divine masculine.

We are here to be the HolyWild Incarnation of the Great Hor!

We descend to the body, taking a pilgrimage into our inner worlds, feeling all that is held here and the thousands of ancestors that support us. Merging the paradoxes in the cauldron of our wombs. The holy and profane, the virgin and whore, the nurturing, loving mother, Agape. The sensual, sexually sovereign queen, Eros. The wound and gifts, the grief and bliss, embodying the totality of our HOR/Womb Alkemy, our sex as sacred, the gift of giving life, our bodies the portal of holy incarnation, of creation.

In the body, we find the soft power of love, the creative flames of our feral nature. In your heart-womb you can rebirth and restore your immaculate essence. Consecrate the land with your feminine waters, your body prayers, your devotion to your ancestors, to life, to love.

Great HOR whispers…

Dance with the mystery of life,
unbecoming to become the sacred pleasure of embodied mater.

Holy in your radiant feminine flesh, full in your expression.
Surrender to the ebb and flow of your breath,
The rise and fall of your heart and womb,
Consumed by your longing for love, union, bliss
Flow with the expansion and contraction of your cyclical healing.
Bathe in the primordial sea of feminine dimension in renewal and rebirth.
Awakening the soft-power of your heart-womb consciousness.
Radiate my/your essence, spin my/your mysteries into the vortex of your creations.

ABOUT THE AUTHOR

NICOLE ISHTARA KATZ

Nicole Ishtara Katz is an international womb shaman, a psychospiritual art therapist, embodied feminine opulence mentor. She is the founder of Womb Bliss and co-founder of EmRahMa Mystery College, Womb Universities that facilitate feminine healing arts advanced training courses, sacred vision quests, ceremonies, and mentorship programs, online and worldwide.

Specialized in womb consciousness and the mystical feminine healing arts, her methods are holistically rooted in ancestral wisdom/reverence and two decades of studies, initiations, and alkemical embodiment. Ishtara weaves ceremonial mysticism with somatic visceral intelligence education to catalyze powerful transformations, transgenerational, feminine, and sexual healing,

Born in the syncretic and multicultural ground of Brazil, Ishtara lived and was initiated in seven countries, and pilgrim to many others. Now residing by the Red Sea with her beloved and her felines, she mystically lives her bliss weaving her medicine in devotional communion with Mater— Great Mother Birther in all her expressions.

Resurrect the sacred pleasure of your flesh, awakening the wisdom of your lineages, embodying your creative sensual flames with Ishtara.

HolyWild Incarnation is a reclamation of your feral feminine and instinctual sensual elemental nature. A pilgrimage into your body to awaken your womb wisdom, alkemy, magnetism, creativity, bliss blueprint, and Quantum DNA. A resurrection of the sacred pleasure of your holy flesh and your divine soul radiance in matter.

HolyWild Incarnation
https://www.wombliss.com/holywildincarnation

Embodying Divinity, Rebirth your Radiance
https://www.emrahma.com/embodyingdivinity.html

Website
www.wombliss.com
Instagram @womb.bliss | @emrahmamystery

SEX AND THE SACRED SOUL

NICOLE MARIE ROSE

HOW DOES ONE EXPRESS THE FABRIC OF THE MYSTERY revealing itself through symbols and feelings? How does one name the un-nameable? How does one put words to the consciousness of the eternal one, continually birthing and blossoming within the womb of the priestess?

To weave the story of flesh and heaven, of spirit and soil, is by nature an art, as the world today has long forgotten what lies beneath the veils of the visible. Our faculties and superpowers, the true capacity of these human vehicles we shepherd, lie dormant amongst the fast-paced buzzing of the age of electronics.

Some cultures, some wise ones, have kept the flame of wisdom going. History is riddled with stories of sacred pilgrimages, groups of devotees protecting the Ones Who Know, as they flee tyranny and countries that threaten to wipe out these sacred codes. Burning the most glorious libraries of human history, smothering the Golden Age of Humanity in ash. Reprogramming with headlines on newspapers, and religion distorted for the power of the few.

Sexuality and the original codes to accessing the Garden of Eden have been stripped from sacred texts. The Inner Alchemies. The Sex Arts. The womb and her gateways and thresholds, the lingam and his penetrative light of transportation to higher realms. The hieros gamos, complete union. In self, and with others.

Once upon a time, we were whole in ourselves and whole with others. The ache for the sacred other is a legitimate calling, because we remember. While there is value to being whole in and of oneself, the codes are held within our bodies. Implied in the structures that the yoni is designed to be filled by something she does not possess...the deep calling for Union is beckoning.

Some cultures...in the East, and those in the jungles of South America... Some have been able to preserve their wisdom. For the Magdalenes, The Mothers, The Marys, the feminine mysteries, we are not as lucky. Wiped out as witches, moon-dancers, whores and hags, there is no intact lineage to trace.

No thousands-of-years-old scripts and scrolls to pass on directly from one woman to another.

And so... we are left to remember.

Bleeding, beating, thrumming and throbbing...in the center of our wombs, in the caverns of our hearts, in the codex of our cellular memory, in the stillness beneath sound... Something aches to be released...

To be re-membered. To be made whole. The Great She. Mother of the Roses. Isis. Mary Magdalene, and the thousand other names the Great Goddess goes by...is pulsing its way into the conscious minds, weaving her way into the fabric of our very existence.

It is an honor to be here today, to speak *as* the Voice of the Womb...
The Language of All Things...
To summon the Great Remembrance,

Just... In... Time.

My sister, my brother, my lover, my friend...

You are the one who knows.

MIDWIFE OF THE VEILS

My story... Mystery... Mm-Ah stir me... Her story... It is all here....

It all began with a death. Life always does. And especially mine.

Some December not so many moons ago, I was happily self-tending after a big and busy year. My partner and I had bought land that March in the beautiful rolling hillsides of Oregon where we were building an eco-village and living our mutual dream.

Since the work was demanding us to be together all the time, and so filled with action, my soul, my body (or something deeper) was calling for stillness and solitude this winter. So when my partner chose to return home to Kenya for the holy-days, I decided to stay alone on the land. Everyone had gone;

our landmates and tenants also went home for the holidays, and so it was just me, and Gaia.

Gaia the land, and Gaia the dog. My sweet shepherd-kelpie wolf pup who was most certainly a soul mate, and my first daughter. We were practically one being. I had trained her to come when I called her, and so rarely called her name unless I meant it. We had an extraordinary trust developed, as I let her get in trouble when it was her lesson to learn from life. She would walk with me professionally-trained while on leash, and as soon as I took that clip off, we would run wild through the fields chasing baby deer, discovering skeletons hunters had left, howling at the moon, and living the adventure of life…together, as one.

So, when she didn't come back for dinner one night, I knew something was wrong. I did everything I could to pray, search, and communicate with neighbors, and one morning I found her… Dead. On the side of the road.

To this day, I have no idea how to name the sounds that came out of my body. Wailing, howling… part wolf and part human, part mother and part death doula.

For the first time in my life, in the midst of the most powerful and unexpected death I had yet to experience, there was no one around to comfort me. To soothe me, to hold me, or *to stop the grieving process.* I was wild with rage, sadness, and confusion. I hit pillows on my bed. I screamed and screeched. I yelled to the heavens. I cursed like a fucking banshee, and I let it ALL out.

What happened during those days… As my heart was cracked open by the heavens, and I was forced to forgo the world and connect with something higher, was a deep, deep somatic release. Lifetimes of pent-up emotion released from my body. Gaia was the sacred muse for a much deeper clearing.

After several days of this, the world looked different through my eyes. I was calm and settled in my nervous system. My mind was surrendered to the power of my heart. My ego was humbled and unwilling to pretend for even a second that it knew what was supposed to happen in my life.

It was as if I had been stripped bare to the core fundamentals of love and truth.

The only thing left to do was to follow the Deeper Listening;

This subtle presence of the Soul, the One Who Knows, that I could now sense and feel as the only thing that mattered.

THE FLAMES OF INITIATION

Gaia's passing was the first of what I call the flames of initiation. In alignment with the beginning of my Saturn return, all that I once knew as working for me seemed to be crumbling beneath my feet.

In my state of not knowing, I reached out to an astrologer for guidance. At this point in my journey, I had not yet developed a network of spiritual peers, and so I followed the Soul's calling to one particular individual who stood out in my awareness. Since he happened to be in my area, he came to my home for the reading.

Going into the experience, I felt that the main things I was solid in were my relationship, and my place on the land. But as we began to journey into the reading, I found myself asking questions about my relationship, about sexuality, about my life purpose, about why I am here.

352

My womb and my heart, my Soul, began to rest into the field of truly being held…by this person and by a majestic spaciousness I now recognize as the Field of Unconditional Love.

Stillness, presence, objective witness – all qualities of the divine masculine - brought rise to sensations and deeper truths within my body. And as he began singing songs in Hebrew after the closing of our session, I found myself completely entranced. I could feel places opening in my high brain centers. Dancing and swirling to the sound of his voice, my body began moving about the space. I felt completely surrendered to this higher power, and I was allowing this deeper impulse to guide me.

MY YONI HAS A VOICE

We spent several more days together over the next few weeks. As friends, simply enjoying each other's company, with light cuddles in a way that was within the agreement field of my current partnership.

One day, I was home alone, and a great Awareness called me deeper into my body. I noticed that I had been having hemorrhoids, that my womb-space was rock hard, and that my yoni hadn't been wet in two years.

I laid on my bed and was guided to give my yoni a voice.

She was furious. As I dialogued between my heart and my womb, she expressed her rage that she had not been listened to, or pleasured in a very long time. And she very clearly stated that I needed to be intimate with this new man who had come into my life. "I don't know what's on the other side of this, but you need to experience it! You can't teach anyone until you have learned, and this needs to happen!"

She began showing me visions of love-making sessions I had had with my current partner, and while we loved one another very much, he would climax within a matter of minutes, which was just as my yoni was beginning to awaken and activate the first gate. She showed me how the life force had become stagnant in my body, and it was actually a risk to my physical health.

It was at this point that I realized the importance of sexual health in our lives, as well as allowing the currents of life force to naturally flow through our systems.

My heart was devastated, but the voice of my womb was clear. It was a power I could not control, and seeing that the bed was drenched in my yoni juices, and I hadn't even touched her, it felt like my body was agreeing with this decision.

So I wrote to my partner of three years—whom I absolutely adored, by the way—told him everything with impeccable honesty and kindness in the best way I possibly could, and in high integrity (though not without pain), and ultimately with his blessing, created a circumstance where I could be intimate with this new man.

THE AWAKENING

The astrologer booked a beautiful rental in the lush rolling countryside for our sacred sensual sanctuary. There were no spirits (alcohol, drugs, etc), no wifi, no books, no phone service and no connection with the outside world.

What happened during that weekend changed my life forever.

Because of the clean space he held as Objective Witness and

Clear Consciousness, the Divine Feminine within me was able to rise. The space we shared was also incredibly natural, spending much of the time naked, with no pressure to be or do anything specific.

Although I had never experienced that before in this life (not with this level of spirit-infused presence), it was definitely second nature to me. So natural, that as my body began to open and surrender and soften into the experience, so too did my energy bodies, my central channel…

And soul codes began simultaneously descending and ascending into the conscious awareness of Nicole.

Memories began flooding through; of past lives in Greece, as One Who Initiates, as Midwife of the Veils (birth, death, life, rebirth) and Priestess of the Intimate Arts throughout many, many lives.

I saw myself facilitating rituals in Egypt; aligning the geometries, timelines and frequency fields of the stars, planets, pyramids, and the inner and outer geometries of the human body-system, to initiate people into the Inner Mysteries.

During our lovemaking, I journeyed through the Origin of Creation itself. I experienced myself *as* the one consciousness becoming two and creating the world, so that we could play and explore ourselves in polarity.

I received downloads of these ancient Sex Arts, along with visions of the Inner Gateways and thresholds, how to walk myself and others through them.

I *remembered* how to live in right relation with them, as them, and how these pathways of sexuality are incredibly sacred, not just because they bring great pleasure, but because it is a technology utilized for our awakening, our returning to wholeness and multidimensional creation. It is an activation of our full potential.

MARRYING MARY

On the other side of this experience, everything changed.

My partnership of three years and our shared dream dissolved, and I left the land that we had been co-creating in surrender to this mystery. Now highly devoted to this deeper impulse within my womb and heart, I was fully in the current of life, wherever it may take me. The visions continued, and the codes began revealing themselves as having always been in place.

I knew that Sacred Intimacy was my path. It was the most important thing I could ever do in my life, and it was the key to our connection with Source Consciousness.

It was the Highest Path to God.

Mary Magdalene began speaking to me and guiding my every action, every day. She came to me in books, in articles, and through other people, but most potently she just spoke directly to me, through impulses in my womb, deep feelings, symbols, omens and sometimes words.

She showed me how the astrologer had held Yeshua codes, and that his singing of the Hebrew was an onomatopoeic activation of my high brain centers. It was designed this way for me to remember. She guided me to information about the three Marys that fled Egypt for France, and how their names were Mary Magdalene, Mother Mary and Mary Jacobi. My original last name is Jacobs. Through a priestess sister, she told me that Mary was a title, not a name. And I then learned that in the olden days of France Mary was actually pronounced Marie. My name is Nicole Marie.

My mother's name is Dawn Marie, Dawning of the Marie. Dawning of the Mary. She showed me how I was born into a Christed line, and pointed out the rose that was on my grandmother's cross she wore every day of her life. "*This* is what that meant," Mary whispered.

In the height of our activation together, she changed the numbers on the clocks. Almost every time I looked, it was some arrangement of 3, 6, 9s, which she told me are the feminine numbers. She showed me how I was born in the 6th zodiac sign, the 9th month of Virgo; the sign of the Virgin-Whore. I was born on 9-21, 9 and 3. My life path number is a 3 and my destiny is as well. I was born on the exact day of the Fall Equinox, without crying, eyes wide and ready, onto the breast of the Mother, Dawn of the Mary.

She came to me this way, working with me outside of myself, until I actually *became* her. One day, as I was sitting on my rooftop balcony looking up at the stars, Mary and Yeshua vibrated into my 3D experience guiding me to become initiated as a Priestess of Divine Union. I was to completely devote myself to these sacred Arts of Union, once again in this life.

At the time, this was monumental to me. I did not feel ready, or worthy, but it was after this, and a series of wild and powerful trials and initiations that tested my strength of character, my devotion to the work, and my willingness to dive deep into my shadows, Mary stopped speaking *to* me, and I began to feel her moving *through me, as me.*

INTEGRATION AND APPLICATION

From this moment forward, the Intimate Arts became my life. I swore an oath to serve the Sacred, and to priestess the Rose Lineage and the Arts of Divine Union. My past lives all came rushing back, and I realized I had even been doing this work within my relationships in this incarnation. The trainings beyond this point gave me a framework and showed me how to apply my spiritual inheritance in a practical way that could be offered as a service to the people.

You see, when code comes barrelling through, we still need to develop the *personal power*, the *language* and the *embodied activations* within this incarnation. We have to train *this body* to channel the energies and clear out anything in the way of the purest essence flowing through.

So I dove in. I did deep, deep excavation within my shadow worlds. Riding waves of torment and liberation, terror and ecstasy, guided by a continual spiral of upward current... knowing that it would one day be cleared. I moved through more major deaths and transformations. I worked on healing the relationship with my mother and familial lines and saw miraculous transformation. I spent thousands of hours in meditation, embodiment, ritual and ceremony in deep devotion to finding the root source of my power and learning to channel the energies through my system to offer the cleanest frequencies for myself, the world and anyone I came in contact with.

I studied with the International School of Temple Arts, completing their practitioner training and started my one-on-one practice right away. I worked with hundreds of individuals and couples to liberate trauma, deepen intimacy with self and other, and have life-changing spiritual experiences. I studied with high priestesses and elder tantrikas who wove their magick into my world by Divine Grace. My life became filled with color and pleasure; helping to organize and assist tantra festivals, facilitate pujas, weekend women's immersions, sacred pelvic healing, yoni massage groups, lingam massage groups, rose priestess rituals, and anything sacred, relational, and sensual I could find. I became fully immersed.

Six years later, at the time of this publishing, I now stand at the center of the center of my own power. My own devotional practices and my own offerings. Always growing, always clearing, always refining, and yet, I have arrived.

The jewel has been discovered, and the seeking has stopped.

Only the quest to deliver it with greater clarity, integrity and attunement continues.

May my story be a prayer and reminder that what you seek is seeking you.

The impulse within you is profoundly intelligent and as you follow it with fervent devotion and deep listening, the day of your arrival *will* come.

HEART ON FIRE

As these sexual energies became active in my life, it was as if something extraordinary happened within my world. Everything went from structure and fact to being filled with mystery, infused with grace and sensuality. Colors were heightened, smells were activated, and all the world became a playground that I remembered I had created for myself to explore and create.

All of a sudden, anything that I was feeling within my body became okay. Welcomed, allowed and listened to. Liberation and freedom flooded my world, and the wildness returned to infuse my cells with her wisdom. The wolves howling at the moon, the winds whispering their secrets through the trees.

As I found this deeper place in my power, synchronicities became not just a fleeting moment, but a rich fabric of communication between myself and nature, the film between inner and outer worlds continually dissolving, ever thinning.
These gateways of the Inner King/Queendoms continue to open within me, within my meditations, with lovers, and with clients. And as they do, crystalline clarity and a heightened connection to All That Is unfurls and unfolds in blessing after blessing of blissful experience. As if petals of truth open to bring experiences that were created from the very fabric of my soul.

Sometimes what's experienced can only be spoken in poetry...

and *experienced for oneself* in the depths of the Temple space.

My friends, my lovers, my sisters, my family...

You do not need me.

You *are* the one who knows.

And yet...

It is my life's purpose and my deepest honor to hold such spaces. For individuals, for couples, and for groups...to come to experience this oneness for yourselves. To be guided into mystical experiences and taste the nectar of ecstasy within.

To feel its healing power.... To witness the miracles begin

to unfurl in your lives. And to rejoice in the experience of the truth of who you are. To come home into your womb, your heart, your lingam, and your soul…

To slip into the space of something deeper…

Where the separateness between self and other, other and god, god and life dissolve into oneness,

your primal nature finds its rightful place at the table of the Divine,

and your soul becomes the guiding pulse for all your actions and choices.

I invite you, dear ones, to come into my world.

To follow me on this journey of ever-unfolding love, consciousness and multidimensional realms.

To join me in my online offerings, in-person retreat, or a personalized immersion wherever in the world I am, or wherever on Earth you would like to meet.

I am your muse, your guide, your lover and your friend.

Welcome to the Temple of the Rose.

ABOUT THE AUTHOR

NICOLE MARIE ROSE

Nicole Marie Rose is a Tantric Priestess, Intimacy Facilitator and Educator.

Skilled at evoking the divine within the human experience, Nicole is passionate about helping people deepen their connection with themselves, each other and all of life. She lives in the space where spirit, science and primal nature meet, and loves to bring logic in for those who need it.

She believes pleasure, authenticity and vulnerable connection, if fully embraced by humanity would be enough to solve all of the challenges we currently face as a species. She is passionate about doing her part to create this reality.

Nicole is CEO and founder of Romantic Endeavors and Of Spirit and Soil. She facilitates high-end private intimacy immersions, as well as a delicious variety of online

362

experiences.

Through guided games, exercises and rituals, Nicole Marie helps breathe life, depth and mysticism back into stagnant relationships and takes solid couples to the next-level depth of their love.

She supports individuals in living a soulful, authentic, and sensual life by facilitating experiences for the true self to be discovered.

She also holds space for groups, offering social lubrication games for weddings and events.

Feeling the pulse? Join her here…

Online Offerings: https://linktr.ee/nicolemarierose
In Person Offerings: www.romanticendeavors.life
Poetry and Artwork: www.ofspiritandsoil.com
Personal Website: www.nicolemarierose.com
IG: Nicole Marie Rose

BLOOM WHERE YOU ARE PLANTED

REBECCA COLLINS

FREEDOM FROM BONDAGE

FOR MOST OF MY LIFE, I NEVER FELT LIKE I BELONGED. I was always grasping at things and people to feel whole. There were the friends who made me feel a part of the group and the cute boys who if I got them to look my way, it made me feel like I was pretty and valued. In high school, I was pretty popular on the outside but lonely on the inside. I remember walking the halls thinking, *If I disappeared no one would notice.* I was hurting inside for many different reasons. I was the baby of five boys and was raised in a middle-class Catholic family. I went through a traumatic thing when I was young, and I never truly grasped how much it would impact my family life and me as an individual. It created a huge amount of shame and a dark shadow that stayed with me. It made me strong, unable to accept help from others, but it also took my innocence away and scarred me forever.

I was born on January 30, 1977, to two parents that truly did not know what hit them. My parents had already had four boys at this point. My dad was a stepdad to two boys that my mom already had plus the two they had together. My parents say that they prayed and prayed for me. My father had eagerly been anticipating his baby girl, but I do not believe either of them knew how much power and might was packed into me. You never truly understand how important birth order is until you get older and family dynamics come into play, as well as the pressures of sibling comparison. My oldest brother was going off into the military when I was practically in diapers, so he didn't really get much time with me. Being the only girl among four boys had its challenges. They never wanted to do girly things obviously—they were all very much boys! They were always climbing trees, surfing, skateboarding and being boys! So when I was able to start having sleepovers I leapt at the chance.

Our family was what I consider middle class, we never really had much extra money, but we never starved. My dad worked very hard, long days and nights for a grocery chain. He was tired when he got home so most nights, he fell asleep in the bath. Some of my childhood was good and some was turbulent, but I do know my parents did the best they could. I know they would have protected me if they could have.

Some background on my folks. My mom was born in Berlin during the war. She was raised partially by her grandmother in very difficult times and with very few luxuries. She would tell me stories occasionally about not having basic things like running water and carrying buckets of water just to have it, and I would cringe. Having grown up in Daytona Beach, that was not one of our struggles; although there were others, that wasn't one of them. My mother is one of the most selfless

365

people I have ever met. For most of my life, she did for everyone but herself. She cooked for friends and neighbors when ill, brought books to jails, and volunteered. She definitely has many qualities that I admire. My dad was born in Pennsylvania and is a devoted father and husband and has a work ethic second to none. I know my dad's childhood wasn't easy either, although he didn't share many details.

So where did my love of numbing out start?

Our family didn't drink much. My mom occasionally had a sip of wine with sprite and didn't like to feel tipsy. My dad had the occasional beer, but I never recall much alcohol in the house. His dad struggled a bit with it, though, so issues with alcohol were in our gene pool. However, I remember my Oma giving me Jägermeister she kept in her fridge when I was sick with a cold and I remember that warm, numbing feeling—I immediately liked it and my brain slowing down, even pausing for a change. I never truly drank my first drink until I was about 13. My older brother had a Rolling Rock and gave me and a friend one to try. I never really liked the taste of beer, but the effect was truly what mattered to me. Your mind can be your best friend or worst enemy.

As life has its way of happening, bad things and good things happened but my family life always felt stressful. Something always seemed to be going wrong. My mom was in several car accidents. Then one of my brothers was seriously injured by a drunk driver. There was trauma that I went through involving a family member that was never truly dealt with. Honestly, I think we all lived in a state of fight or flight. With five kids there was always a lot of yelling and someone needing discipline who was not following the rules. It was never perfect, but it was way better than some people's family lives.

We were a Catholic family that attended mass most Sundays plus Sunday school. I remember sitting in the pew thinking *if* there was a God why did he pick me for this family? They never seemed to understand me, and I always wished I could run far away. Although, I had a lot of "friends" I felt misunderstood most of my life within friendships. When I started dating, I think I finally felt like my boyfriends might get me. They seemed interested in more than just the temporary physical stuff…or at least I hoped it was that way. Growing up near the beach was awesome, especially as a teen. Summers were spent at the beach and MTV was usually in town for spring break so that was always cool. After I got to college, I remember people saying they hadn't drunk until they were 18 or 21, but in Daytona I had access when I was very young.

CHAOS

I grew up in a popular Florida spring break destination, and I had many experiences one should not have had by the age of 15. My parents tried to intervene and put me in counseling but there were deep-rooted family secrets that weren't being addressed so I ended up being the one with the "problem" instead of them addressing my acting out as a symptom of pain and addressing what I'd been through by properly keeping me away from the person. Instead, they just moved forward. Back then you just didn't talk about stuff. I drank to hide my fears, I drank to be the girl I always wanted to be, I drank to not feel and to be a part of something. I graduated high school with honors and took a year off to "find myself." What I found was wherever you go there you are…yup that familiar saying is true. Moving to another state far away from my family did not heal me, but it did create a fierce desire to be successful and gain my family's approval. Deep down that is all I have ever wanted from any of them.

367

To be loved. To be valued. To be accepted.

DEPENDENCE

Now I am not going to sit here and say I was an angel, no way not even close, but I will say that I do scratch my head and look to the skies and sometimes think what is God thinking when He picks our birth family? I told my husband recently that this choice was for my maximum growth and to grow in patience and learning, to not expect much from people. I never seemed to receive what I needed on an emotional level and always felt sad, lonely, agitated, and forgotten. I turned to alcohol in my youth for coping, but what I have learned in the past few years is that dependence was always in my life in many forms: dependence on people, places and things. My coping skills were not great. No one really in my family ever exercised regularly or explained to me how important living a balanced life spiritually, physically and emotionally was. I think between the emotional turmoil and lack of parenting I was kinda left to grow up too fast in some ways. I do know now that I am raising children in a healthy, involved way, I know how hard parenting is, and that I was not an easy teenager. I think I had much anger inside of me that I didn't really know where to direct, so I started numbing my feelings from probably about age 15 to my early 20s.

I used all of the tension inside to become a go-getter, someone who wasn't going to let bad things bring me down. My home life was less than perfect, but between the raging hormones and things I had been through, alcohol became a big coping mechanism for me. I always had a successful job and was driven to succeed but had to cope with life in not always the healthiest ways.

CONTROL

Our family had a strain of toxic communication in many forms. My mom taught me the art of control. So yes, even though they were not big drinkers, my parents had their own unhealthy coping skills and generational patterns.

The question I ask is "Why did I allow this toxicity to lead so much of my life and create so much pain for me?" Conditioning is a big part, I thought you were there no matter what for them because this is your "family." For many years I continued to try so hard to be liked by my family. They were incapable of showing the affection and type of relationship I always craved.

In hindsight, I have always had a very high need to both give and receive love. I guess I was dependent on others to be more than they are capable of being. I really just wanted to be accepted and loved. Also, I often felt needy because I looked at other people's families and craved one like they had. I know why—because my pain body and shame kicked in repeatedly telling me something was wrong with me because that ideal family is not what I got. And add to it siblings who are all men who are not the most sensitive, saying things like, "Stop trying to want more, this is how our family is." It stung worse because my pain body was so impacted by approval. Approval that unfortunately no one in my family was ever equipped to give. They were and are incapable. I'll say that, again, they were incapable of loving me like I thought I should be loved.

COMMUNICATION

None of us was really told or shown what a healthy family was like and since we rarely saw extended family due to distance—both sides lived far away—so I didn't really know the definition of family or actual love. Family: "A group of persons of common ancestry." That is the basic definition

369

but, as I have learned through therapy and having close friends, a family should be there for one another not just when you are in the hospital but to say, "Hey, I haven't heard from you in a while" and check in. To maybe even see each other more than only on special occasions. Who want to take an interest in each other's lives and ask how things are. Unfortunately, my parents didn't really have those types of relations, so how would I think they would teach all of us how to function that way? I am the caring, persistent, thoughtful one; some of them still see it as too persistent, but oh well. I try to get together with my siblings even though they often do not make the time. I try to send texts. I no longer call much because it seemed that phone calls were an inconvenience when they seemed grumpy or rushed, and that drained my energy. I have started meeting people where they are. I started being aware that the more I restrain from control and try to have what type of relationships I think I need, the more they show up in different ways.

"You will be aware that each moment of each day is unfolding and you neither have control, nor crave it." *The Untethered Soul,* by Michael Singer.

AUTHENTICITY

All those years of showing up for people, being a good mom, daughter, sister, putting others before me…and I had finally had enough. All of a sudden, I knew I had an inner voice that was telling me to speak my truth. I remember when one person said, "You are too loyal, Becky, and sooo devoted. Stop being that way if others are not showing you the same loyalty and love." This hit me. You mean I could actually choose not to be there all the time for my family of origin to the extent my mind told me I had to be? Yes! I could choose how the story moved forward in a healthy, more balanced way for my relationships and sanity. This was the beginning of my shadow work. When you get down to true work on yourself, a lot of who you thought you had to be may not even be who you want to be anymore.

"The butterfly is only beautiful because the caterpillar is brave." –T.m.t.

I remember the first time I spoke truly authentically after 40 years of backing down or wishing I was different and hiding what I really wanted to say. I called my mom out on a behavior she kept doing that I didn't like. I said it once, then I said it again more firmly. At first, she seemed surprised like a kid who had been scolded—mind you at this stage in my life I have learned a lot. Been in therapy, support groups and read A TON of books!

Next, I tried my new behavior when a sibling said something along the lines of, "You take things so personally. Stop acting like a baby." Instead of the old me crying or drinking or shutting down, I spoke up and said, "We had different experiences growing up. You will never understand my life or what I have been through. Please stop telling me to feel or be anyone different." Say what??? Did I just do that!!! This felt AMAZING! Then I started placing boundaries where there were none, telling even more people both in my family and outside it what my true thoughts were. I stopped allowing people to take my power away from me. I snatched it back and lit it up like a firework.

What is MY definition of family within my household is now based on just a few things:

Unconditional love
Supporting each other
Lifting people up when they are down
Acceptance

Trust

I read a lot, and many times I have read that you get to be the parents you always needed growing up. So I have had to parent myself and choose to be the exact parent I needed when I was growing up and unfortunately did not get. I had to stop thinking there was anything wrong with me, or that I was someone broken or unlovable, and truly heal my inner child.

AWAKENING

In my early 20s, I felt something was missing. It was definitely a belief in a higher source. I was successful, graduated with my bachelor's degree, was pretty okay looking, had a great job, and always dated the cute guy—but I felt like my life wasn't the one I was meant to live. So I decided to stop relying on alcohol to cope with the good days and the bad days. I made the choice to get sober.

At that stage in my life, it was the best decision for me. It made me grow up and learn self-discipline as well as self-control. I had many beautiful, strong women come into my life who taught me much about life and God and growing your connection with a higher power. I was always the weekend drinker, not the daily one; so although I had made some poor decisions when alcohol was involved, I thankfully stopped on my own with the help of meetings. I was able to graduate from college and support myself and learn healthy coping skills. Things I may not have accomplished if I was still binge drinking.

ANGELS

I have had many wonderful people enter my life right when I needed them. There was the one who said maybe alcohol isn't good for you, at least for now. There was the one who pushed me to become a yoga instructor. There have always been little angels in my life that God has sent to nudge me along in my journey. I can tell you during some of my hardest times, internally if I just flip the script and said I am not that hurting little girl...what is it I really need and want? I have all of the answers within me.

I have learned that dependence is a tricky little thing. Most recently at this stage in life, I realized I just want to be me—a 45-year-old woman who is raising beautiful, emotionally strong girls who know how loved they are. We didn't hear this a lot growing up. Unfortunately, there was often a lot of stress going on in our family and not always the joyful stuff in my house. My mom never quite got the memo that it was most important to take care of herself before others and has struggled with a lot of health problems now because of it. But she is and always will be one of the strongest, most thoughtful people I know. I love her dearly. She is my biggest cheerleader even though she isn't one to say it much I know it in my soul.

ACCEPTANCE

I currently have experienced a freedom and love of self I never have had in my life, which is very God and family focused. I do a lot of service work and will forever be grateful to twelve-step meetings for pulling me out of the pain I was in and teaching me that regardless of what life throws at you, you always have a choice in how you want to process the pain. I have the utmost respect for them, and they are what brought me to peace within myself during the most anxious and overwhelming years of my life. I am currently in a state of life after many sober years where I have an occasional beverage and I barely have one. I have learned strong self-control and coping mechanisms that I didn't have in my teens. I am no longer dependent on anything or anyone but God. I think my teens and early 20s were some of the most lost years from who I am currently. I read that the adolescent brain is in a developing state until around age 25, and the part of the brain that responds with good judgment is not fully formed until 25. That absolutely makes so much sense in my life, because by 25 I'd made some less than great decisions due to that immediate reward response. The "feel good" one.

GRATITUDE

I currently maintain balance in my life through teaching and taking yoga, daily exercise, energy work, being outside with my husband and kids, writing, reading, and traveling. I have realized that I am loveable exactly as I am—and whether that love shows up from a friend or family member, I know there is nothing wrong with me. I am a child of God. "Be still and know that I am God" will always be one of my favorite Bible verses. Being a mother is truly who I was meant to be, as well as making an impact in the world through helping others improve themselves and shine their authentic spirit for the world to see. I love working with people to help them see that regardless of what they have been through they are capable of greatness.

ABOUT THE AUTHOR

REBECCA COLLINS

Rebecca Collins has a Bachelor's in Marketing, and after spending 20 years in the Healthcare arena in various sales positions, she found her true calling in helping others. Currently, she is an international bestselling author and freelance writer. She is also a 200-hour certified yoga instructor. She loves helping her clients tap into their truest selves with energy work, journaling, writing prompts that aid in changing patterns, and allowing self-healing. She also loves to help her home decor clients rethink a room using items they already have.

Rebecca has a strong belief in a higher power whom she calls God and believes everything that happens in our lives happens to bring change about for both us and the universe. We have to peel back the various layers of who we think we are to find our authentic self.

She is a happily married mother of two beautiful daughters who loves being near the mountains, ocean, boating with her family, traveling, and most of all helping others see the beauty within.

She currently teaches both adults and children yoga and is available for life coaching, freelance writing assignments, and help with home décor advice.

"When you recover or discover something that nourishes your soul and brings joy, care enough about yourself to make room for it in your life." -Jean Shinoda Bolen.

She resides in New Smyrna Beach, Florida, and looks forward to working with you to help you align with your highest self.

You can find her at:
https://www.facebook.com/rebecca.collins.5201/

Website: www.soberfemale.com

Instagram: @bestillyogawithbeckynsb OR @rebeccacollins5805

Email: beckymohn@yahoo.com

WISDOM IGNITED WITHIN MY SOUL'S IMPRINT

SAMONE MARIE

OUR CONNECTION BEGAN MANY LIFETIMES AGO. I am the descendant of a long line of Soulestial healers sent to earth to awaken humanity to the universal language of unconditional love. With each new incarnation, we are guided on a journey to activate the light from within and awaken the souls from their galactic slumber. This process has been happening for hundreds of thousands of earth years which in the spiritual realm where time does not exist would be equivalent to a blink of an eye.

This lifetime I came in through the portal of a queen, whose vessel was striffed with scarcity, pain, shame and fear. She, like those before her, had experienced many levels of abuse as the tangled web of ancestral karma bled across many of earth's oceans and carried its camwood-stained markers across my lineage. The markers that would pave a road of compassion, strength and determination.

My story began long before I was aware of its great importance to the evolution of humanity. I would only learn about it as I was awakened by my siStar Mary of Magdalene during a shamanic journey while attending a mediumship course at Lightsong School of 21st Century Shamanism and Energy Medicine, where I had the pleasure of meeting Mary herself, where she chose me to be the conduit to share her wisdom. The turn of events that would lead me to her had been written in the stars upon my incarnation, and I had no clue of the beautiful journey that would unfold as she took my hand and pulled me through the cave where she spent much of the end of her lifetime.

A turn of events that would change my life forever...

Lying on my bed, staring into the screen of my phone during my nightly ritual of perusing Facebook, a Facebook live of Ashley Bradley, an Intuitive Business Coach who was pulling cards for business owners, emerged almost out of thin air. I typed my business name Tru2We, saying hello and asking for a card pull with the blue butterfly emoji. Ashley of course said that she loved the butterfly and felt drawn to me. She spoke about my business and how she could see that the business I had launched would be shifting more towards assisting those through my story and life experiences on a much deeper level than I had already been called to do. She mentioned that she could feel deep ancestral energy around me. I was intrigued by this message and so wanted to learn more, as yes, the work that I had been doing was all about connecting with ancestral lineages, and at the time I was providing life path sacred oracle readings.

I then went to follow her Facebook group The Practical Mystic page she had listed in the live feed. She was freaking amazing, and I was intrigued by the work that she was doing.

I finally would come across an invitation she put out for a Power of Eight Circle she was offering and eagerly signed up and waited for the group to meet. My intuition screamed at me to be sure to attend this. As I logged onto the Zoom call, I was so excited to be connecting with Ashley and the group of healers that showed up to the circle. The energy felt so calming and supportive of those in the group. We were asked to set our intention for our business and the outcome we had desired. I really was looking for more clarity on this new avenue and was open to whatever messages that spirit had to share with me. Yesssss, I was called to sit in the love seat. Everyone in the group channeled messages for me related to my business. Many people could see the energy around me and spoke of how my work was that of the angelic realms and that they could see a beautiful bright light surrounding me. How I was stepping into the next phase of my life, and many things would be opening up for me as my spiritual gifts were expanding and being awakened. I was in awe and lost for words at all the information shared during this session.

Immediately following this session, I received my first paying client, Emily, who had been one of the healers in the circle. I had been providing readings, coaching clients, channeling spirit guides and relaying ancestral messages for years but had always done it for free. I was so excited and couldn't wait to connect with her. On the day of the reading, a friend of mine Athena stopped by and we discussed a new program I had started and was excited to share it with her because I was health coaching at the time. We always found ourselves talking about spirituality. She told me how she had recently spoken with a friend who had mentioned to her to read about Mary Magdalene and that she hadn't done so but it had come back up. At the time, I didn't think anything about the conversation, hugged her goodbye and prepared for my reading with Emily.

I shit you not… The first thing that Emily said when the Zoom call began was that Mary Magdalene had wanted to be a part of this reading. It was definitely a first for me, as I had never really worked with Mary Magdalene and didn't know much about her other than she was somehow connected to Jesus. Also, the Life Path Readings were opening the sacred IFA Oracle portal and connecting with the ancestors and Yoruban African Deities. Nonetheless, my shamanic background reminded me that I had just called in all the benevolent spirit guides that were looking to work with Emily and guide her on her life path, sharing their words of wisdom. So Mary Magdalene must be one of her guides. I completed her Life Path Reading. I asked her if she had any more questions and she shared with me about a book that she had been reading, the Sophia Code, and that she was most interested in the chapter about Mary Magdalene. I was intrigued and decided to also order the book on Audible. I downloaded it and didn't think too much about it.

The following week I received an email from my shamanic teacher Karen Hefner, MA, MS, ShD asking me if I would like to continue my shamanic journey at Lightsong and sign up for the next level that was beginning in a week. This class mentioned embodying the mystical energies of the divine, immersing yourself in sacred ceremony, learning mediumship and channeling, discovering the hidden mystery of your True Self, shifting your frequency of vibration, transcending your ego and experiencing the divine. I was very excited and felt that the invitation was an energetic YESSSSSSS, *sign me up.*

DISCOVERING THE CLOAK…

My ex-husband at the time was living in Texas, so we would FaceTime from my iPad in the evenings. This particular evening, I had been standing next to my ancestral altar as I video chatted with him. He froze as he stared at me...

I asked him, "What?" And at that very moment, my whole body became a bone-chilling cold as the hairs rose on my arms.

He said, "You're not going to believe this... It looks like you have a deep purple cloak that is glowing with what looks like Egyptian symbols."

"Huh?" I asked. He is very spiritually attuned and I didn't have a clue what it meant or why I couldn't see it but trusted what he said as I definitely felt something.

The next day I yet again was perusing my nightly Facebook feed and came across Shannon Van Den Berg live as she was sharing about an upcoming book project that she was accepting applications for authors to be a part of her book *Magdalene Rising, Feminine Leaders Guided by Her Fierce and Unconditional Wisdom.* I felt called to apply, and at the time I had no clue how I would afford to pay for my share of the book cost as well as make my payments for the class I had just committed to. But yet again it was a huge energetic YESSSSSS. So I reached out to Shannon, completed the Kiva Publishing application, and when I received the email saying I was accepted I was so excited to have signed my first book deal. I had never written before other than in my journals and had no clue what the heck I was going to write about for 3,500 words–all I knew was this is what I was being called to do.

I remember a time that I was journaling my New Year's affirmations back in 2005... Saying that by 2007, I would be debt free and married to the love of my life. In 2007 I married my husband and became debt free for the first time in my life. The details that I had written two years prior were uncanny how they lined up exactly how I wrote it down to owning my first home. So I knew that writing was definitely a gift of mine. It would come up in almost every reading for me, telling me to write.

BECOMING AN INTERNATIONAL BEST-SELLING AUTHOR

As I began to write, the words would just flow from me. Not to mention that I was being guided on a beautiful journey by my amazing publisher Shannon Van Den Berg, creating a sacred space with an opening ceremony for my sister authors and me in the book, being fully supported by the journey to connect with my spiritual book guide. And for the first time, I felt seen, heard and witnessed by the sisterhood that had formed through this magical experience that was just unfolding before my eyes. I had no clue that this book would be an initiation that would activate the evolution of my being and release me from the bondage of my past. I was awakening Samone Marie, the Soulestial Spiritual Guide that had been suppressed deep within the scrolls of my subconscious mind. Each week meeting with the amazing fierce feminine frequency keepers illuminated my being.

Simultaneously, while writing, I would continue my studies at LightSong and one evening during class she emerged during a journey to connect with my regalia spirit. She came through like a vibrant green vine of spiritual life intertwining past my gatekeeper and stood before me in her cloak peering out. I asked are you my regalia spirit? She replied yes, as she reached out her hand for mine. She instantly transported us into a cave. Within this cave she then began to share with me the importance of the cloak and the symbolic meaning of the hieroglyphics transcribed on it are those of protection. She told me that the cloak protects the vessel of my physical body preventing it from being hosted by others as I travel the

382

galaxies and the many Spiritual realms as a light being. I was speechless and really didn't know what to say. She grabbed my hand and pulled me through the wall of the cave and we were standing in the living room of my friend Athena. I instantly had this overwhelming feeling of ALERT ALERT ALERT …we are in Athena's home standing in front of her herb cabinet without her permission. She assured me it was okay and told me that Athena was an alchemist and hadn't stepped into her true power yet, that she would be teaching me about the power of plant medicine.

We then popped out of Athena's house and the vibrational call from the drum to return pulled me back into my spiritual room, back into my body. I started writing my experience as fast as I could in my journal to not forget the details and was so excited, I immediately called Athena to share with her what had happened. She shared with me that she was wondering why her little boy, a little miniature black dog, was growling intensely looking over at her herb cabinet. I was like, "Omg omg omg it's because I was in your living room with Mary Magdalene…" And shared what she had told me. We were both so excited and shocked. I apologized to her, saying omg how embarrassing I was in your living room without your permission. She laughed and said, "You guys can visit me anytime, haha."

It is all starting to make sense as to why Athena was there at my house the day telling me that she was told to read a book about Mary Magdalene, I shared with her the story about my client who told me about Sophia Code, which I hadn't read or listened to yet. She was so intrigued she purchased it. Just when I thought things couldn't get any more interesting, I also shared with her about the cloak my husband had seen me wearing during the video call and that Mary Magdalene has chosen me to work with during the shamanic regalia and how I had just had my first session channeling her when all of this happened, not to mention that I was just accepted as an author in the book Magdalene Rising which all started from a business reading. Omg Omg Omg ….. I was really working with *the* Mary Magdalene.

SUMMONING MYSELF FROM THE FUTURE TO RETURN TO THE PAST

I would then continue my journey writing my story and attending my classes. In each class I would be so excited to reconnect with Mary Magdalene. She started to share with me the work that she, Jesus and the disciples were doing. How they were raising the consciousness of humanity by igniting the light in all those that they connected with, teaching about the universal language of unconditional love. How I had summoned myself from the future to return to the past to share the messages of the wisdom. Huh… Yeah, you heard me, "I summoned myself from the future to return to the past to share the wisdom and hope for the future." Right?!? I am still in shock by that. Does that mean that one of my incarnations was that of Mary Magdalene? Am I a descendant of Mary Magdalene? I had so many questions running through my head and every time I would get ready to ask them the call of the drum would summon me back into this reality, back into my body.

With each merge it would become easier and easier to connect and hold the frequency of her energy. I recall a time when I physically felt my soul standing outside of my body while I watched almost like I was on standby while she hosted my body and performed healings on my classmates. During these sessions I learned to imbue objects with the energy of waterfalls, stars, spiritual places and make them sacred objects to be used during ceremonies. I was shown the objects she wanted me to collect and wear during the upcoming regalia…the meeting of the benevolent spirits in a sacred ceremony. Each object that I was to imbue held this beautiful cooling energy similar to the energy that I felt when she hosted my body. She guided me in curating a special Siberian eye curtain to wear made of chain, sea shells, crystals and feathers, a white linen dress, feet jewelry with coins on them, and my seashell necklace used in another ceremony. I was in awe of all that I was learning and my level of ascension.

I remember a time as we reached closer to regalia, she instructed me to call back all versions of myself to merge with me and hold the energy of all of the versions. I practiced this and held the energy. It was remarkable that this was possible. I remember during this time taking pictures of myself and seeing someone very different each time. I would alternate from a young woman to middle age and older woman in the pictures. If you go back and look at my bio pics from each of my books you can see the different women in each image. I was very intrigued by this and how I felt being merged with all of these versions of myself at one time. Things would seem to instantly manifest seamlessly and I was cautioned to be careful of my words, thoughts and actions as I was truly creating reality in real-time.

This journey continued and Mary Magdalene began to tell me her story and her beautiful connection to Jesus. She told me that she was a wealthy woman, who lived during a time when women had no rights, and were persecuted for their spiritual gifts. So they hid them. She had traveled all over the world growing up, awakening the spiritual gifts from within her while attending many spiritual schools. That her parents knew her purpose, as did she, from a very young age. She was the one who funded Jesus and the disciples as they traveled and that there was a misconception of her being a prostitute that was created due to the fact that she was affluent and didn't have a desire to marry a man to care for her. She was a powerful healer and light worker and some around her created rumors about her to discredit her. Many were afraid of her and her gifts, and she often camouflaged them for her own protection and the protection of those she loved.

MARY'S VOW AND PROMISE TO HUMANITY

The day of the regalia approached just as the book *Magdalene Rising* was launching and, to my surprise, became an International Best Seller overnight. I was so excited yet very nervous at the same time. On the day of the regalia, I prepared myself with all of the sacred items and logged onto the ceremony. I spent the first part of the ceremony channeling Mary Magdalene and performing healings for those that rotated through my virtual healing room. Holding her frequency was absolutely invigorating and the first time I'd held the frequency for so long, for several hours.

It came time for the meeting of the spirits, where the teachers of the school asked the panel of benevolent spirits questions. I remember this experience like it was yesterday. Another classmate was channeling Jesus and as we both entered the room, I could feel this deep love, joy, excitement. I thought I knew what unconditional love felt like across all time and space, but I never knew until this exact moment. They asked Mary Magdalene if there was anything that she wanted to say to Jesus. She replied, "Jesus, my love, I miss your presence and the feeling of your touch here on earth but hold my unwavering love for you within my heart." The deep feeling of love was something words could never explain as I felt the warmth of tears just stream down my face.

That was the moment I knew for a fact that love definitely is universal. Her soul longed for his soul and felt this comfort and warmth as they were reunited for a brief time during the ceremony. I felt so honored to have been the vessel that allowed her to have that feeling once more. It really inspired me to continue my journey and assist in the evolution of humanity which I had begun many lifetimes ago. My unwavering love for humanity has never changed and will continue to be a driving force in my life–assisting all those I meet to discover the true essence of their soul's brilliance, energetic connections to one another, the earth, the universe, the galaxies and awakening the universal language of unconditional love by igniting the light within.

As I walk through the portals of life, I am awakened to the truth that is me... Samone Marie, Soulestial Ancestral Medium, Shamanic Healer, Spiritual Teacher, Mindset Facilitator, and Yoga Teacher.

Are you ready to begin your journey to awakening and empowering you? I encourage you to reconnect within, giving yourself permission to discover the brilliance that is you. I am currently accepting new siStar clients in my program Unfuck Yourself: a 12-month program that shares the spiritual prescription to awakening the version of yourself that is free of shame, pain, scarcity, fear and unworthiness. Leaving you feeling empowered, inspired, ignited and ready to navigate life's experiences using the spiritual toolkit gained by attending the program.

ABOUT THE AUTHOR

SAMONE MARIE

Samone Marie is the Soulestial Ancestral Medium, International Best-Selling Author 5 times over and creator of the Soulestial Starseed School.

She guides her clients deeper into their soul remembering, why they're here and how to expand their gifts so they can be of greater service during this ascension of humanity.

She's the initiated embodiment of Yemonja (yeh mow jaa), Yoruban goddess of the oceans, expressing her frequency of unconditional love to raise the consciousness of humanity. As a founding member of the Jaguar Council, she illuminates the ancient wisdom of the ancestors, honoring their practices and activating the 21st century medicine within.

Your Soul's Path is already a blueprint sketch on your heart. Awaken. You are a divine being incarnated to be and share your light, love, and co-creation.

Traveling through time, to channel the messages, and align your frequency.

An Oregon native, she followed the calling of her soul and resides in South Florida with her husband and twin boys.

Are you ready to begin the journey to reclaiming the power within?

She invites you to book your free connection call via the link below.

Learn More: https://linktr.ee/SamoneMarie

Connect With Me: http://www.samonemarie.com

DAUGHTERS OF THE ROSE

SHONA KEELI ROSE

THE LAYERS OF RECEPTIVITY IN OUR COLLECTIVE consciousness are finally softening enough to receive the true essence of the Rose. As we begin to allow the pristine perfuming of her presence into our lives, we can slowly, ever so gently, and ever so softly unfold into the multidimensional aspects of who Mary Magdalene was and is to this day. I still feel she is a mystery, and that's her true magic.

Mary has been whispering to me for years, "Shona, there is no need to rush but not a moment to waste. "

Over the last eight years, I have decoded this message. The time is now to drench ourselves in the devotional discipline of The Venusian Rose Temple Arts. These are the temple arts teachings that were once forbidden but never were they forgotten.

I genuinely believe there wasn't just one woman that has carved out the way of the Rose but a whole lineage of women that are now returning at this time, and this is who the Daughters of the Rose are to me.

Humanity is currently in a process that I like to call "The Great Softening." These are the times we have been preparing for, for thousands of years. However, much suffering, disasters, and poverty are currently sweeping the Earth, we must remember there is also a lot of healing. Miracles and deep layers of magic are being revealed to those with eyes to see, ears to hear, a nose to smell, a mouth to taste, and hands to touch.

These words I am sharing with you on these pages are an invitation to move beyond the original sin that has been programmed into us since birth—inviting you into full reclamation of the pure remembrance of the untouched template of Erotic Innocence that is within your body.

I imagine if you have found yourself here reading this, you are a powerful woman leading the way with your sacred services to support the masses in this Great Softening that is upon us. Over this past decade, I have understood that no matter how much I anchor into my Magdalene codes, I must also honor the Christos codes.

As powerful, awakened, and conscious feminine leaders, the reality is that we are being tricked by false religions, the feminist movement, and broken lineage lines to emasculate our men. To compete, overpower, fear, abuse, and even hate the masculine by projecting our unprocessed trauma, weaponized pain, and unrealistic love stories upon them. We have become a by-product of hundreds of years of planned indoctrination–it's not truly who we are!

When we invite the true essence of the feminine into our beings, we activate the full codex of the embodiment of

391

Divine Union. It is time for us to restore The Land of Rose Milk and Honey by honoring the oracular fertility of the pure feminine principles of the Ancient Origin Mother. To not push away what we feel, but to feel it all and surrender to God with our deep longing to be a bride of Christ.

It is a privilege to be here during times of such great change. In this lifetime, we will see the restoration of the Holy Mother/Father Rose Line; the Covenant of the Holy Family will prevail.

Embarking on a path of embodiment is not for the faint-hearted. Still, it is what will save our world...dreaming, seeding, and creating from an inner sovereign Union is what the ancient mystics mastered—bringing the worship of the womb back into the home, merging the Mother and the Priestess, the Father and the Priest, and the Mother and Father as one with God. You can't create a lasting legacy by having one without the other. The ancients knew we would keep winding around in circles without embodied Divine Union.

There is no world to save outside the Union you create with the Divine!

We do this for ourselves, our lineage, and humanity's healing. We honor those who have walked before us and those who shall walk after us on this sacred path of the Rose.

We are the Daughters of the Rose. We are daughters of the Holy Father and the Holy Mother, God and Goddess. We seed in the still point of immaculate conception as we walk the way of Union. We are now arriving at a new era of Trinity-Based Consciousness.

WELCOME, BELOVED

Thank you for being here with me; I am profoundly humbled and honored to walk this way of the Rose with you.

I invite you to place your left hand on your heart and take a deep breath into your heart. Allow yourself to breathe out through your heart as you anchor into the purity of Love, truth, and innocence that you are by simply being here with me.

I invite you to place your right hand on your womb, take another deep breath but now into your womb. Allow yourself to breathe out through your womb as you trust the intuitive process of your unique blossoming, blooming into the most in-depth remembrance of the ancient unraveling of The Rose Lineage.

I invite you to slow down even more with me now and ever so gently, ever so softly, breathe deeply in through the nose and out through the mouth.

Invite in these long, deep, and devotional breaths here, in through the nose and out through the mouth. Soften your mouth open as you exhale and relax the jaw.

Continue to do this three more times, each breath in through the nose and out through a relaxed open mouth.

With each breath, you are resting a little more into yourself and all your cells.

Inhaling fully and exhaling completely.

I invite you now, as you exhale, to allow yourself to sound and make an audible sigh. Once more.

And finally, the biggest breath you've taken thus far today

in through the nose and out the mouth, allowing a full-body sigh or any sound to release.

Take as much time as you require here to receive yourself.

We are softening, listening, feeling, healing, forgiving, setting boundaries, befriending our inner thorns, and fully appreciating the exquisite beauty beckoning from within.

What a gift it is to share my story with you. I pray you can feel me and that you get to know yourself through my words.

I long to witness you in your sensual sovereignty, feeling stable and safe to be fully embodied in your pure essence as I share a snippet of my mythos of the Rose with you.

I believe that we are all born of the Rose. My lineage is of the Rose, and if you have found your way here, your lineage is of the Rose, too. We are all devotees of the Divine Mother, Holy Father, and Daughters of The Rose. Together we honor the beauty way, walking the path paved in rose petals and dripping in honey.

My arm is outstretched to you, and I want to remind you of the power of fully stepping into a path of reclamation of your erotic innocence. May you feel at home in this vibration. May your heart continue to serve the strongest desires of your rose womb heart.

May you know your strength in the madness and the baptism fires upon us. May you return to the sacred holy waters of the womb and be baptized by its pure Love. May you receive the codes of the Rose so you can rebirth through this world of calcification with grace and ease.

I am Shona Keeli Rose, and I live in the ancient

Grandmother Garden Island of Kauai, and this is where I came home to myself and the Lineage of the Rose. Although I just had my eight-year anniversary living on these sacred lands of Kauai, my soul chose to incarnate into form in the beautiful Mother Land of Australia.

I was born with a scarlet letter, a child created in Love but outside the traditional confines of what was socially acceptable. This scarlet letter has colored my life experience beautifully.

I want to rewind for a moment and start at the beginning, at the center of the Rose, when she first called me.

I remember frolicking and playing in my grandmother's magical rose garden when I was a little girl. Little Shona formed some of her fondest memories growing up in those magical gardens. I was in a state of consistent wonder, surrounded by the Queen of the Flowers and communing with the fairies.

Some of my closest friends were the roses, her thorns, and the fairies. They would whisper ancient secrets to me and bring me comfort when nothing else in the world could!

I remember my Grandmother Dennis winning the "Rose Gardener of the Year" awards yearly. My Grandmother remarried, and her last name became Gardener.

When I was just over two years of age (my daughter is the same age today), my mother left her hometown to be with my father, leaving behind the magical rose garden my grandmother had created. While I was forever grateful to be living with both of my parents, I remember feeling very lost without the rose garden or my grandmother's wisdom.

Fast forward to just before I lost my virginity, we moved back to the town my grandmother was living in, and I slowly began connecting to the magical rose garden again. When this happened, I was at the very ripe, young, and impressionable age of 12, and I was still trying to understand how to remain present and aligned with myself.

My first sexual experience was without consent, which harshly altered my relationship with my erotic innocence. The transition from being a girl to becoming a woman felt deeply influenced by the outside world.

Still, to this day, this has been one of the greatest gifts I was given from God, as it put me on the path of consciously healing myself and my lineage at a very young age.

I first began to study traditional tantra, yoga, mantra, meditation, and reiki in India when I was 19. Being steeped in Indian culture opened the temple doors for me to some incredible teachers, guides, and gurus, which today would not be possible.

I was blessed to dive very deep into experiential and hands-on learning in a traditional setting over the six years of traveling back and forth from Australia to India, which continues to influence my life and work today.

Amidst all my studies, traveling, and growth, I found myself choosing a path of an exotic dancer to support my studies and travel funding. In my early twenties, I learned how to walk between the worlds, choosing two paths that seemed extreme opposites but somehow made so much sense for my sovereign way of healing the inner child.

I started to understand that I was bridging two worlds, just like Mary Magdalene had done most of her life. I was merging the two into one: the saint and the sinner, the light and the dark, life and death, Eve and Lilith.

I started to understand that we have been taught to fear our sexuality, shadow, the void, and the unseen. Despite what our cultures have taught us, the darkness isn't something to be scared of: it is the yin state, the true fertile grounds of the feminine.

Through my early twenties, I uncovered that false religions and dogma have been using the darkness to control us for eons. They knew that if they kept us separate from our sexuality, our shadow, and our innocence, they could control us with it.

Through becoming an exotic dancer and studying traditional tantra, I slowly learned how to take up full residency of my inner Throne. Even in the darker places and spaces within, that is the power of becoming a true Queen of your realm. True Queens embrace their shadow and alchemize it into simultaneous softness and power.

I continued to deepen my studies; I sat with shamans, drank plant medicine, and trained with grandmothers in ancient womb religions. I explored the jungle in South America, all searching for how to heal my connection to my sexuality and integrate myself deeper into my body.

By age 26, I had traveled worldwide, and my spirit guided me to Grandmother Kauai, where I began training as a birthing, postpartum, and death doula with a beautiful elder named Barbara.

Within five months of being on the ancient island of Kauai, I was pregnant with my son Isvara Jasper Skye. The ever-unfolding initiation of pregnancy and early stages of motherhood began to draw me more deeply inside. I was no longer roaming the world looking for my teachers and lineage. I was wandering the depths of my soul, remembering that I am my teacher and my lineage was the Rose.

It was through connecting with my womb and becoming a mother that my path as a priestess was fully activated and continues to unfold. Through my womb, I have received my oracular gifts, connecting directly with the energies of Venus, Mary Magdalene, Yeshua (Jesus), Mother Mary, and Isis as my direct guides. They have shared visions of their ancient work on this planet and guided me to create The Rose Lineage Mystery School and, finally, The Rose Lineage Ministry to reignite their teachings and lineage of Love.

My deep connection with the Avalon mysteries and the Rose Dragon Lay-lines between Avalon and Grandmother Kauai have ignited even more profound memories that I continue to explore. My understanding of how these beautiful Dragon Rose Lay-lines weave together has grown stronger after birthing my daughter Astarte Sophia Rose onto the earth plane just over two years ago.

Connecting to my womb and Mama Gaia through Grandmother Kauai has been a sweet Rose healing balm to my mind, body, and soul. Daily I continue on my healing journey, calling all parts of myself home, and I am blessed to support other women to do the same with the sacred teachings I am being entrusted to carry in my womb and heart, birthing them back into remembrance here and now.

We are all of the Rose, ever-unfolding into the infinite bliss of pleasure encapsulated in every moment.

We are born of this sacred essence from the pure erotic innocence that lies within every form, facet, phase, and fiber

of our beings, opening and dissolving into existence.
Who Is Mary Magdalene:

Mary Magdalene is divine by design, human, and holy. Mary is both a Mother and a Priestess. She unites the spirit and the flesh and is obtainable and applicable to all women. Mary was the wife of Yeshua (Jesus) and the mother of his children.

I have studied Mary Magdalene consciously for many years; she made it very clear to me repeatedly that I will not find the true essence of the Magdalenes or the devotional feminine in scriptures, books, and or anything to do with the mind. Although I have been writing a full manuscript about her for many years as she continues to channel her temple arts teachings through me.

You won't just find Mary in quiet places, in beautiful temples and caves, and within exquisite altars and all sorts of pretty things. You will find her in the most sacred of temples, the body, and within the bodies of the beloveds we devotionally keep near us.

She awaits you in the sound of your screaming children longing for you and only you. Mary was on the streets of the homeless and starving, helping the sick and those preparing to enter the sacred rite of death.

There she is again, in the middle of your biggest messes, supporting you to pick up the pieces with grace and ease. She is a true friend reminding you how to turn your suffering into solid gold for your soul.

Mary Magdalene is a mistress of the awakened heart, a devotee of pure exalted devotion, a midwife to our individual soul's authentic remembrance, a doula of death, grief, and sorrow, a member of the council of the Rosa Mystica, a highly trained Priestess of Isis. The Isis-Magdalene Rose Line that many women carried in secret through the Middle Ages had to go underground to stay alive.

She is one of the primary and current embodied goddess energies of The Sisterhood of the Rose, or as I call them, The Daughter of the Rose. She is an over-lighting healing presence for women's sexuality for the fallen woman: the woman who has been shamed or cast out as a result of infidelity, prostitution, wedlock, or sexuality. She also carries within her financial empowerment key codes and ancient wisdom for women serving the sacred eternal flames of the feminine.

Mary initiated women into the path of the sacred sexual priestess and mother priestess arts by aligning their sexual energy with the purity of an awakened heart.

She midwives us through past-life trauma, supporting us to anchor back into the remembrance of the healing powers we each individually possess through our own two hands.

"Thank you, Mary Magdalene, for enriching my life with your glorious presence. Thank you for helping me understand the ancient wisdom of my soul. Thank you for helping me master forgiveness. Thank you for helping me perceive and receive the wellspring of wisdom and wealth within me. Thank you for restoring my body temple's original and erotic innocence template. I welcome your white rose transmission into my heart now!"

She is a protectress of the sacred Venusian Temple Arts, and I am honored to be entrusted to steward these teachings as her as my primary guide.

400

WHAT ARE THE VENUSIAN ROSE TEMPLE ARTS AND VENUSIAN ROSE CYCLE?

The Venusian Rose Temple Arts are a temple template that restores the original and erotic innocence to the whole world's consciousnesses. This sacred temple template is a transmission from the trinity of teachers (Heart, Womb, and Yoni) that live within your body–it has the direct blueprint on how to awaken into the highest version of your feminine form.

Currently, eight physical Venusian Rose Temples activate the eternal flames of the feminine. An energy that cannot be possessed, bought, claimed, or destroyed; it is an eternal hearth fire of the Divine Mother, Sophia's and Shekinah's pure essence of unconditional Love.

These Venusian Temples are the wombs of the Earth carrying the seeds of light, the bringers of the codes for the new Earth to birth. Our womb carries these codes, they are not outside of us, and we are the origin point within the center of the Rose.

The origin point of the Rose Lineage is Venus. Our beloved planet Venus is the sister twin guardian of our solar system, Earth–the Blue Pearl. Venus is here to support us as we transition into the New Earth Star.

A new woman is being born through the breath of her beauty!

Venus, or how I like to refer to her as the orbiting star of remembrance, traces a pattern in the sky that looks like a five-pointed star or five-petaled wild Rose. This eight-year Venusian Rose Cycle is woven in sidereal space. It comprises five synoptic periods that take 19 months long each to complete.

The Sun and Venus align every 9 ½ months. Each time Venus crosses paths with the Sun, she alternates between descending into the Morning Star phase (Greek Phōsphóros, meaning "light-bearer") and the ascending Evening Star phase (Greek Hésperos, meaning "western").

There are also two subphases; the Reset Phase where the Interior (inferior) conjunction takes place. Meaning Venus is between the Sun and the Earth, this is when Venus is closest to the Earth and they kiss. Venus appears as a Morning Star after going through an Interior conjunction.

The Underworld Phase is where the exterior (superior) conjunction takes place. Meaning Venus is behind the Sun, furthest away from the Earth. Venus appears as Evening Star after going through exterior conjunction.

The patterns of Venus are gorgeous–they are the heart of the Rose. They reveal Venus's essence in her role as celestial guardian of the sacred Rose Garden of Eden.

The dance of the Sun, Venus, and Earth: their retrograde motions, synodic periods, distance, and orbits present us with patterns that resonate so deeply with the ancient origin point of the pure mythos of the Rose Lineage of Solar Masculine and Feminine Christ.

Syncing with the Venusian Rose Cycle supports us to soften into the opulence unfolding from within the safety found within our skin, free from any traces of sin.

Embodying these teachings in the body as opposed to just learning about these teachings with the mind is why I align all the teachings that I share in Daughters of the Rose

Training (online) and The Venusian Rose Temple Arts Training (in-person) with the Venusian Rose Cycle.

Are you a Daughter of the Rose?

We would be honored to welcome you into The Rose Lineage Collective. We offer multiple ways to support all women to remember and embody their true essence of the feminine.

Radiating Rose Love,

Shona Keeli Rose,

Xx

ABOUT THE AUTHOR

SHONA KEELI ROSE

Shona is the found-her of The Rose Lineage Mystery School and Ministry for The Venusian Rose Temple Arts; She is a Mother Priestess, Rose Empress Initiator, and Gifted Womb Oracle.

She is present in this time of the great softening to support the budding, blossoming, and blooming of the true essence of devotional feminine expression and exploration of inner power.

Shona holds an impeccable space for hands-on healings, group and private mentorship, and temple arts training in person and online. Supporting women to soften and surrender into revelation as she assists the full reclamation of the Feminine Face of Christ.

She is a Venusian Rose light bearer and shadow dancer, an energetic midwife to the wave of Rose Consciousness that is currently birthing.

Shona's wisdom is drawn from ancient tantric teachings and womb religions. She practices and teaches traditions spanning thousands of years, including Gnostic, Egyptian, Mayan, Vedic, Lemurian and Atlantean.

You can find her in domestic bliss stewarding the Rose Lineage Temple on the Grandmother Island of Kaua'i, caring for her two Starseed children, temple, and garden. Always stopping to smell the roses as she continues to humbly learn the dance of weaving the Mother and the Priestess together as one.

Website: https://theroselineage.com

Free Grounding Rose Lineage Meditation:
https://theroselineage.com/rosemeditation/magdalene-codes/

Instagram: @theroselineage

Facebook Group:
https://www.facebook.com/groups/roselineage

A PRIESTESS IS A PRAYER

STELLA GRACE

A PRIESTESS IS A PRAYER IN THE SHAPE OF A woman. AS soon as she enters the room, you can taste her energy. Her perspective is POTENT and provocative. She either triggers you or turns you on. Sometimes both at the same time. She is detached from everything and devoted to the divine in a way that confuses the average mind. Her vision is edgy. Her truth is embodied. There is nothing she cannot be, do or have. And she knows it.

When you hear her speak, you can feel it. Her certainty. Her courage. Her conviction. She's dripping in divinity. Her voice sounds like honey and heaven making love in the rain. Her highest service of all is the way she tends to her own garden. Her body. Her temple. She is a living, breathing mystery school. When you walk with her, you become more of who you really are. She leaves you unrecognizable to yourself and everyone around you. She turns you all the way on.

I activate life force for a living. Always have and always will. It's who I am. It's how I serve. It is my gift to the world. My energy wakes up the part of you that has been asleep at the wheel. Because you've got big things to do here. And there's no more time for hiding, playing small and avoiding the responsibility of your power.

To the women who know deep in their bones that they are here to protect the land, restore the grid, open the portals and birth the codes... I'm calling you forward. With my hand over my heart, I am asking you to stand up, take a stand and reclaim your royal seat. You can no longer pretend like you are not what you are. It's time to be brave with your life.

PRIESTESS IN BUSINESS

I am here for the ancient ones. The ones who don't fit into any of the boxes. The ones who were born to serve the restoration of humanity. The ones who are here to create and lead in a way the world has never seen. The ones who know on a cellular level that they are here to bring heaven to earth with their voice and their vision.

A priestess does business the same way she does life. With grace. With Gaia. With God. Her heart beats in the earth and in the sky above. She walks between the realms with power and precision. Her business isn't a business, it's a sacred offering, a potion, a song.

She holds space masterfully. She receives exquisitely. She is a birthing machine. Because when Shakti is truly embodied, you vibrate at the frequency of Creatrix. The work that you are doing on this planet is a cosmic co-creation with Spirit. And everything that you share with the world is medicine and art.

The women I serve give me full-body chills. They are the entrepreneurs that are actually medicine women. They are the coaches and mentors that are holding high-level priestess codes in their blood and in their bones. They are otherworldly and extraordinary in ways this world is finally ready to see.

When you are truly *a Priestess in Business*, you are not "creating content," you are speaking fire into the heart of humanity. You are channeling divinity for a living. You are in a devotional relationship with your highest heaven on earth timeline. So your standards need to be high and your boundaries need to be clear. Because the only thing that could compromise the integrity of your mission is your unconscious energy leaks and the fear of your own power.

You hold the most steady space for your clients to unravel and come fully home to themselves. You think about them all the time, not just on their weekly calls. You open your heart, your womb, and your channel to receive high-frequency downloads for them. Your clients aren't clients, they're soulmates. They are men and women whom you are coded to co-create new worlds with. It's so damn beautiful.

If you are truly walking the priestess path, you must learn how to keep your channel clear, your energy clean and your intentions pure. It's the only way you will be able to trust yourself with this much power...and it's the only way that you will be trusted by those you are here to serve.

A lot of people think that this work is airy and fairy. But that couldn't be further from the truth. This level of devotion to the divine requires roots and wings. What it took for me to cultivate the level of safety and stability within to truly hold my mission is unlike anything I've ever known. This is not only about taking flight in this astral. This is grounding down to the vibration of the earth.

Priestess, you are being called to the frontline. And the bottom line is that there is simply no more time to pretend like you are just running a business online.

MOTHER MAGDALENE

She enters your field on the exhale. Mary Magdalene travels through the breath. Into the body and all the way down into the core of the earth. She has been showing me that the medicine of this collective crisis is about refusing to be controlled by fear. And that those who know how to safely navigate and trust the sacred fires of transformation are leading humanity into the next golden age.

She slows us down, invites us to our edge and shows us exactly how to heal every part of ourselves. I love her with my whole heart. She is my light in the dark, my multidimensional mentor, my sister, my ancient mother, my guide. She reminds us that we can do hard things. And that we all deserve the life of our dreams.

Mary Magdalene taught me that womb work is wealth work. That the body is the portal into our heaven on earth timeline. And that this timeline is happening here and now. Our job is to learn how to align with it and allow it in.

As women, we were all programmed to feel guilty and ashamed of our beauty, our power and our desire for more. This keeps us trapped in a frantic, desperate, anxiously attached energetic state of dysregulation, guaranteeing that we will never break free from survival consciousness in this life. I've got two words for you. FUCK THAT!

When you are no longer seeking permission or praise, you

are free to be who you were born to be. Without apology.

The divine feminine codes of creation have been unlocked on this planet by the women who truly embody The Magdalene. We are here to lead in the areas of energetic + emotional + erotic intelligence. Our work supports our clients and communities around fully reclaiming their multidimensional gifts, healing their relationship with their yoni's, opening their hearts, restoring their womb space, liberating their lineage and sourcing their wealth from their wellbeing.

A true Magdalene is not a martyr. She is here in service to the liberation of the feminine and the earth mother. She understands that to truly support this sacred mission, she must be relaxed, receptive and resourced. So it's important that you know that you will not ever see a spiritually mature woman shaming the rise of feminine wealth on this planet. You will see her celebrating it and encouraging it.

TURNING WOUNDS INTO WISDOM

Wounded maidens project their pain around men and money onto the world around them. But a woman who is truly walking the priestess path has healed her core wounds, regulated her nervous system and sees beyond the drama of our current cultural climate.

When a woman rises into mother. When the maiden becomes the mother of her own life. You can feel it in her field. How deeply she has faced herself. How committed she is to what she is creating. How devoted she is to bringing through her deepest desires and biggest dreams. How anchored she is to her purpose.

The ancient mothers of the earth had to mother themselves.

They were typically born into chaos and have suffered more than most in this life. What they survived by their first bleed would have destroyed most. But these women were born to rise. To lead themselves, humanity, and the earth mother out of the wastelands of our time. They walk with a grace that was earned in the fires of their own transformations.

A priestess is a sacred mirror for everything and all. Her frequency shifts every single room that she enters. Her medicine reminds you that you are responsible for what triggers you and what turns you on. She is Magdalene embodied. A safe/sacred space for those ready to be initiated into their fullest potential in this place. Her presence commands reverence and respect. If your intention is not pure, she'll know. If you seek to siphon her life force, she'll know. If you are casting the evil eye in her direction, she'll know. And she will send it back tenfold in the form of an opportunity for you to clean up your own energy. She doesn't cast stones but she also doesn't wash anyone's dirty dishes. Everything that is not God is transmuted by her fierce, loving presence. But she's no one's doormat or dumping ground. She is not a martyr. She is MOTHER. Her vibration feels like heaven on earth for the ones that are truly ready for liberation. And the ones that aren't will typically be repelled by her potency and her power. Either way, she's unbothered and unattached from the programming and conditioning that seeks to enslave humanity. She vibrates at the frequency of "come correctly or do not come at all." She is embodied goddess consciousness. She is priestess. She is power.

The journey from the fragmented feminine to the mature feminine requires a complete and total rebirth. And that rebirth requires the deepest faith you've ever known. To trust the divine timing of all things, even when it's not what you would prefer, is holy hotness at its finest. To be lifted from the illusion of comfort and control. To trust the moment enough to relax into it. This is how we bring heaven to earth through our leadership and our love.

PRIESTESSES OF GAIA

The Earth speaks to/through women like us. She prepares us for what's coming before it comes. She appreciates the way we listen. The way we see her. The way we honor her. When you are equal parts BOSS bitch and ancient priestess, you require a very unique style of support. All those previous experiences with subpar coaches, courses, and mentors served a part of you but ultimately left you feeling thirsty and hungry for a flavor that is more aligned with the most secret and seductive aspects of your being.

That's where I come in. That is the space that I fill with my multidimensional medicine.

Who you are matters just as much if not more than what you do and it's officially time to ALIGN with that deeper part of yourself PERSONALLY and PROFESSIONALLY. You're not just leading a global movement, you're leading a sacred mission You're not just scaling a business, you're scaling a sacred business. You're not just sharing your message, you're channeling the divine's message.

Your journey to wealth and abundance beyond your wildest dreams gets to be a co-creation with Spirit. And that's exactly why I took my time while birthing the PRIESTESS IN BUSINESS membership, mastermind and podcast. I wanted it to be my most sacred offering thus far. A temple experience for the Sacred Feminine Leader who is ready to step all the way into the deepest embodiment and fullest expression of her soul's mission. These containers are equal parts practical and magical. Because in order for you to fully ground your mission, there needs to be a celestial style to your marketing. And for your message to penetrate the hearts of those you are truly coded to serve, your brand essence needs to feel like home to your most ideal client.

As an artist, I fell in love with business when I realized that the most creative thing I will ever do with my life is create the life and business of my dreams. This took grit. This took grace. This took vision. This took conviction.

I walk with the women who have done the work. The ones who are committed to the journey no matter what kind of challenges or setbacks show up along the way. The ones who put the mission on the altar, prioritize the healing of their deepest wounds and the regulation of their nervous system. We create masterpiece after masterpiece. I show them how to shift from running an online business to birthing a boutique brand that is irresistible to their people. Because impact and income are two sides of the same coin. Every penny that comes into your business is a symbol of a life changed and transformed by your commitment to your purpose.

I deeply believe that birthing a new earth has to include birthing a new economy or else what are we actually doing? And that is going to require as many heart-centered, mission-driven entrepreneurs in their power as possible. We don't have time to sit around feeling guilty for putting a high price on our work anymore. When your offer is life-giving, the sale is sacred. And it's officially time to own it!

My work is alive and dripping in eros. My medicine is a FULL POTENTIAL ACTIVATION through the lens of divine feminine ascension. I was born to turn you and your genius all the way on. In the body and the business.

I walk the most powerful women on this planet through the

thresholds. The big ones. Into their fullness. Into their depths. Into the most potent aspects of their divine assignment.

My medicine is about divine feminine desire and devotional business coming together to provide the exact experience my most ideal client has been combing the earth looking for. I am not a business coach, I'm a business Oracle. I'm here for the entrepreneur who cannot work with traditional business coaches without feeling like their soul is being sucked out of their bodies. If that's you, this is the beginning of something really beautiful.

ABOUT THE AUTHOR

STELLA GRACE

Stella Grace is a divine feminine leadership + sacred wealth embodiment mentor. She guides women who resonate with the priestess path into their highest evolution by reclaiming their peace, their pleasure, and every single drop of personal power that was ever taken by force or unconsciously given away.

Her divine mission was forged within sacred fires of her own rebirth. A survivor of narcissistic abuse and a traumatic suicide attempt, she deeply understands the darkest and most painful parts of the human experience. Her work in all its entirety is a journey of reclamation and liberation. She teaches mission-driven + visionary women how to bring the goddess into the business.

Stella believes that the journey to embodied wealth is about deep healing and divine service and that the world has never been more in need of awakened women who are emotionally, energetically and financially empowered. She is also the owner of goddess medicine, a ritual perfume + ceremonial body care line.

If you feel called to connect more deeply with her work, this is the perfect place to begin. Rose Codes is a sacred feminine activation portal in the form of a monthly membership. If you are ready to reclaim the fullest expression of your divine feminine essence, I invite you to click the link below.

Facebook: https://www.facebook.com/profile.php?id-100016644483500

Instagram: @goddessmedicine

Website: www.goddessmedicine.life

Website: www.priestessinbusiness.com

JOURNEY INTO ACCEPTANCE

VICKI LATTER

I SPENT A LOT OF MY LIFE FIGHTING TO FIT IN, TO FIT WITHIN the constraints of a box that I imagined would allow me to be accepted by my peers.

As a young girl, I shed many tears as I believed I had to be a certain size, speak a certain way, wear a certain brand, or look like everyone else to be one of the girls. The young, carefree girl who would run through the mud as she fought dragons and saved princesses lost the sparkle in her eyes, and she became obsessed with finding ways to fit in.

Have you ever felt trapped in a box, limited by the expectations you have put on yourself? Those expectations you assume everyone else has about you and your life. Thinking that was the only way someone else would like you, or it was the only way you would be included by others?

I tore myself apart spending many nights crying myself to sleep, just wanting to feel I was accepted by someone. Anytime something in my life happened that made me feel I was different, I would hide or pretend it wasn't true.

I mean, if anyone knew I was different, how could I ever show my face?

Would anyone ever accept me?

JUST TO BELONG

The fear of never being accepted overwhelmed my childhood memories.

From a very young age, my life was spent as a people pleaser. I just wanted to belong. I wanted to be invited to the popular girl's birthday as much as I wanted to be asked to play red rover on the playground or picked to be on the team. Not the child teachers had to ask other kids to play with. Many nights I would come home in tears feeling that I was all alone in the world, and no one liked me. I felt that no one even knew I existed.

I grew up to believe the more I bent over backward to meet the demands of someone else, the higher the chance was for me to be liked. I mean if I helped someone with her homework, there was a chance she might like me or include me in a game of cat's cradle. Or the days when I shared the treats of my lunchbox in hopes someone would talk to me at recess. I had days I would try anything to be noticed or to be part of any group.

There was a time I attempted to be one of the cool kids. I had taken a ring, one of those prizes from the dentist and

418

thought it would make a beautiful nose ring. Yes. I had stuck the ring up my nostril, hoping that the sparkle it had when my head moved would at least encourage one of the girls to speak to me. Maybe even see me in the light of someone who was cool, not just someone who sat in the shadows.

That bright idea did not turn out the way I had hoped. No one noticed, except for the teacher who had to deal with the continuous nosebleed I ended up with and my mother who caused insurmountable pain by removing the ring that night. A lesson learned at the age of six, dentist rings are not to be shoved up your nose and they don't make you part of the cool crowd.

Other moments came and went throughout my childhood, those moments of ingenious ideas all in hopes of feeling accepted. There were days of exaggerated stories, stolen treats from the cupboards at home and birthday presents for the kids that didn't know I existed. There were days of being a punching bag where children would call me names or tease me because of the clothes I wore or my body size. Comments I would sit there and take, hoping I could fade into the shadows and be forgotten. Always hoping the words, "Sticks and stones may break my bones, but names will never hurt me," were true.

The box never seemed to be my size. I would put a foot in and never be able to fully step inside it. I felt that the expectations creating the limitations kept evolving, almost like the target kept moving just outside of my grasp. Any time I felt that I was closer to my goal of being accepted, it seemed like the rules changed. The saying "one step forward, two steps back," described my challenge to fit in.

I forgot who I was at my core. I was so focused on the hope that someone would want to be my friend or like me, I forgot the magic that was hidden inside. The little girl who wanted to run wild in the meadows and dance the night away as she told the most enchanting stories about faraway lands and mystical creatures. The little girl whose smile would light up the room, her eyes would dance with excitement on what was next in the world.

This little girl attempted to hide in the shadows in hopes that somebody someday would see her and shift the boundaries, making it just her size. Since fitting into the box would equal acceptance.

PRESSURE TO BE ACCEPTED

The belief that a box of expectations existed followed me into adulthood. The extremes to which I would go to fit in expanded and continued to take me further away from what my heart wanted. The fear of never fitting in overwhelmed the need to be an individual. The rules that appeared as part of the expectations started to include all aspects of life, such as: who to date, where to shop, what to wear, who to associate with, and even what to eat. As the rules became more complex, the desire to fit in increased. As I felt myself lose aspects of my personality and character, I felt trapped inside a jail cell, and the experience was more painful than I ever could have imagined.

There were times I would bust my ass to make a basketball team or join a club, simply to be a member of the team–yet never feeling like I was part of the team. There were many times I was told I didn't look like an athlete, that I had to be the team manager. Every time I joined a new team, I felt that I was always on the outside looking in, wishing I could be part of the inside jokes or just be one of the girls.

When life handed me challenges, I was afraid to share my

struggles. I feared I would be judged and excluded from the limited opportunities that I had fought so hard to find. Almost like the idea of fitting in was a fleeting dream that wasn't mine to keep.

To fit inside the box, I found myself dating men who were not the man of my dreams. I convinced myself to date the men who I felt society dictated were the only ones I was good enough for based on my physical appearance and financial situation. I allowed myself to believe that no man would accept me unless I was able to meet whatever their wild request was or find a way to provide for them, as opposed to expecting them to provide for me.

I fought tooth and nail to keep fitting inside the box. I allowed society's ideals to define who I was and the life I was living. I believed that if I lived a quiet life under the radar and never spoke up, I would have to be accepted. I would jump through the never-ending hoops, hoping it would then equate to the life I was expected to live.

For many years, I felt that the box was defined by the expectations that as a young woman I was to get married to my college sweetheart, have two kids, live in the suburbs as the president of the parent's council, and walk the family dog past green lawns with white picket fences. Nothing outside of that was allowed to be seen or shared.

Being married was the first step in that equation. As a young woman, I decided to marry the first man who told me, "No one will ever accept you. I am the best you will ever find." Craving acceptance from anyone, I said yes and agreed to an emotional rollercoaster. I threw myself headfirst into a relationship with a man who plotted how he could exploit me next, without having to give anything in return. I grew to believe love was running myself ragged while ensuring my partner was living his best life.

It confirmed that I did not love or accept myself as a woman, and I would settle for crumbs of attention from anyone who might love me. Now, it was no surprise that the marriage did not last.

The relationships that followed were very similar in dynamic. Instead of standing in my self-worth and knowing the amazing woman I was, I continued to pursue men that might accept me in between the days they would degrade or belittle me. These thoughts led to me chasing an idea of what a good man was, the man who never seemed to appear.

The pressure continued to mount on how I perceived a young independent woman should be living her life. The idea of fitting in the box of "married with kids" was overwhelming and all-encompassing in life. I continued to believe I could live that life, and someone somewhere would want to be with me. Being embarrassed by my choice of partners, I eloped for the second time without informing my family and friends. Knowing that if they had met my partner before we were married, they would have an opinion and not approve of the union, more than likely being disappointed in me. The weight of the perceived expectations took me onto another rollercoaster in life.

Then the day came when I was potentially going to be twice divorced by 30, and I couldn't navigate what step was next. The fear of how I would be seen. Being a strong independent woman, who had two failed marriages all before I was 30 years old. That image did not fit in any box that I had ever seen or explored. Who would accept me after? How would I ever explain what happened behind the closed doors of my relationships and took me into the darkest days of my life? The days when I lost all thought of who I was and let go of all my dreams for someone else. It was like living a life for someone else and not knowing anything about who I was.

After struggling for so long fighting to be accepted by anyone, the idea of acknowledging that I was never going to fit inside the box was heartbreaking. Who could I be if I could never meet the expectation of another? Was it worth hiding behind closed doors? Continuing to hide the emotional turmoil that was overtaking my life and the self-doubt that consumed me? Was that all I was destined to do in this lifetime?

The fear of not living life was real. The idea of pretending I was living the expected life exhausted me. The pain of loving the idea of a man who would never accept me as his only love defeated me. The pain far exceeded the fear of the unknown and what judgment could be coming my way from being twice divorced by 30.

For the first time in my life, I saw that the box wasn't solid. I saw that the need to choose myself far exceeded the need to be accepted. Cracks started to appear in the logic I had perceived around all the expectations in my life. There was a glimmer of hope. A glimmer of hope that the acceptance I had been chasing throughout my life didn't look the way I had imagined it did.

ACCEPTING MYSELF

Acceptance started to look different in my eyes. All those years of standing on the outside craving to be part of the group seemed to appear differently. All those dreams and thoughts of the things I wanted in life started to become clearer. I no longer felt the need to limit myself on what I craved to experience in this life to meet the expectations of someone else.

I started to see that the box I had used to define my worth was just an illusion I created out of my need to belong, my need to feel I fit in and to feel that I was accepted.

I started to navigate a new world, standing on my own two feet as a strong independent woman who was carving her own way in the world. I learned the value of living life for myself. I learned that acceptance was not defined by someone else or by how well you fit into the box you had chosen to define yourself. Acceptance was how you choose to define it.

I was finally open to exploring a whole new life. I stopped feeling I would be defined by a relationship or that I had to stick to a decision I made because of the pressure I assumed from others. I learned who I was. I realized I had dreams, and I had opportunities to live an amazing life.

I had spent years convincing myself that single women did not travel the world on their own. The world had convinced me it was not safe for independent women to be abroad alone, and it was so expensive when you travel on your own. And strong women would never meet a nice boy to marry. Those false stories had turned into expectations on how to live.

Life presented a beautiful opportunity for me where I was able to take 100 days and explore Oceania on my own. These 100 days allowed me to see my inner strength and the gifts I held within. I was living my adventure and learning all about who Vicki really was.

I found my resilience on the Yasawa Islands in Fiji during a cyclone, where I chose to hunker down with the local family in a bungalow through the storm. I found I trusted myself in a country without a map or a plan. I realized I love spending time alone and my heart craves adventures to feel fulfilled. I learned I have the tenacity to never give up, and through personal pain, I can climb volcanoes.

All lessons I never would have discovered if I continued to live under the pressure of someone else's expectations. That fear of being different would have stopped me from getting on the plane, and discovering what an amazing person I am. I knew I needed to go and live my life for myself.

I spent three weeks in a camper van driving all over the north and south islands of New Zealand. I had arrived with no itinerary other than a flight home, and no idea what to see, where to stay, or what route to travel. It was the best decision, learning to fend for myself and create my own journey in the unknown.

During the first week I was on the North Island, I allowed the pressure of expectations to take over my trip. I felt pressure to travel the "expected" route that most tourists were posting on social media. Now, I had no interest in Lord of the Rings, Hobbiton or the glow worms, but the pressure mounted and led to me feeling overwhelmed. My heart was calling to the coast, the wineries, and the little towns with so much depth to explore. It was at this moment when I reminded myself it was my adventure. I could go and see anything I wanted, and no opinion mattered but my own.

From that moment on, it became clear to me that I was a person who loved adventure—and it could look like anything I wanted, as long it felt right to me.

The box continued to shrink and fall apart as I discovered the world of healing modalities along my personal journey into who I am. I learned about energy healing, NLP, hypnotherapy, soul exploration, and the importance of finding myself and honoring my needs and desires. I started my adventure within. The adventure that led to discovering that strong women don't need to be defined and they never need to fit into society's ideals.

ADVENTURE WITHIN

As I dove deeper into the exploration of who I was and redefined my adventure within, the idea of acceptance shifted more. It became clear that my struggle to fit in had been my own lack of self-acceptance. That adage that "you can't accept someone until you accept yourself" was now very clear in front of me.

All the years of turmoil and feeling like an outcast that had plagued my thoughts, dragging me into the depths of depression and loneliness, started to fade away. They no longer had a place in my world to dictate what came next.

Time passed, and I slowly embraced the adventurous lifestyle as I struggled to accept it was okay to live a life different than everyone else. It was okay to be a career woman chasing her dreams without a life partner and children. It was okay to never want to put down roots and own a house in my hometown. It was okay to be motivated by feeling excited and pushing yourself out of your comfort zone. It was okay to live life on your own terms, no matter what those terms were.

This all sounded great in theory. In real life, though, this was extremely tough. That lifelong fear of never belonging was deep within my being and never seemed to fully disappear. I would find moments of my own truth and power and use my voice only to be knocked back onto my heels. Feeling like the little girl who just wanted to fit in. This tug-of-war continued, as did the feeling of returning to one step forward and two steps back. It almost felt that no one took me seriously or believed that I could live a life outside of the box and on my own terms. I would never be anyone amazing if I didn't find my place within those boundaries.

The sense of losing my power overwhelmed me. I craved adventures that light up my soul, and yet I felt that familiar feeling of paralysis and a downward spiral into the darkness of depression. I went from a cheerful, gregarious woman to the girl who couldn't find the energy to step outside of her house. To the outside world, it appeared I was living a great life, and yet I was just going through the motions of life.

That continued until one fateful day when a friend asked about moving to Central America. I had never thought about leaving the good corporate job I had to get a plane to find myself again.

Plans were made to travel with my friend and have an adventure. To both escape life as we knew it at home, and to discover what was next in life. Well, the day of our flight came, and I was the only one on the plane. My friend had changed their mind, and I was going for six months to a new country alone.

And I was excited.

I was told by friends and family I was brave and courageous. I was doing something many dreamed about and would never have the courage to do. To take a risk and rediscover their magic.

For six months I was on my own in a new place. I was able to reflect and find what lights up my soul.

I found my light within. I found pieces of life that excited me. I found genuine connection. I found comfort knowing I was different. I found my sense of adventure and inspiration to share with others.

I found self-acceptance.

Walking the beaches day in and day out allowed me to explore life on my terms. I realized I am free to create my own path into the future that doesn't come with a box. I was reminded that I am free to be whoever I want and there is no external opinion that matters.

The day came when I realized it was okay to be different, to be unique. I was free to adventure deep within and discover what was waiting for me. It was okay to show my scars, to own my choices and to look however I wanted. Those expectations I used to agonize about just disappeared. No longer did the voice of anyone else matter, as I stepped forward into my own power and learned to trust my gut. To trust that I was a strong woman who was here to live life on her terms.

I gave myself the greatest gift of my life. I accepted myself exactly as I am.

ABOUT THE AUTHOR

VICKI LATTER

Vicki Latter is the Freedom Catalyst, International Best-Selling Author and creator of Adventure Alchemy. She walks side by side with her clients seeking freedom from their self-imposed prison.

Vicki adventures with her clients, igniting their soul compass and eradicating the hurdles sitting in their way, so they can be liberated in living the life they crave. Adventure Alchemy takes you from feeling restrained and stuck to feeling light and free.

She embodies the lessons frustration and limiting her soul have taught her to guide others through their journey into peace and freedom.

Currently residing in the Foothills of Alberta, Vicki spends time paddle boarding, rockhounding and chasing waterfalls, always finding new ways to feed her adventurous soul.

Now is the time to free your soul and release the self-imposed constraints on yourself.

Adventure Alchemy:
www.vickilatter.com/adventurealchemy

Learn More: https://linktr.ee/vickilatter

Connect With Me: www.vickilatter.com

FB: https://www.facebook.com/vicki.latter.5/

IG: www.instagram/smileyvicks

ABOUT THE PUBLISHER

SHANNON VAN DEN BERG

Shannon Van Den Berg is the CEO of Kiva Publishing and High Priestess of the Jaguar Council, International Bestseller 10 times over and Feminine Leadership Mentor for over two decades.

She founded Kiva Publishing to provide a platform to quantum leap courageous feminine leaders into their highest potential by sharing their story and message with the world.

She specializes in activating her client's Inner Creatrix and Divine Storyteller so they can cultivate an epic life, bring in the New Paradigm and unlock deeper levels of service, impact, and wealth in their business.

This is what sparked the creation of her signature program, the Jaguar Council which is designed to activate fierce feminine frequency leaders rising into their power, purpose and prosperity.

She lives on her ranch in the sacred Four Corners area of Hesperus, Colorado with her husband and four homeschooled boys.

Shannon's powerful multi-author books are the heart of Kiva Publishing, initiating authors into their clarity, expression, impact and soul mission. They're also an accessible stepping stone to birthing your own book with her.

If you feel the call to share your story and become a bestselling published author in a highly supported and guided collaboration of like hearted women, you're invited to join our next book project.

Contribute to Kiva Publishing's upcoming Multi-Author Quantum Creatrix Oracle Deck: Fierce Feminine Frequency Leaders Merging Ancient Wisdom and New Earth Sovereignty.

Join the Multi-Author Oracle Deck Here: https://shannon-van-den-berg.mykajabi.com/quantum-creatrix-oracle-deck

Step forward into your leadership in the Jaguar Council: https://linktr.ee/shannonvandenberg_\

Website: www.shannonvandenberg.com

Let's Connect:
https://www.facebook.com/shannonlvandenberg

Follow Me:
https://www.instagram.com/shannonvandenberg_/

Join my Creatrix Coven Community for complimentary weekly activations and bonus free masterclass:
https://t.me/+uTOo7Ov8Nyg2NzE5

Feel the fierce feminine rising and expanding through your heart, radiating liberation and sacred disruption through every part of your being.

Agnieszka Golasik
Allie Marie
Anca Lavinia
Angela Rosenow
Caryn Terres
Cassandra Finch
Cathy Ho
Chelsea Boissonneault
Colleen M Coyne
Crystal Lynn Privett
Daina Gardiner
Dhyana Kluth
Ehrin Parker
Ilona Poka
Isabel Morales
Jenna Brown
Jessica Sage
Juliana Lavell
Kathy Eller
Lisa Curtis
Márcia Dáromck MerMa
Melissa Ann
Monique Vette
Nicole Ishtara Katz
Nicole Marie Rose
Rebecca Collins
Samone Marie
Shona Keeli Rose
Stella Grace
Vicki Latter

Made in the USA
Middletown, DE
02 March 2023

26069955R00245